HERBERT ROSENFELD
AT WORK

HERBERT ROSENFELD AT WORK

The Italian Seminars

Edited by

Franco De Masi

Foreword by

Riccardo Steiner

KARNAC

LONDON   NEW YORK

First published in 2001 by
H. Karnac (Books) Ltd.
6 Pembroke Buildings, London NW10 6RE
Reprinted in 2003.

Translated by Adam Victor.

Italian edition: *I Seminari Milanese di Herbert Rosenfeld*
Copyright © 1997 Centro Milanese di Psicoanalisi

British Library Cataloguing in Publication Data

A C.I.P. for this book is available from the British Library

ISBN 1 85575 264 6

Edited, designed, and produced by Communication Crafts

www.karnacbooks.com

Printed and bound in Great Britain by
Antony Rowe Ltd, Chippenham and Eastbourne

CONTENTS

PREFACE TO THE ENGLISH EDITION   vii

FOREWORD *by Riccardo Steiner*   ix

PREFACE TO THE ITALIAN EDITION   xv

INTRODUCTION   xxi

PART I
Theoretical seminars

1   Psychotic transference diagnosis and treatment
issues in the analysis of a psychotic adolescent   3

2   The relationship between psychosomatic symptoms
and latent psychotic states   24

3   Communication problems between patient
and analyst in psychotic and borderline patients   45

4   The analyst's use of phantasy   64

PART II
Clinical seminars

5   Traumatic infancy   77

6   Transference in psychosis   118

7   Persecutory anxiety   160

8   A primitive psychic structure   181

9   Crisis situations   202

REFERENCES   227

INDEX   229

PREFACE TO THE ENGLISH EDITION

F irst of all, I would like to thank Karnac for publishing Herbert Rosenfeld's Italian Seminars, particularly in the face of the difficult conditions in which psychoanalytic publishing finds itself today. Karnac has done all that is possible in continuing to promote and disseminate texts of high psychoanalytic value.

And this book is of high psychoanalytic value. In our particular discipline, a part of scientific communication takes place during seminars, in discussion with colleagues, and in the act of teaching students. We well know that, when transmitting psychoanalytic thought, the written text carries only a part of the ideas and intuitions that can be found in oral communication.

Words penetrate in the communication between colleagues and weave the specific structure of the analytic community, but, alas, they may be forgotten, and many a precious intuition runs the risk of being lost.

This book tries to fix, spread, and transmit to new generations of psychoanalysts a part of Rosenfeld's final thought that was not written but was communicated by him—passionately—to an audience of colleagues. What this book is trying to do is to fill the gap that exists in creative minds between the depth of thought that can be expressed by means of the written word and the spontaneity and personal intuition that are brought out only in oral interplay.

This imbalance between the new ideas expressed in writing and those that are only spoken is, in the case of Rosenfeld's final thought, particularly evident. So this book might be the one that Rosenfeld himself might have written had his indefatigable energy not suddenly come to an end.

A final word on the reasons that Italian analysts had in listening to Rosenfeld and in considering his clinical work. The Italian psychoanalytic movement has original characteristics that are intertwined with the cultural and social life of a country that has enjoyed a rebirth in knowledge, and in which psychoanalysis itself has appeared, after the fall of Fascism, as one of the tools of fundamental confrontation.

At first, a characteristic of Italian psychoanalysis was that of developing some widespread analytic topics of a philosophical or epistemological kind or, yet again, that were based on Freud's work.

Even though there were in our own country important colleagues, such as Gaddini and Fornari, who were also appreciated abroad, there was in us younger ones a need to refine our clinical skills. For this reason, we invited and listened to a number of British analysts, who helped us reach a deeper approach with our patients in the analytic room. This book also stands as witness of our gratitude to these foreign colleagues—Eric Brenman, Martha Harris, Betty Joseph, Donald Meltzer, Irma Pick—who were present in Italy together with Rosenfeld. They have been a major influence on the growth of our Italian group, whose scientific presence is now stronger than in the past and is also able to make a contribution, together with other colleagues, to the psychoanalysis of the future.

Franco De Masi

FOREWORD

Riccardo Steiner

"*Ich bin kein Theoretiker*"—"I am not a theoretician." Those were the words with which Rosenfeld, during the first interview I had with him (which now is lost in the night of time!), underlined his way of working as a psychoanalyst.

I had arrived in London from the Continent just the night before. That Saturday morning at the beginning of March, it suddenly started snowing, and, while he was telling me this, for a brief moment Rosenfeld looked outside the bay window of his vast consulting-room at 36 Woronzow Road, London, NW8, where he was living at the time. In the front garden there were some branches of already blossoming bushes and a magnolia. Rosenfeld seemed suddenly worried about the weight of the snow on them, and he glanced intently at the flowers for a fraction of a second. Then, slowly, he turned his head and eyes towards me, as if curious to see the effect that his words were having on me. His face lit up with one of those smiles that everyone who has met him must still remember—a smile that seemed never-ending, wrinkling his spacious forehead, his lips and the whole mouth broadening, beginning to reveal rather strong teeth. At the same time, his eyes, half open, but in which nevertheless one could sense a sly glimpse of ironic undertones, were softly but in an extremely penetrative manner exploring my face and expression, making eye contact with me without being too intrusive, with a sort of benevolent patience yet full of curiosity for this new arrival, as if he were saying, "Well this is me . . . it is up to you to make up your mind and decide what you want or to choose to do."

I thought I would begin this Foreword to the English edition of Rosenfeld's clinical seminars and supervisions in Milan—which he had started presenting also in Rome, invited there by E. Gaddini— by recalling my experience of his personality and way of dealing with potential patients, colleagues, students, and so on, because the way our Italian colleagues have managed to transcribe and publish verbatim their meetings with Rosenfeld seems to contain "in action" what I have tried to describe as Rosenfeld's spontaneous way of speaking and being with the other.

I personally do not always agree with our Italian colleagues' statements concerning Rosenfeld's enthusiasm, which at times, especially during the last years of his life, could be really rather excessive and too optimistic in dealing with some of his patients. I also do find rather questionable Rosenfeld's latest views concerning the need to respect the patient's idealization of him as a therapist. At times, to me they seem too excessive—although it is true that Melanie Klein stressed the importance of the baby's need to idealize the mother's breast, to a certain point. Like many others here in England, I also have slight reservations concerning the differentiation Rosenfeld made between "libidinal defensive narcissism" and what he called "destructive narcissism". After all, one could say that both forms of narcissism are defensive, and at times what lies behind "libidinal narcissism" can be quite difficult to handle, too, because one can never exclude the presence of envy even in the case of libidinal narcissism. But in spite of all this, we have to feel enormously grateful to our Italian colleagues for their initiative to publish this book, because with their act of love and admiration towards Rosenfeld they fulfilled a wish that he had expressed to many of his colleagues and ex-students here in England, Germany, France, and South America, to which he travelled quite regularly during the last fifteen years of his life.

Rosenfeld had wanted to write a book on supervision and had collected an enormous amount of taped material, but, as our colleagues rightly reminded us in their introduction to this book, he died too soon, while still in the process of planning and finalizing, between other works, a kind of book like this one—a book that is, incidentally, quite uncommon in the psychoanalytic literature.

To edit and publish such a book is not an easy task. As I reported from my first interview with Rosenfeld, he claimed in his rather modest and even slightly ironic way that he was not a theoretician of psychoanalysis. By the latter he meant someone who would deliberately abstract from the clinical material in order to build up sometimes even too sophisticated and anodyne theoretical systems, hypotheses, or definitions, or someone who would write about psychoanalysis while ignoring the clinical and unique experience with patients.

Prima facie, therefore, dealing with what Rosenfeld said, wrote, or left unpublished could seem much easier than in other cases. But it is a false impression, because, as this book shows, Rosenfeld had an extremely complex and at times inimitable approach to his work, which, *per se*, is a theoretical position that emerged from close attention to patients' material and is organically rooted, one could say, in his vast and sometimes unique experience with borderline and psychotic cases, spanning more than forty years.

Therefore, Rosenfeld's particular theoretical approach is a combination of his clinical experience and his capacity for—or, one should say, art of—observation and interpretation. He had the gift of an astonishing capacity for identification with psychotic sufferance, defences, and ways of thinking and was able to spot psychotic processes—or "psychotic islands", as he also calls them in a marvellous, detailed clinical vignette of a psychosomatic case reported here in seminar two.

Rosenfeld could remind one of a sort of "browser" of psychotic states who was naturally able to perceive at times, in an almost uncanny way, the most disturbed unconscious areas of his patients. He had a particular capacity to understand the non-verbal, the verbal, and the pre-verbal communications of his patients, particularly through their body language.

Those who worked with him as patients or supervisees or listened to his seminars can, I think, still remember the intensity, the total listening to the material of the patient, which Rosenfeld had developed during his whole career and particularly during his latest years. He was participating with his whole body, at times closing his eyes to better feel and immerse himself even in the intonative pattern of the speech of his patients or in their body movements—in all aspects, as far as possible, of the communications of the patients, as well as those of the analysts during his supervisions with them. I think many can even remember the movements of his arms during his long interpretations, or even the long, flexible fingers of his hands, which together with his amused or extremely focused eyes, seemed bodily to comment on his words. It was as if at times he literally wanted to grasp and put back together, integrating into a whole, the fragmented and often awkward communications of his patients and also of his supervisees. The particular nature of this book allows the reader to experience very vividly this kind of intensity, or at least to get near to it.

What is so unique about this book is its dialogic nature, which grows bit by bit between Rosenfeld and his group of students, through the extremely detailed clinical material, stressing what the patient said and then what the analyst said and also Rosenfeld's comments. This detailed exploration of both the patient's material and the analyst's interpretations was a condition *sine qua non* of working with Rosenfeld, and the examples we find in this book constitute *per se* an extremely rewarding and rare teaching and learning experience.

All this has maintained the spontaneity of a *"parlato"*—a spoken dialogue—which allows us to observe Rosenfeld really at work, with his passion for working so intensively and on the micro-sequences of a session.

Of course, at times one is also tempted to question the inevitably didactic nature of some interventions, reminding one of a master-class given by a great musical interpreter who intervenes and corrects the student performing in front of an audience. Rosenfeld, as it is possible to see even in this book, could be quite cutting and even rather absolutist in his viewpoints concerning what was right and what was wrong, what one should tell or not tell to the patients, and when and how. But on many occasions this was also due to his enormously subtle and quick grasp of the unconscious intentions and problems of the patient, particularly when dealing with acute psychotic anxieties and acting out, where the analyst needs to be acutely aware of what could happen and how to intervene. And the reader can find in this book an extremely illuminating example of all that, when Rosenfeld discusses with his supervisee the case of a manic patient in danger of committing suicide.

There is something else that I think should be pointed out. Particularly in the last fifteen years of his professional life, Rosenfeld became increasingly interested in trying to clarify the difficulties inherent in the psychoanalytic encounter between patient and analyst. An area of research on which he insisted more and more involved the hidden or even not so hidden black spots of an analyst who cannot grasp, understand, or put into words the often extremely subtle communication of the patient, who is at times pointing out those black spots to the analyst in various ways. If this complex process is misunderstood as destructive aggression or if it is only the patient who is blamed for those difficulties, this can lead to difficult impasses, to further traumatizations of the patient—this time of an iatrogenic kind—and to the breaking off of the treatment. Particularly important are Rosenfeld's observations on the use of countertransference by the analyst as a defensive rather than an exploratory tool, which can lead to the typical attitude that can be expressed verbally as: "Look what you do to me, I who am so good and am containing you." This is a dogmatic moralistic consequence of the at times extremely useful technique that focuses on the here-and-now, which nevertheless can become too narrow-minded and obsessive if based only on what could be defined, paraphrasing the famous Cartesian motto, as *"sentio ergo es"*—"I feel it, therefore you are what I feel" in the here-and-now. Rosenfeld emphasizes more than once in this book the necessity to use, in the clinical encounter, reconstructions in addition to constructions.

The reader can find Rosenfeld at his best in those pages where, at times with a great sense of humility speaking about his own difficulties, he points out the multifaceted aspects of the analytic encounter and dialogue. Like a patient "talmudist" confronted with a by-definition living text, he describes at times with an astonishing phenomenological attitude his way of interpreting a dream or trying to enumerate all the questions that came to his mind while listening to the material of the patient and using his capacity to identify both with the patient and with the supervisee as an extremely mobile sounding-line that constantly has to change the direction in which it is to be launched. And the reader should also note Rosenfeld's constant attempts to save the libidinal, creative aspects of the personality of the patient, acknowledging them and differentiating them from the more destructive or self-destructive ones. At times, one can even catch through this dialogue some traces of Rosenfeld's proverbial sense of humour, which, like smilingly touching not only the psychic skin of the listener but what could perhaps be defined as his or her psychic "epithelium", was never too heavy or irritating.

More than once in his seminars, including those he gave abroad, Rosenfeld referred to psychoanalysis as being an art. Well, what should one make of a statement like that, particularly today, when the neo-positivistic era in psychoanalysis does not, in the name of empirical research and scientific proof, seem to allow a great deal or room for such an attitude? Of course, it is up to the reader to decide.

In reading and studying those seminars, I was reminded of what W. Benjamin—perhaps the greatest interpreter of the cultural Diaspora of the German Jews of Rosenfeld's generation—once said about poets and poetry: confronted with a genuine poet, one can never use the past tense in speaking about him or her or about his or her work—one always has to use the present tense. *Mutatis mutandis*, this is true of every genuine creative work in all other fields of human activity. Of course, it is difficult to anticipate how many readers will use the present tense in speaking about Rosenfeld and his work after having read this book! One fact seems to me indisputable, nevertheless. Nearly twenty years have passed since Rosenfeld gave those seminars and supervisions in Milan. They seem to have preserved a sort of intact pristine freshness of something still extremely alive and usable even today. I personally am persuaded that the dialogue we become part of in this book will continue for many years, both in the mind and in the clinical practice and experience of many readers.

PREFACE TO THE ITALIAN EDITION

This publication, part of the *Quaderni del Centro Milanese di Psicoanalisi* series, contains transcripts of a number of theoretical works and clinical supervisions, taken from the seminars that Dr Herbert Rosenfeld gave in Milan and Rome between 1978 and 1985. This material presents only a small amount of what the English analyst covered during his regular visits to Italy, invited by a group of Società di Psicoanalisi Italiani members who were keen to find out more about his thinking and method of working with patients.

During this period, a number of other English analysts gave clinical and theoretical seminars in Rome and Milan: of these, I wish to recall Eric Brenman, Martha Harris, Betty Joseph, Donald Meltzer, and Irma Pick. Analysts of my generation owe a large part of our psychoanalytic training and identity to these colleagues.

Herbert Rosenfeld made an enormously significant contribution to clinical and theoretical psychoanalysis.

Forced to emigrate to London immediately before the Second World War to escape racist laws, as a very young man Rosenfeld came into contact with the thought of Melanie Klein at the Tavistock Clinic, where he began working with psychotic patients.

Analysis with Melanie Klein and the reading of her works, especially "Notes on Some Schizoid Mechanisms" (1946), enabled him
to undertake a sequence of pioneering clinical and theoretical
studies on the treatment of psychotic patients. These have remained a model of analytic care and rigour. At the same time,
Hanna Segal (1956, 1983) and W. R. Bion (1954, 1956) were producing further significant contributions on psychosis.

Rosenfeld firmly believed in the possibility of entering into
contact with psychotic patients by using transference and interpretations of the content of unconscious feelings and fantasies, the
understanding of which promoted insight. His work during this
time, much of which appears in his book *Psychotic States* (1965),
makes use of Melanie Klein's theoretical framework regarding
persecutory anxiety, projective identification, the impossibility
of splitting, and the resulting confusion between destructive and
libidinal impulses, primary envy, and the archaic and persecutory
superego.

Rosenfeld made a further significant contribution to psychoanalysis with his research into the psychopathology of narcissism,
most broadly dealt with in his work "A Clinical Approach to the
Psychoanalytic Theory of the Life and Death Instincts: An Investigation into the Aggressive Aspects of Narcissism" (1971). Further
exploring the difference between libidinal and destructive narcissism, Rosenfeld demonstrates that in seriously disturbed patients
treated analytically it is possible to uncover a particularly malignant form of narcissism, which coincides with a very powerful
psychotic organization that prevents the libidinal part of the self
from coming into contact with relations and objects capable of
helping. He postulates that this psychopathological organization,
connoted as destructive narcissism, appears during treatment of
patients who assert their superiority over the analyst, attempting
to devastate the analyst's work as well as the analyst's ability to
comprehend and obtain gratification from the relationship.

Rosenfeld continued to pursue this theoretical insight of his,
though in later works (as may be seen in the book *Impasse and
Interpretations*, 1987) he toned down its significance and blended it
with an interpretative approach.

A further contribution equally worthy of note concerns his concept of narcissism and a clear differentiation between libidinal

and destructive narcissism. The former is an idealization of the self through an omnipotent projective identification with good and protective objects; the latter, on the contrary, derives from idealization of destructive parts of the self. In the realm of post-Kleinian psychoanalysis, Rosenfeld and Segal take opposing stances on this point: for Segal, narcissism is always a defensive structure against envy, a distortion of a sense of reality, the perception of truth and of feelings of dependency functional for development. Rosenfeld, however, even in his late works, insists on the utility of maintaining and valuing idealization of the analytic couple as a significant element in the handling of certain infantile or passionate transference.

* * *

The emergence of a new interest, a new phase in Rosenfeld's theoretical approach and clinical practice, evident to those listening to his Italian seminars, dates from the last part of his life.

In my opinion, this change commenced with the paper he presented at the Jerusalem Congress, which was published in the *International Journal of Psycho-Analysis* in 1978, entitled "Notes on the Psychopathology and Psychoanalytic Treatment of Some Borderline Patients". Working from the premise that there are some borderline patients whose disturbances are dependent on external rather than internal factors, to the extent that normal development of primary anxieties has been impeded, Rosenfeld tackles the theoretical and clinical issue of the consequences of the original trauma on the patient's psychopathological structure, and how these factors re-emerge during the course of psychoanalytic treatment. Traumatized patients are dominated by confusional anxieties and pathological splitting processes rather than by destructive narcissism. Because of the presence of a highly sadistic superego, with these patients it is not possible to formulate interpretations that take into account aggressive or destructive aspects. In the final analysis, this superego is said to be responsible for the formation of a transference psychosis in which the patient develops a delirious experience centred upon the analyst. From this moment onwards, Rosenfeld considers transference psychosis—and, in less seriously disturbed patients, an impasse or negative therapeutic reaction—as consequences not of the patient's aggressiveness, but of repeated and systematic misunderstandings in communications by the analyst.

During his visits to Italy, Rosenfeld covered a number of topics that he was developing in great depth: infantile trauma, the importance of the patient's history in the analytic process, the distortions of analytic communication that lead to impasse. During his seminars, I recall his insistence on the importance of the ever-modifiable history—or, rather, hypotheses—that the analyst must formulate on the patient's past, on how the patient is equipped to tackle conflicts, and on how the patient was deprived of fundamental relationships. This is all for the purpose of structuring a specific analytic setting, functional for that given patient. Hypotheses on the past assist in comprehending the nature of the impasse, when it occurs, and in emerging from collusive relations in which the past is recontextualized in transference and countertransference unbeknownst to both participants. Rosenfeld insisted a great deal that at certain times the here-and-now could only be understood if one bore in mind how the past could continue to exert its influence. He ascribed a similar importance to patient–analyst interaction, considered as a potential element for development of the therapy. Regardless of how serious their condition, patients always communicate: not just their own anxieties in the relationship with the analyst, but also their observations on the analyst's mental state and the analyst's abilities and failures. Analysts should listen carefully, make the most of these remarks, and differentiate them from aggressive attacks.

Rosenfeld demonstrated to us how one may fully understand the patient by bringing together two fundamental elements: listening to emotional forms of communication, and being attentive to countertransference. He brought these elements together in a very coherent, persuasive, and never abusive theory of development and object relations.

Colleagues of mine who listened to Rosenfeld over the years still retain a vivid memory of how deeply he could listen, and of his truly unique ability to shift coherently between the clinical and theoretical levels, while keeping them united.

He had an exceptional capacity for work; even when his listeners were tired, Rosenfeld still wanted to go on working, talking, and debating. A number of his Italian seminars were collected in his final book, published posthumously, *Impasse and Interpretations: Therapeutic and Anti-Therapeutic Factors in the Psychoanalytic Treatment of Psychotic, Borderline and Neurotic Patients* (1987).

The present book contains four hitherto unpublished theoretical seminars. We have still further recordings of supervisions which could not be included because of space constraints. All of these works, particularly when compared with his output during the early part of his scientific activities, demonstrate how Rosenfeld continually enriched his approach of listening and working analytically, and how his theoretical position became increasingly valuable.

During the 1980s, post-Kleinian psychoanalysis was in great ferment, and Rosenfeld's thought was influenced and enriched by other significant ideas from many colleagues who worked alongside him, especially Bion. It is my belief that during this period a veritable revolution took place in methods of working with patients, a revolution that continues to stimulate us to this day. I believe that the long shadow of that great ferment of ideas continues to be cast, and that many of these insights still need to be fully developed. It is my hope that this book, illustrating the fruitfulness and relevance of the thought of one of the most creative minds, may help to take us more deeply into the difficult issues raised by the analytic comprehension of seriously disturbed patients, stimulating us further to research, explore, and develop.

At a time when psychoanalysis appears to be in danger of losing its own identity, with some practitioners attracted by the sirens of intersubjectivism and hermeneutic relativism, Rosenfeld's work stands as a salutary anchor for our specific difference, for the originality of our clinical and theoretical approach.

I wish to thank and extend my gratitude to my colleagues Paola Capozzi, Edgardo Caverzasi, Angela Galli, Patrizia Gammaro Moroni, Ronny Jaffé, and Michele Stuflesser, who have worked with me to produce this Centro Milanese di Psicoanalisi publication dedicated to Herbert Rosenfeld.

A final, heartfelt thank you to the colleagues who have granted permission for the use of material presented during the seminars.

Franco De Masi

INTRODUCTION

The purpose of our work group is to investigate and disseminate knowledge about Herbert Rosenfeld's thought, as expressed and defined during seminars he gave in Milan and Rome.

It is common knowledge that Rosenfeld dedicated his working life to the understanding and treatment of borderline narcissist or psychotic patients so difficult that in the past—and, indeed, often today—they have been considered untreatable with psychoanalytic instruments.

The rise of the neurosciences, which would appear to rule out a psychoanalytic approach to serious pathologies, makes this issue of great relevance; given the growing demand for analytic assistance by patients who at times have recourse to symptomatic therapies of a pharmacological nature, psychoanalysts are increasingly involved in this field.

One of the problems that has fed the crisis imputed to psychoanalysis could find a solution in further theoretical development that would tailor an approach to this type of patient. Rosenfeld is indeed a forerunner of this approach.

During the initial process of transcribing Rosenfeld's seminars we have endeavoured to maintain his colloquial and narrative style in order to convey his vivid and lively way of communicating. The text should be considered akin to a spoken text, like a conversation in which we are a participant, prompting questions, raising doubts, and undermining taken-for-granted certainties.

We have attempted to convey the emotion so many of us felt on hearing Rosenfeld's voice, listening to the comments and questions that analytic material prompted in him. Our goal is to stimulate interest in the methods with which he sought the most appropriate interpretative hypotheses, applying the experience of a man capable of uniting empathetic listening with scientific rigour and psychoanalytic knowledge.

In order not to crystallize an approach in evolution, dense with theoretical implications and technical comment, we do no more here than underline a number of points that Rosenfeld returned to on several occasions during his theoretical and clinical seminars.

Rosenfeld adduces the impasse or failure of some analyses to problems of communication and misunderstanding between patient and analyst. Striving to avoid or overcome these difficulties, he often emphasized that an analyst needs to listen to the patient with an open mind, free of prejudice, with the intention of seeking comprehension and scientific truth, which must compulsorily take place through awareness of an initial not-knowing.

It follows that it is necessary to listen attentively to all of the patient's forms of communication, verbal and non-verbal. This encompasses not just tone of voice or gestures, but also the projection of strong emotions. Projective identification strongly influences the analyst, who must be in a position, via use of his/her imagination, to understand his/her participation in this process and to differentiate between his/her own feelings and the feelings projected onto him/her by the patient.

Rosenfeld emphasizes that often the patient communicates his/her perception of the mental workings of the analyst when the analyst unconsciously refuses to accept and contain an emotion from the patient that is too intense, violent, or laden with anxiety.

Fundamentally, the patient's history must be retained in the background as an interpretative hypothesis, held in reserve and drawn upon when it may be tolerated by the patient. Connecting this with what is actually going on in the analytic situation helps us to understand what in the analytic relationship may be rejected, forgotten, omitted, or misunderstood.

The importance of the patient's history and past brings us to Rosenfeld's final theoretical formulation regarding the importance of traumatic experiences in serious pathologies, understood not just as external events but above all as a damaged or wholly insufficient maternal containment—that is to say, a lack of the function necessary for developing normal capacity for thought and mental functioning.

A lack of primary containment sets off violent anxieties that can only be tackled using old, evacuative defences, such as denial, splitting, and projection. This leads to formation of splits and separated parts of the self. Psychotic parts of the self may hinder, invade, or block mental functioning or may remain enucleated as "psychotic islands" which often house psychosomatic illnesses.

In all such cases the analyst must provide the patient with the missing or damaged containment. This entails putting up with the establishment of transference psychosis, which is sometimes necessary to reach the patient. The analyst may therefore "flow into" the patient, blend with the patient, in order to be in a position to withdraw in such a way as to understand what is happening, and then offer to the patient this comprehension.

A vast range of methods can lead to psychoanalytic insight between patient and analyst. Rosenfeld generously illustrates these methods during the course of his seminars.

One of the methods that should characterize the approach to serious pathologies is constantly to maintain the ability to receive patient communications with a strong feeling of empathy. This concept is far removed from its Kohutianesque meaning, which foresees the creation of a communicative environment which can take on elements of a contrived ability to help repair a traumatic flaw in the self.

Rosenfeld does not have in mind a child patient who seeks from the analyst a response empathetically harmonious with any narcissism wounded at too early a stage; on the contrary, he ascribes to the patient a competence in communication which requires from the analyst a well-considered and complex method of listening, an ability that is always placed under a strong dialectic tension. The empathy Rosenfeld propounds is totally different from complaisance, even complaisance when used for a salutary purpose; it derives from what we may term a deep feeling of sharing and solidarity with the patient, with the ways the patient communicates his/her own struggle to emerge from the illness and move on. The analyst should feel internally enriched by the patient; it is equally important for the analyst to communicate to the patient not just the full understanding of his/her point of view, but also the extent of the patient's contributions during moments of evolution and progress. Lack of acknowledgement of moments of progress and the lack of acknowledgement of the patient's con-tribution are one of the causes of impasse and negative therapeutic reactions.

If projective identifications are not returned appropriately, the result is rage and envy, the consequences of relational failure. It is thus important to respect and engage with the forms of communi-cation with which the patient chooses to enter into relations with the analyst; secret, allusive, and metaphorical language must be picked up on by the analyst's intuitive powers and find resonance in his/her imagination. It is also important to seize upon and make use of infantile transference, an ensemble of intense and primitive emotions which must be constantly kept alive in order to allow development. Through communications and passionate feelings that may be perceived as disturbed, a child whose vital emotions are repressed comes back to life in the analytic relationship.

In his seminars, Rosenfeld constantly refers to defences that cannot be considered only as a rejection of relationship, but, on the contrary, provide a means for survival. These defences, he says, may not be modified or transformed until the patient is in a posi-tion to equip him/herself in a more effective manner.

After his death, a number of British analysts ventured that Rosenfeld's later theoretical and clinical contributions seemed to be coloured by optimism. For those of us who heard him when he came to Italy, and who are now engaged in this work, it seems that the most striking thing about Rosenfeld was his focus on new, continuous developments in psychoanalysis, allied with his com-plete faith in the tool of analysis. It is extraordinary to see this in an older person, a man who is seemingly approaching the end of his career. But enthusiasm is not exactly the same as optimism, and it should be said that Rosenfeld still had the same enthusiasm as Freud when he was working on his very first clinical cases.

This is but one more reason why Rosenfeld's death, after a long and successful career, seems to have come before its time.

Paola Capozzi, Edgardo Caverzasi, Franco De Masi,
Angela Galli, Patrizia Gammaro Moroni,
Ronny Jaffé, & Michele Stuflesser

PART I

THEORETICAL SEMINARS

Psychotic transference diagnosis and treatment issues in the analysis of a psychotic adolescent

I have selected the case of a 16-year-old psychotic adolescent to cast light on certain aspects of psychotic transference which often remain concealed and therefore insufficiently diagnosed and interpreted in the analysis of psychotic patients. This not only slows down the progress of treatment, it can produce an acute psychotic situation inasmuch as the concealed and split psychotic parts escape control and overpower the non-psychotic elements in the patient's personality.

The therapist who presented the patient in a seminar was very keen to speak with me about this; the patient's state had suddenly deteriorated after three and a half years of analysis and after both the analyst and the supervisor thought the patient had improved considerably.

It suddenly became clear that the patient was rapidly producing a schizophrenic situation. This was a real blow to the analyst, and without doubt, to the supervisor as well. Given that the analyst was not in a position to tackle the intense negative transference that had emerged, a transference which did not respond to any interpretation, it was necessary to terminate the analysis.

Nevertheless, the analyst continued to be very interested in the patient and was keen to find out if I could somehow explain what had gone wrong with the treatment.

In the analysis of psychotic patients one expects psychotic transference to develop sooner or later, and when this happens it should be diagnosed very rapidly. Often signs of either positive or negative psychotic transference appear early on in therapy, but usually the patient attempts to suppress and conceal the most destructive and violent aspects of his psychosis; it is nonetheless essential as soon as possible to reach the emotions and fantasies connected with the split part of the self, to stop the non-psychotic parts from being overpowered later on by an acute and sometimes delirious psychotic attack.

I do not intend to spend much time on details of the analysis, which had been conducted with skill, sensitivity, and empathetic and affectionate comprehension. Rather, I shall focus on the more significant aspects of the concealed psychotic transference, which progressively became more and more intense until it got completely out of hand, precisely because it had not been recognized and interpreted by the therapist. Another important factor in the analysis was that the patient openly displayed significant aspects of a strong negative transference accompanied by very powerful destructive and sadistic feelings. This, however, concealed the fact that his dangerously destructive aspects were highly split and that there had been an attempt not to reveal them—something in which the analyst was unconsciously colluding. It was very clear from the clinical material, and it is precisely this that I will attempt to demonstrate, that the above factors were responsible for the malignant evolution of the psychosis that took place after the patient had clearly made considerable progress under analysis.

The patient—Bernard, as he is called—is an elder son, with a sister who is four years younger. His American parents went to live in France a year before he was born. His father, a writer and journalist, travels a lot on business and is often away, sometimes for a couple of months at a time. His mother, a rather fragile and infantile woman, does not work. Bernard had previously gone for a consultation with an older psychoanalyst. Bernard says that he came to the clinic because he is unhappy, does not like himself, and feels that he is bad. He would like to purify the world, and he would like to be helped in this. The future frightens him; he is scared of becoming poor and not coping. He fears that he is stupid and that his sister is intelligent. He thinks that the world is mean and nasty to him. One day he leaves a note for his parents: "I hate myself—destroy me."

He imagines that his parents are going to abandon him; he has hallucinations in which he hears them saying that they are going to abandon him. Bernard says he is very jealous of his sister, but from his mother it is learned that he has never done anything mean to her. He is afraid of cataclysms, and he dreams that he has lost his bearings. On two occasions he draws maps because he likes geography, but then he makes a kind of completely shapeless scribble which he calls the infinite and the eternal. He has a nightmare in which *he is attacked by a swarm of bees while his mother tries to protect him.*

The conclusion of this consultation is that the boy, aged 11 years at the time, is suffering from depression; also, there is still the problem of an infantile psychosis. It is decided to commence therapy; a psychotherapist is selected for him, to see him three times a week, with the supervision of an older analyst.

The psychotherapist notes that he met the parents together once, and that he agreed that they could meet the supervisor, as they were requesting. According to his report:

"The father struck me as an intellectual, a man rather detached from reality. He is a long way from understanding the seriousness of his son's condition: for him, Bernard's problems are down to bilingualism; he considers him extremely intelligent and sometimes encourages him to take part in political discussions with his colleagues. But father and son do not get on well, and the father seems worried, perhaps even hurt and unhappy about this. The mother is young-looking and fragile. She expresses herself with great difficulty in French and starts by talking of the problems that arose after Bernard was born: she acutely felt her inability to speak the language, and the lack of friends and relatives around her was extremely disturbing. She was very anxious and completely disoriented when she left the clinic. She did not know how to look after the child: she looked up books on the topic and fortunately received affectionate help from an American neighbour of hers, a woman of Greek origins.

Her mother had planned to come and stay with her for a few months around the time of the boy's birth, but she had to cancel the trip due to the unexpected death of a relative. The woman admires her son and protects him a lot."

In a later meeting, the therapist met Bernard:

"Unlike his parents, he has no accent and expresses himself perfectly in French. He speaks in an unstoppable flood of words, listing all his symptoms, most of which are of an obsessive nature. Every day he bangs his head against a ruler to punish himself. Before crossing the road, he has to count to 12. There are also worrying rituals to avoid poor marks at school, which is one of the main dramas in his life at this time. He is very unhappy and he cries a lot; despite his intelligence, he is not doing well in his studies because he is so disorganized. He sits down and writes political tracts and short stories; he is seeking a style and closely studying his personality; he thinks that therapy might be a rather quick process, because he knows himself so well. Nevertheless, he finds it very tough to fix times for the sessions. My unyielding attitude is of considerable relief to him. I am struck by Bernard's intelligence and also by his physical restlessness, as well as his need to rationalize everything. One perceives a thousand different things jostling around inside him, a thousand things he desperately tries to control and dominate through a considerable flow of words, which, however, leave little room for a real exchange."

Observations on the diagnostic interview

It is clear from this account that the mother clearly understands, following the birth of her son, that she does not feel capable of providing him with any security in the initial part of his life. She feels hopelessly lost; she does not know the local language and is overwhelmed by anxiety. His very mother, therefore, feels like a little girl, a little girl abandoned by her own mother who had promised to come and help but could not keep her promise. It really seems that the mother felt that she and her newborn baby were two lost children, until the friendly neighbour came to give them a little help. The child's birth is obviously very traumatic for the mother, and, we may suppose, for the son too. In this diagnostic interview the patient expresses a fear of being completely lacking in organization, a situation he defines as infinity-eternity. He also recounts the dream that is rather common in psychotic patients *of being attacked by a swarm of bees, while his mother tries to protect him.*

From these observations one may conclude that the patient is conscious of infantile psychotic anxieties, occurring very early in his personality, and he does not know how to handle them.

Continuation of the therapist's account

Bernard says that he has come because there is no alternative, but in reality he finds it hard to accept asking anybody for help. In fact, he needs somebody. His refusal to recognize or to experience a dependent relationship or simply his need for help was practically constant throughout therapy. "It really is too humiliating and degrading," he says. During the positive phase of treating this patient, there is evidence of a psychoanalytic process under way. Nevertheless, the therapist never has the feeling that real internalization takes place. There is still a major risk of the patient's personality disintegrating; this is confirmed three and a half years later when therapy is broken off. The therapist divides the therapy into four phases. The first lasts roughly a year and a half. There is an atmosphere of violence in the relationship; for the patient, the sessions are a place for expressing his "craziness"—he often says, to reassure the therapist, "Don't worry, I don't act as crazy as this out there, but in here I can explode." For example, he confides that it is his opinion that every fruit has its own personality, an idea to which he subscribes completely. Fruits are actors in his phantasy world: kiwis are like contemptible, sadistic Chinese—they fascinate and scare him; they gang up to attack pineapples, which are weak creatures.

"One day he turns up with a kiwi and asks me to touch it so that I can feel its slightly hairy skin. He feels this need. For me, it is as if I had agreed to touch him. During the sessions he is extremely agitated; he laughs, grimaces, throws chalk and even his school-bag up into the air. On more than one occasion I am forced to protect myself from projectiles. He cannot keep himself under control and he knows it, so he says sorry. He attacks me a great deal with words too.

"He displays a significant paranoid element, and this remains constant. Sometimes even the most positive moments are interpolated with phrases such as, 'What do you want from me? I don't want to come any more.' He feels attacked, threatened, he asks what I do with what he tells me. He thinks I am studying him, examining him to write a book or tell my supervisor. He himself constructs a set of tests to assess his parents and his sister's intelligence, something he considers to be great fun. He hardly ever speaks about his real life. On the contrary, he invents imaginary countries peopled by extra-terrestrial monsters with hooks for limbs."

Discussion

First, I would like to discuss the structure of the patient's personality: intellectually he is capable of understanding that he needs to be treated, and yet this need provokes considerable resentment within him. It therefore becomes difficult for him to feel that he must be treated and that he must seek help from somebody. The need to be treated is perceived as being too humiliating and degrading; this narcissistic denial of his need to be treated combines with an attitude of strong paranoid rejection of the analyst, which is expressed in the following manner: "What do you want from me? I don't want to come any more." This attitude remains unchanged and is manifestly not analysed at any time during treatment. The patient feels not only not accepted, but also mistreated and exploited by the analyst, who is described as a totally narcissistic personality treating him only for her own ends. It seems possible to link with the projection of his narcissistic organization onto the analyst the fact that the patient feels completely in the hands of a therapist exclusively interested in herself: this is an aspect of the psychotic narcissistic transference. It appears to be vital in this situation to bring more to the surface the patient's fantasies of omnipotent self-sufficiency, which conceal the infantile structure of a very small and omnipotent child who does not need his mother, and allow him to delude himself into thinking that he can get by on his own perfectly well.

Bernard wishes to prove to himself that he was born without any particular feeling, or difficulty, and to be able to face life without finding himself in the humiliating situation of acknowledging that as a baby and as a boy he needed a mother, and that he has had to face the jealousy deriving from sharing her with another baby, his younger sister.

It is very important to tell such an intelligent boy that it is the voice of his omnipotence within that prompts him to believe that a little baby can do without its mother and be independent and mature. This is obviously an illusion. But if the boy insists on believing what this voice is telling him, he continuously treats himself as being stupid. This is the reason why he feels stupid and why he is concerned with stupidity. It is essential, it follows, to help the boy work through the feeling of stupidity that comes from the absolutely unrealistic claims of his omnipotence. The healthy part of him knows it is unwise to continually follow the suggestions of omnipotence; it is very stupid to do so. Yet Bernard is not strong enough to oppose these continual stupid suggestions. Naturally, if a part of the patient is convinced of the truth of his omnipotent self and what it suggests to him, another part of him understands that it is all evil folly; it is inevitable that great confusion results, sometimes even a total mess, with the result that he feels that he can never know the truth.

Usually, psychotic patients such as this boy feel enormous relief when they begin to understand that there is a conflict between this omnipotent and often completely mad part (which says: "I do not want to be treated, I am perfectly fine and independent.") and the part that understands that this is madness and that he must learn to stand up to this madness. When, during the course of analysis, he begins to understand this difficulty, at first the patient can admit that there is at least a little truth in what has been pointed out, and he can start to be more honest about this point and acknowledge to himself, not to mention to the analyst, that he is in difficulty with this omnipotent part of himself. Later on, he may recognize that there is no point in continuing to pretend that his omnipotence is always right, as the analyst knows what is going on.

Naturally, this comes a great relief because at this point Bernard wishes to be controlled by the analyst and, if the analyst is helping him with what he knows, he begins to feel that he becomes less stupid and can think with greater clarity. This evolution in the transference relationship is of prime importance because the boy becomes less diffident, much more inclined to listen to the analyst; what emerges is a patient who truly wants to collaborate with the analyst.

It is also important to understand that the humiliation and degradation that are crushing the patient derive essentially from the part of him that is suffering the delirium of omnipotence, that tells him he knows everything and can do everything and therefore does not need to depend on anyone. This is why the omnipotent part of the patient feels humiliated and insulted by everything—situations and people alike—and contradicts his omnipotent assertion that he has always been able to look after himself since his earliest infant days. This part of the patient does not know what it means to learn or take something inside oneself for the purpose of growing. The omnipotence stands in the way of a process of introjection, which would weaken the self-sufficiency thesis. Therefore, a patient dominated by an omnipotent self is not capable of introjection. In describing how analysis proceeds, the analyst shows understanding that the patient is not capable of introjection, but perhaps does not understand the root of this problem, which only becomes clear when the strength of the omnipotent narcissistic structure begins to decline as a result of detailed analysis. The omnipotent structure is also responsible for constructing a false self, given that it has nothing to do with the real process of growth, which takes place when a child grows thanks to a relationship of dependency with an understanding and sensitive mother. Humiliation, degradation, and the idea of going back to infancy also crop up when the narcissistic omnipotence is projected onto the analyst and the patient feels that the dependent and healthy part of himself is incessantly denigrated by the omnipotent parts of his self, which have taken the place of the analyst. But there is also a chance that a real omnipotent adult has produced the same effect on the patient. Naturally, it is very important to distinguish between the patient's own omnipotence, and the omnipotence of past and present figures, just as it is essential for the analyst not to feel omnipotent and not to act in an omnipotent manner. This is not, however, the case here. It would obviously be silly of the analyst to address an omnipotent patient, who in reality is only an omnipotent child, as if he were an adult: this would only greatly augment his omnipotence. But the omnipotent self cannot be ignored—it too has the right to be helped in analysis, although so very easily it can feel wounded and rejected. It is therefore important, as early as possible, to make the patient aware of the struggle between the part of himself that is rather infantile, closer to the conscious, more inclined to dependency, more realistic, and, therefore, healthy and the omnipotent psychotic aspects of his personality.

If, in the analyst's position, you feel that all of the different elements of the patient tend to establish a relationship with you, then you can show this to him, and little by little he will feel more secure and better accepted. When the omnipotent part of the patient says to the analyst, "I do not want to be treated," a possible answer is, "Probably you feel you don't need to be here, you feel that you know everything and want to stay as you are. But I have noticed that another part of you feels differently; it is this part that perhaps wants something from me, and we must see if it feels free to speak to me."

It cannot be said that there are hard and fast rules for practically handling this kind of situation, but the analyst should grasp every opportunity to maintain a balance. I'd like to remind you that when the patient said he wasn't going to come any more, and expressed the idea that the analyst was studying him and perhaps was going to write a book about him, he was working out a set of tests to measure the intelligence of his parents and sister, something he enjoyed enormously. I consider this to be an absolutely certain indication of the fact that he was continually measuring the analyst's intelligence and the analyst's ability to understand, using a secret method; this enabled him to feel greatly superior to the analyst and seemed to make her ridiculous. But I am also certain that he was afraid that the analyst would notice and take retaliatory measures. It would have been very important to interpret this situation, for these omnipotent fantasies encompass an intrusion into the analyst for the purpose of belittling her and looking down on her; on the other hand, there is a great fear of talking to the analyst about real flaws, which he may have noted in her way of proceeding. Naturally, many elements of the transference situation were not sufficiently clarified by the analyst.

Continuation of the analyst's exposition

The analyst continues:

"In the last session before the holidays the patient wants to break everything, for example the telephone-socket connector; he imagines that he is in a satellite which is bombing and destroying galaxies, represented by the walls and ceiling. I tell him that the room represents me and my body, which he prefers to destroy, destroying both of us, rather than tolerating a separation, even if it is a temporary one. In spite of the extreme violence of certain sessions, I am never afraid, nor do I feel that the situation is getting out of hand. The following winter continues much as before. Bernard is fascinated by dates and numbers, which often act as a sign. He has invented a secret language, and he sometimes writes words or sentences on the blackboard which I have to guess, just like a mother who has to intuit the language of her little baby, as I tell him. He spends much of his time wandering the streets of Paris, attracted by the chaotic districts where there is a strange atmosphere of disorder that provokes a sensation of fear in him. He says that some of these Paris streets are good, others are evil and alarming. This topic soon becomes omnipresent; at the same time he asks me where I'm from, who I am, where I live and what my origins are. He looks up my name in various directory books."

Unlike before, he attends regularly, no longer just turning up for the last five minutes of the session merely to check that I am there. One day, wishing to depict himself, he draws geometric shapes in place of a human body. When I point this out to him, he explodes, screaming that he does not have a body, that he rejects it and finds it horrible. Nevertheless, some time after this, with great unease he tells me of a childhood memory he hates and rejects:

when he was 1, 2, or 3 years old, he soiled his trousers, a long way from home. His mother was upset and did not know what to do, so he had to stay in that state for a long time. He comes to the next session with a record that he insists I listen to. It is a sequence of groans, sounds of retching, 'a gross thing', as he defines it. After he turns the volume up, he thinks I must be nauseated by the noise, which he really likes but which also worries him. This moment, however, between the two of us, is all a put-on: he wants a real relationship, a friendship, but feels that I do not take him seriously. I am sincerely struck that despite the therapeutic relationship, he cannot imagine or expect that I could have really positive feelings towards him. I feel that this lack of faith undermines the progress of the therapy. He says he has had enough and, for what it's worth, wants to finish up within the next few months because he can't go on like this for the rest of his life; he wonders, from a crime-and-punishment point of view, what would happen—i.e. whether or not he would be charged—if he killed me."

Observations and comments

From this material it clearly emerges that the patient does not usually have difficulty in expressing very violent, aggressive, and sometimes even sadistic feelings towards the therapist. She states that she has not been scared by his violence at all and has never felt that the situation is getting out of her control. But I cannot be certain what she has truly felt up to now regarding such violent sentiments. I understand that she thought that the violence focused on destroying the ceiling and walls of his home before the holidays was connected with the patient's inability to stand any separation, to the point of destroying himself and her rather than tolerating even a temporary separation. But the patient imagines himself in a satellite that is bombing and destroying a galaxy, the universe.

He certainly wants to impress her with his powers and hopes to entertain rather than destroy her with these fantasies. Even when he insists on saying that he is crazy, inasmuch as he is so aggressive towards her, he is attempting to excite her and arouse her interest in him. Should we therefore be surprised that he asks her what she intends to do with the magnificent and exciting material he has given her?

Isn't he a more interesting and exciting patient when he expresses himself more violently than her other patients? I think he feels disappointed because she does not openly acknowledge the excitement she gets from his stories; he therefore accuses her of studying him purely to become famous by writing a book about him, or telling her supervisor all about his crazy fantasies in order to improve her standing; not surprisingly, this makes him very jealous. I do not regard the violent fantasies as really where the craziness is. Many of them are aimed at making himself look important and interesting in her eyes.

I believe that the truly mad part of him is what he conceals, the part that does not want to be treated; this is the very dangerous part of him. When he asks her what she intends to do with his sadistic fantasies, he is probably advancing a criticism because she has colluded in his conviction of analysing his craziness, whereas in fact she was not analysing it. I believe that she was not sufficiently clear about this mistake. Now, in this material the violent and secret attacks are much more evident; but since these have not been interpreted to him, the secret attacks are rapidly getting out of hand. At this point we should recall that it is the psychotic, negative, and secret aspects of the transference that have not been analysed. The patient's secret paranoia surrounding her increases, just as does his fear that she might understand thanks to him; but she does not use what she knows to help him. There really is something in this accusation and suspicion, and this must be interpreted for the patient. When Bernard invents his own secret language and writes on the blackboard, she considers that this is part of the idealized mother–child relationship and that she must guess the same way as a mother does with her baby; but she does not understand that the patient also wants her to find out a terrible, hidden secret—that secret that she describes, immediately after the reference to an "ideal situation", when she says that the patient spends most of his time roaming the streets of Paris, attracted especially by disreputable districts with an odd, chaotic atmosphere that provokes great fear in him. This situation becomes crushing and intrusive, as she tells us; it is connected with a secret and unknown factor associated with the analyst's personality, as the patient continually asks her who she is, where she lives, and where she is from.

It seems at this moment that there is something absolutely frightening and chaotic associated with her that throws him into confusion. She simply interprets that the good aspects of the city are connected to his good aspects, the bad aspects to the fear that she is using him for her own ends. Although I am certain that these interpretations are partially correct, they do not, however, contain the element that it is she, as an analyst, who is secretly exploiting the patient and thereby becomes an increasingly dangerous figure. What is secret and unknown increases the terror he has of her and of her secret purposes. Here lies another very serious error, for she interprets this material as if she knew what it meant. On the basis of what she has said thus far, however, the therapist cannot be in a position to know this. This is much more clearly visible from the way the patient brings this secret material to analysis, material of which she knows nothing. Bernard is worried about this, which could be of enormous use. He attempts to inform her about this problem, a problem that is very worrying. But her interpretations about the material refer simply to a split between his good and bad parts; this turns her into somebody who still does not know, but who omnipotently asserts that she does know. In this way, once more she is colluding with the patient's omnipotent self, which asserts that it knows everything. When he draws himself as a geometrical shape, he attracts attention to something absolutely dead and inhuman regarding his image of his body, and also the image he has of the analyst, whom he believes has transformed into something absolutely deadly and horrible. He explains this after recalling his infantile memory, when he was a couple of years old and defecated in his trousers a long way from home, and his mother did not know what to do, so they remained like this for a long time: this is the situation he is experiencing now with the analyst in the sessions, when he loses control and heaps her with dirty and terribly disgusting material. The patient vividly illustrates this with the horrible noises on the record which he forces her to listen to. He obviously feels that these anal attacks on his mind and his body are very concrete and disgusting; they transform his body by making it seem sterile and unattractive. At this point, the patient feels that the analyst's positive feelings are a simple pretence. But he effectively insists that he wants a real relationship with her, no longer just an analysis, and this is the most urgent problem he has with her. He says that he has had enough and that he wants to finish within the next few months. At the same time, he wonders if he would be charged if he killed her. It would seem likely that at this moment of the analysis a frightening and destroyed image of the analyst has formed, which is therefore dangerous and which arouses strongly criminal feelings in him. This is when the psychosis seems to get out of hand. The patient has made an enormous effort to show her how this terrible image came about, but I think that not even at this moment does the analyst understand what has happened and why.

Continuation of the analyst's account

The end of this first phase is remarkable for a session in which the tenderness of the atmosphere clashes with what has gone before. They are sitting next to one another. He draws his face and describes himself very delicately, but the therapist in fact has the impression that they are both there, leaning over the cot in which he is lying, a baby. The second phase shows development of a negative Oedipus, which seems to bring him greater cohesion. He idealizes the intellectual abilities of the therapist just as he does his father's. He asks her what her father's first name is. He is hurt by not being appreciated, held in low esteem by his father, whom he rarely sees. He is no good at anything, he is useless, weak. He is a symbol of trouble and mishaps. He writes stories about this. He eggs her on: "Go on, go on, work," he says, "Analyse, analyse away." He says he wants to end the therapy because he is fine now, he has some friends, but he doesn't say who, because it is not the therapist's business. She feels that he really is stronger. He has a secret and no longer wants to come to the Saturday session, out of respect for this secret. The problem of his origins torments him; he is of Russian and Polish origin, with a little German blood mixed in too, but the Russians and Germans have always been enemies. He talks about war a lot, he imagines countries with far-Left or far-Right governments, where prisoners are tortured, insulted, and brainwashed. On this topic, he feels that this is what the analyst is doing to him when she wants to make him normal, in the process killing his personality. This is her unavowed goal. Here the therapist feels that the patient is truly persecuted by his ideas, and that she really is wicked. The patient is less than nothing, the lowest of the low, a disgrace and a failure—how could it be otherwise, given that he was a mistake. Though his parents did not marry for this reason, he was their first child, he was a mistake. This is why sex is disgusting and humiliating. "I want to kill feelings, I hate them," he says. He cannot imagine coming out of his mother's body. He twists and squirms as he says it, he sometimes scolds the therapist for her lack of sincerity: "You only care about me for money, and all you are concerned about is holding onto your job." He tells other people that he hopes the therapist will help him in his intellectual achievements.

Discussion

The session in which the patient and the analyst suddenly find themselves sitting side by side in a very tender atmosphere, and the patient slowly begins to realize that a real and affectionate mother–child relationship could exist but could not last long because of the great intensity of his persecutory feelings, clearly demonstrates that he is certain that his violent anal attacks on the mother-analyst have destroyed and transformed her. He feels that he cannot put her back into shape and repair her because there is too much confusion, and the image of the analyst and of the mother seems to change into that of a horrible persecutor. In that particular moment there may still be a chance of saving the situation by going through with him, step by step, what has happened and what has created this terrifying image. So, during this second phase, the patient enacts a split and projects all his bad feelings— including the feeling that the analyst is an idiot who has disappointed him—onto his mother, who becomes an idiot. This makes it possible to continue to idealize the analyst for a little longer, particularly for her intellectual abilities. Now the analyst has become an idealized intelligent father, whom the patient attempts to use, investing her with all his father's good qualities; but the good image of the woman, the mother, seems to have completely vanished by this time. Unfortunately, the overestimation and idealization of the analyst as father leaves the patient rather empty, but this is something we will only see further on. With this split he attempts temporarily to save himself; he manages to look stronger because all of his nastiness and anxiety has been linked to the destroyed image of the mother and his unconscious fear of driving the analyst crazy as a female figure. At times, it seems that there are psychotic attempts to repair her, as he says, "Go on, go on, work, analyse away," but in fact the patient feels extremely dubious that his analyst can still work and function as an analyst.

There are also hints as to how horrified he is at his mother's body and his analyst's body, at what happened inside these bodies; the idea of coming out of this horrible body is completely intolerable to him. He naturally feels terrified that the analyst will not allow him to exist, or have his own personality, and he very explicitly states his conviction that she wants to kill his personality: this is seen to be the analyst's unspoken purpose. He feels awful because he has come out of the analysis with nothing; a disgrace, a failure. This analytic birth seems to be a truly horrible mistake. Even now he feels he is a mistake; after he starts to idealize the analyst as a father, he finds he cannot support this for long, and so once more he returns to the horror of the analytic mishap, of being a failure. In effect, at this point the analyst seems to be completely paralysed: the impression is that she does not know what to do with the material that has emerged—for example, the birth material.

There is no interpretation of the description of the horror of what has happened in his analysis, his mother's body, and the analyst's body. It really does seem that the therapist has totally lost control of what is happening in analysis and, therefore, is clearly anxious and depressed. I believe that it would still have been possible to rescue the analysis at this point, by going back over part of the preceding material which was so significant and vivid. In my opinion, this material clearly shows that the patient was capable of contributing to the comprehension of this problem. It is worth remembering that psychotic patients hide and split the dangers of psychotic processes not out of evil but out of fear. They are terrified that nobody wants to or can understand them. Unfortunately, this happens frequently, not just in the case of the patient we are discussing. Here, for example, the material related so vividly is extremely communicative, regarding his wanderings around Paris, particularly its chaotic districts filled with a strange atmosphere of disorder, filling him with a feeling of fear. When one listens to the patient, it is essential to follow him empathetically, with one's phantasy. One should not be afraid of the patient's desire to take us to this place, which is so frightening for the patient because he fears that it is frightening for us too. Both the analyst and the patient must face the situation if the analysis is to survive. When, soon afterwards, he ceases to draw a human body but instead geometrical shapes, he acknowledges that his body has become intolerable to him. He finds it horrible, it is another horrible place, a horrible and frightening part of town. Soon after this, feeling great unease, he brings the analyst his infantile memory, when he defecated in his trousers, a memory he hates and rejects. Here, he still has faith in her: he brings her his innermost and most disturbed feelings. To start with, the therapist must share his horror of losing control of his mind and his guts; this is the shit his mother is not able to deal with, the situation he is going through once more with her. He vividly illustrates and communicates this point by playing the record, making sure that this horrible anal attack is fully experienced in session. Very clearly, he says that he is afraid that the therapist is nauseated by the noises, because he has done something terrible to her by putting her through this experience; he therefore fears that she will be dragged in, have to be there and feel dirty and crazy with him, and unable to contain the situation. Here, containment means a detailed mental working-out of the meaning of each of these three very vivid situations. Indeed, he fears that these lie at the root of his madness; he does his utmost to bring them out into the open.

Clearly Bernard must have always lived with the horror of this psychotic world, unable to share it with anybody and incapable of tidying it up. At this point, we, and he, would have hoped that this concrete experience was understood. The fear of destroying a good relationship with the analyst and with his mother could then have been tackled, averting a disastrous conclusion. Step by step, he has translated concrete experiences and projected them onto her; this time, into phantasy thoughts and words that could have been recognized and understood to the point that, in the relationship of containment, the poison of the concrete experience could slowly have turned into something less malign. I understand how distressing it must have been for the analyst to tackle the pain of not being able to help this patient; I also believe that it is necessary to examine all the details with great precision in order to learn from the mistakes made here; we all make mistakes, and we all wish to learn.

Conclusion of therapist's account

During this period the patient talks a lot about his father. He brings up memories of a few rare, long walks he took with his father through the city streets: these are among his fondest memories. The analyst notes that his desire to identify himself with his father is very clear. Bernard regrets that he is not like his father was at his age; he would like to be a writer, but he knows he will never reach his father's level because he feels that everything he himself writes is rubbish. At this time, masturbatory feelings and homosexual inclinations emerge. One day a man follows him in the Metro, and he allows himself to be fondled in exchange for ten francs. The analyst realizes that this experience is traumatic for him: indeed, the patient often feels that people are looking at him in the street, that men follow him especially when he is on his way to a session. He continually insists that he wants to be like his father and, when he is 15, meet the woman of his dreams, as had been the case for his father when he was this age. The analyst feels that the patient is in the grip of a conflict that is very hard to handle. Even while defending himself against an intense desire to have homosexual relations, he must also defend himself against the desire or the fear of a closer relationship with a woman by calling upon this homosexual inclination. These anxieties prompt him to smoke hashish with a friend; he also starts to smoke cigarettes during the sessions. He starts to rebuke the analyst, accusing her of being frighteningly possessive like his mother. He also fears that she might push him into having sexual relations, a situation that terrifies him. On occasion he also seems to defend himself against erotic feelings towards the therapist. But more often, at this stage, he strongly insists on his request to finish the therapy. He wants to run his life on his own, he wants to be independent and face reality single-handedly. In therapy, he feels passive, when what he wants to be is active.

When the therapist agrees that they can finish the therapy, after sending him to the supervisor—who felt he was progressing towards a more neurotic type of structure—the patient reacts violently with panic and says, "You're leaving me in the lurch. Now I know you don't care about me, you're sending me to my death." When the parents make a request, the supervisor sees the patient again and finds him extremely disorganized and seemingly well on the way to schizophrenia. He prescribes pharmaceuticals, which Bernard does not take. When the analyst sees him again, she is surprised and upset at how far his condition has deteriorated. Nevertheless, certain things he says reveal his suffering and give her some hope. Bernard bitterly complains about the emptiness he feels; he realizes that he does not really understand what depression and emptiness mean. Faced with his agitation, the therapist simply suggests that they go on; however, following this he skips a large number of sessions. The therapist attempts to interpret the meaning of these absences without much success; the patient comes even less frequently. For the first time, the therapist feels irritated by this behaviour. It seems to her that the patient is attempting to destroy the contact between them. Analysis then becomes so difficult that, in the end, she advises him to quit. She suggests that since Bernard doesn't want to have anything to do with women, he could try analysis with a man. This is how the analysis ends.

Discussion

If we now look at the analyst's concluding remarks, it is clear that the patient is still trying to rescue himself by addressing the father, by wishing that the analyst was the father.

But on his own the father can do very little: how can he be successful, how can she as father be successful when his confusion is so great? Yet Bernard is terribly afraid that if he shows himself to have a greater ability to understand than her, then her frightening possessiveness would make her stand in his way and stop him from succeeding. It therefore seems that we also have the image of an envious therapist who cannot stand him being successful. Once again, understanding this is of great importance. Interpreting this would diminish his castration anxiety, his fear that she will not allow him to be a successful male. This is the problem that prevents him from handling any rivalry with her as a man or as a father. To avoid this difficulty, he withdraws once more and thinks of her as an attractive woman, but in fact he feels completely blocked in analysis, incapable of moving. In effect, he has not been able to bring up this problem of his father with the therapist as father, because he has not been able to undergo the infantile maternal transference necessary for normal development. Bernard fears that she can tell him nothing; he feels so incredibly empty and fears that she does not understand that his depression is, in fact, emptiness, and that this emptiness is completely intolerable. His omnipotence is gone now, and, given that his omnipotent structure was never worked through, he immediately collapses into the chaos of his disorganized infantile state, without being at all prepared for it. I would say that his request to end treatment is, given the circumstances, completely understandable. At a certain point he must have hoped that there was a positive part within, and a relationship upon which he could build something; but, unfortunately, he most probably falls back into his narcissistic organization and psychotic structure.

When the therapist calls a halt to the treatment, he feels lost because he suddenly realizes that he really needs her—though this had been evident for the last twelve months. He realizes that his psychotic narcissistic organization has become weaker. When she leaves, he suddenly ceases to feel omnipotent, he experiences it as being a baby abandoned to death. At the same time his psychosis, which has always tended more towards schizophrenia than depression, comes to the surface. Of course, he knows he needs more help, but at this point he has no faith that anyone can help him. He can more openly acknowledge that he has always wanted to show the analyst that he has always been empty, something that she does not understand. He is acutely aware that depression is not the right word to describe how he feels within. At this point, there is no longer any real contact between patient and analyst; this manifests itself in his absence, which has always been an expression of the omnipotent psychotic parts of him, and which now have prevailed: "I don't want to come and I don't want anything." The analyst attempts to understand the patient's absence, but, obviously enough, the patient might return to analysis if he feels that the analyst really recognizes what has gone wrong and what the problems are. This is an impossible task for the therapist, who herself has a greater need of help to understand what has gone amiss with the treatment.

Many patients who experience a failure in the analytic process do think only of death because they feel as if they have been cast into a terrible position from which there is no escape, a situation in which nobody can help them. It is interesting to note that in the final stages of treatment the patient becomes increasingly angry, and that there is a feeling that he could more clearly reveal what he feels inside. It is my belief that he was afraid of dependence on the analyst; becoming dependent without receiving any help from her: this is completely intolerable and so he wants to end it once and for all. Rightly, the analyst feels that she cannot continue with treatment; given that at this point the supervisor wants to treat the patient with psychodrama, this is what he suggests, and his suggestion is accepted. The patient goes to the psychodrama, though I do not intend here to discuss the value of this for patients of this type. What I am interested in understanding is why the treatment of certain psychotic patients, who basically have a good prognosis, goes wrong, and I am grateful to the analyst who brought us this very enlightening case.

It is always extremely testing to have to work in a sea of details when it is too late to do anything. But there is much we can do in future. It is only by understanding our problems, difficulties, and failures in treating schizophrenia and other psychotic conditions that we can gradually achieve greater successes.

TWO

The relationship
between psychosomatic symptoms
and latent psychotic states

Such has been the boom in literature on psychosomatic illnesses that it is impossible to summarize it, let alone even read everything that has been written on the subject.

A number of authors have attempted to describe specific psychic conflicts or specific character structures for each individual psychosomatic illness (Franz Alexander and Flanders Dunbar). Others, such as Felix Deutsch and Adolph Meyer, posit the existence of strong interactions between body and mind in all psychosomatic conditions. There are also those who highlight that multiple factors underlie psychosomatic illness, including genetic factors, the existence of traumas at an early age, inability to resolve a situation through behaviour, symbolic representation and even psychosis. The ideative level can lead to a direct physiological expression manifested via the autonomous nervous system. In 1964 I hypothesized that mental conflict, especially early confusional conditions (which are particularly intolerable for the infantile ego), tend to be split and projected, evacuated into the body or internal organs, in such a fashion as to cause hypochondria or psychosomatic illness, or sometimes a combination of the two.

Given that there are many factors capable of bringing about a psychosomatic illness, only a detailed analytic inquiry into the specific psychosomatic problem can clear up what has caused the psychosomasis in an individual.

In this seminar I shall attempt to develop the concept that when, for professional reasons, anxieties are touched upon in neurotic patients or people in analysis, these often have what, following Melanie Klein's terminology, we could term the quality of psychotic anxieties. Klein investigated and described in detail the earliest infantile anxieties and the mechanisms of the paranoid-schizoid position and the depressive position. Specifically, she highlighted both the damage to an early ego that has to handle primitive destructive emotions and the early defences erected to avert invasion of the self by the by-products of the destructive impulse (death instinct), a problem that had occupied Freud in his work "Analysis Terminable and Interminable" (1937c).

In our so-called normal patients, we often find "psychotic islands" that are well encapsulated or concealed in psychosomatic symptoms or in other types of symptoms. It is clear that this capsule is created because the psychotic areas are so cleanly split from the psychic self that they are initially completely inaccessible when revealed. Moreover, the psychotic problems about which one does not have knowledge are solidly lodged in the body organs they have penetrated. A damaging influence is spread by the destructive "psychotic island" lurking in the body organs. The penetrating quality of the "psychotic island" is linked to the omnipotent projective identification, which has probably withdrawn inside after an attempt at projection onto an external object. This problem becomes evident in analysis and can therefore be analysed, but only after the "psychotic island" has to some extent moved from the organs and the conflicts have appeared in the transference. At this point, it becomes clear that the patient is using projective identification to communicate and, at the same time, to free himself from his intolerable psychotic problems by projecting them onto the analyst. When the area in which the psychotic anxieties are lodged or encapsulated responds to analytic treatment, we often see an apparent cure, especially when some aspects of the patient's anxieties are made clear; but often the "illness" or "psychotic anxieties" are shifted into an unknown place, and the patient makes sure that this area remains unknown. Should the patient consider himself cured and suspend treatment, given that his symptoms have disappeared, there is most certainly a greater risk that some illness return in future. In my experience, I have been able to verify that psychotic areas or islands are rather common.

* * *

I will be using the clinical material of a young married woman who was in analysis for a depression resulting from repeated miscarriages and a premature birth which resulted in the death of her newborn baby. What I wish to highlight is the existence of a "psychotic island" in this patient's uterus. After a brief clinical summary, I will present dreams and a description of the intense interactions between analyst and patient, in an attempt to trace the development and explosive appearance of the "psychotic island" in the analytic situation, which created a brief transference psychosis. After dislodging the "psychotic island", the patient was in a position to conceive and give birth to a healthy baby. In this case, it was possible to broadly bring the psychotic process to the surface and work it through in the transference situation. In describing the "psychotic island", I also wish to differentiate between the patient's traumatic experiences and her deep-seated fear of parts of herself as genetically unacceptable and deadly, a fear that had been completely immured for much of her life. I also wish to clarify the more or less successful attempt of the analysis to integrate the "psychotic island" into the patient's self.

In this anamnestic case history, I only wish to mention the presence of a younger brother who, from a very young age, had been completely ignored and then, subsequently, strongly protected by the patient.

For many years the patient's mother suffered from a cardiac disease which left her extremely vulnerable. From earliest infancy, the patient experienced her as being very fragile because she was incapable of tolerating aggression and loud noises. The father wanted his children to be top of the class at all costs. My patient had attempted to satisfy him by achieving excellent results, but though she had become the best in the class, she never felt that she had satisfied him and made him happy. It is probable that at home there was unacceptable pressure, which forced the patient to split and project part of her intense desire to be herself and to be able to express herself. As a child, she suffered asthma and eczema.

In discussing her gynaecological problems, she recounted that the gynaecologist thought that there was a physical problem connected with the miscarriages; as well as the probable existence of a physical weakness, the patient was aware of needing my help. She was highly intelligent and extremely skilled in her profession as a researcher. Though appearing to be somewhat rigid and restricted in our preliminary interview, from the very first session she developed strong feelings regarding communication of an experience that had upset her a great deal: in hospital, after the death of her newborn baby, she had felt inconsolable and suddenly had a vivid phantasy of jumping into the breast-pocket of an older and esteemed friend. This experience seemed to illustrate her feelings towards me at that moment, consisting of an almost instantaneous transference. From that moment onwards in analysis, she operated at both an emotional and intellectual level. In this session it was clear that she had consciously identified with her newborn baby and that, aside from the anxiety and depression she felt over the death of her baby, she was also conscious of her fear of feeling repressed, controlled, and put upon by the baby if it had lived.

I would now like to bring together several fragments of this analysis connected with the problems I wish to discuss. The patient did not want to become pregnant again before having worked through at least some of her problems. She had clearly relived paternal rejection at the height of the oedipal phase at the age of 5 years, when her mother was pregnant with her little brother. It clearly emerged that the patient had vowed to avoid situations in which she risked being humiliated by a man, or by her mother and father, who had made her feel that she was only a little girl incapable of making a baby herself.

Gradually, she began to feel better about her father and started to become more confident, and she attempted to fall pregnant again, something that had never been a problem for her; on the contrary, she had complained of becoming pregnant too easily, and hence the previous miscarriages. Nevertheless, despite repeated attempts, and (after) following medical advice, she still did not succeed. My suspicion at that time, given that she had never had infertility problems before this, was that she was suffering a hormonal imbalance. When she saw a specialist, it was found that the endometrium was not growing in such a fashion as to make conception possible. After the clear improvement that came about following her experience of the intense oedipal conflict with her father, I suspected a deeper mental problem.

During this period, the patient had a psychotic, egodystonic, and destructive dream. In this dream *she was sitting on the banks of a lake, watching a man who was swimming. All of a sudden she realized that the man was swigging from a big bottle of whisky: he was trying to drown himself. It was clear to her from the triumphant expression on his face that the man was drinking to make sure his suicide attempt succeeded. She yelled at him to stop drinking, that she was ready to help him, but he kept on drinking, looking at her with an expression of triumph; he began to sink deeper and deeper underwater. In desperation the patient ran to a phone box to summon the emergency services, but she noticed that the telephone wires had been cut and there was nothing she could do. Nevertheless, she felt that in the end somebody would have helped to pull the man out of the water and bring him back to life.* Even though the patient didn't associate anything with the dream, I began to suspect that what was at work was a part of her destructive and self-destructive personality: she was desperate and was seeking my assistance.

Soon afterwards she had a similar dream which was more closely focused and was associated more clearly with her uterus and her fear of not being able to have a child. In the dream, *there was a newborn baby who was so ill that he couldn't be looked after properly and was unable to grow normally. In fact, in the end it was necessary to take the baby into a psychiatric hospital for electroshock treatment. In the dream, the cause of the baby's illness was traced back to the fact that the baby's legs had been bent and squashed in the uterus.* On this occasion, too, the patient had not made any associations. I interpreted her fear of having a serious depressive illness that would fail to respond to analysis, and of her projection of this fear of mental illness onto her uterus. I was unsure about the meaning of the baby's bent legs, apart from the fact that it seemed like a studied, violent detail.

Immediately after this, the patient told me about another dream she had. In the dream *she spent the morning in bed, so her mother-in-law (who lived with her) had to do the household chores. After feeling guilty about staying in bed so late, she got up at midday to give her mother-in-law a hand. Her mother-in-law, however, angrily told her that she was tired and had decided to go off on holiday.* Normally, she and her mother-in-law got on very well. The patient always got up very early, even on weekends; it was her husband who got up late and arrived late at sessions, whereas she was always on time. Her reaction to the dream was extremely particular: although she usually offered many associations herself, she stayed silent after telling me this dream. I attempted to verbalize some of her feelings connected with the dream, dwelling on the contrast between her behaviour in the dream and in real life. After complete silence, I pointed out that that day she had been rather inactive and (unusually for her) non-collaborative with me in the analytic work. I concluded that she was behaving in analysis as she had done in the dream, with the consequent fear that I would get annoyed with her and abandon her. I connected the dream with her fear that I was not capable of tackling her difficulty in conceiving, and that I would behave like a weary mother who is incapable of doing anything for her child. In the next session, she arrived several minutes late and told me that she had almost not made it—she had decided not to come at all. She added that I had behaved in such an incredibly clumsy way in the previous session that it had made her furious. How could I, an analyst, lose my control so badly? She seemed cold and furious rather than outwardly upset.

I had already had an insight that the patient had been behaving far too well up until then; as a result, she was now allowing herself to express part of her aggressive feelings through dreams and behaviour. For my part, I felt no anger whatsoever. On the contrary, the dream had struck me as highly significant. I stressed that, for some reason, the preceding day's dream had become a reality for her today. I understood that she had undergone a temporary transference psychosis. I told her that I understood that she was absolutely certain of the fact that I had been angry and had lost control. She may have forgotten or not heard some of the things I had said to her, so I told them to her again. Given that I knew she had always behaved well in analysis, I told her that at that moment she was obviously convinced she was right and I was wrong, but that we could gradually clear up what was happening. I asked her what led her to believe that her view of things was correct. I felt that at that moment she probably wanted to attack me, make me feel like somebody who has had a miscarriage, but I thought that something specific in the previous session had irritated her, and that she did not want to tell me what it had been. For the next few days she continued to be coldly angry and aggressive towards me, but then gradually she began to loosen up, and she told me that she thought she was rather tense at that time and had probably been mistaken. Only much later did she explain the reasons for her anger. She had not told me that in her dream the sheets had twisted tight around her, so that she felt tied up in the bed, almost as if the bed represented a uterus. Moreover, that day she had felt particularly isolated, she hadn't wanted to go out, and didn't want me to upset her.

During this session, she had had the impression that I was talking as if I wished to intrude on her isolation. This behaviour brought back memories of the dream of the baby whose legs were forcefully bent in the uterus. Indeed, she had acknowledged that in the dream her staying in bed represented isolation in the uterus and refusal to come out. Like the behaviour that was to manifest itself many years later, and which would hinder analytic progress, this intense block, representing a taking of refuge in the uterus, signified a hostile projection of being alive, of becoming a patient dependent and in need of me. This was the issue that she had not wanted to broach.

With hindsight, it seemed to me that, in the weary mother-in-law dream, the central point was the issue of maternal inability to contain her. The transference psychosis demonstrated that she had been helped to act out part of her anger and resentment towards her parents with me, for she had always felt obliged to please them, out of fear of the likely violent rage that would have been set off in her mother if she had expressed the need to be looked after and taken care of, given her mother's inability to do this. However, the transference psychosis had also expressed the fact that deeper anxieties were about to overwhelm her because, blocked in the uterus, she had felt like an intensely destructive self that could not be helped by anybody; this was what she had to keep concealed. With my clumsy insight into the uterus, I had invaded this extremely dangerous area. She feared that I was going to open up an area that I would not be able to contain, because her feelings were too lethal and terrifying.

Expression of this intense fury and resentment brought her relief, she felt less blocked and could speak more freely. She was stunned that I had not responded to her communication of intense hostility with anger and argument. Several months later, however, she recounted a dream that had upset her a great deal. In the dream was *a rug with a very thick weave in which a horrible creature lived. It was so horrible that she could not bring herself to look at it, and yet she knew that it had a greenish and death-like appearance.* Despite the horror pervading the dream, I felt that it was extremely revealing; she, however, was not capable of offering associations. It was clear in my mind that the description of her uterus, on which a thick membrane had grown, meant that she was ready to become pregnant. At that time we did not know of this factor, as her most recent medical report had been rather pessimistic. It was clear that she felt herself unable to control her deadly, horrible destructiveness, but in fact the destructive influence on her uterus had diminished, as was shown by the rug's thick and healthy weave. I think that the dream should be considered a precise revelation about her psychosomatic state and psychotic violence (in the uterus). Despite her reluctance to look at the horrid creature in her dream, her psychotic state was evidently represented as a psychogenic manifestation. The isolation and split between psyche and soma had been reduced, as was abruptly manifested in the transference psychosis, in which she was very concerned about what was happening. The improved functioning of her uterus, which had not been destroyed by the deadly creature, seems to imply that the patient had not hurt me with her violent attack during and subsequent to the transference psychosis, and that she trusted my containment function. Nevertheless, the persistence of this creature, which she did not want to look at, warned us of the existence of a problem we would have to tackle in future. I did not mention this to her at that time. During the session I interpreted that she seemed to want to inform me that her uterus was much improved and that in all likelihood she was ready to conceive a baby; I added that she felt that inside herself was something horrid she did not want to see and that I was not meant to have glimpsed. The patient did not have her period, and four weeks later a test confirmed that she was pregnant. During the nine months of the pregnancy she focused on following her doctor's advice to protect the foetus, which also involved a number of months' hospitalization; the doctors did not want to run any risks, as her cervix was a little weak. In due course, she gave birth to a healthy little girl, to whom the patient completely dedicated herself for several months. She delighted in her baby's behaviour and communications, and in her ability to understand the baby so well; she talked to me of this in detail, and her problems seemed to have vanished.

I allowed things to continue like this for a certain time; it seemed natural that she would be full of happiness and joy at looking after her little girl, and sharing her observations with me. But after a few weeks, I pointed out that it was difficult for her, during that period, to come to analysis; in response to this interpretation she had a dream in which *she was a 6-week-old baby, in a newborn baby's tiny clothes, trying to walk and talk.* She had explicitly said that she felt very sympathetic to her baby and felt pleasure looking after her and watching her. This meant that for a certain period it was hard to admit her need for analysis. The other meaning of this dream revealed something of her psychopathology, her tendency to idealize herself, associated with a certain pseudo-maturity which, at certain times, led her to deny all her problems. The dream could therefore be understood as a sort of caricature of this situation: she represented herself as a 6-week-old baby who was growing up too quickly and already wanted to walk and talk. This idealization and superiority had always been known but never openly acknowledged. Now it had increased because she had proven herself to be the ideal mother she herself had always wanted. This idealization and its associated denial soon began to cause considerable difficulties in analysis. It was evident that she had made progress—she confided more in herself and in me—but it was also evident, in the appearance of that horrid creature, that the analysis had only made partial progress and that there was a risk that some of the psychosis could remain concealed for ever. It was also clear that the patient was extremely intolerant of her own feelings of envy, and very sensitive to the envy of others.

For example, one day she invited a number of colleagues to her house for a party. One of these colleagues accidentally broke a large vase of which she had been especially fond. This friend behaved in a peculiar way: she did not say anything to the patient, who found the vase in pieces in a corner after the event. Another friend later told her who the culprit had been. The woman concerned did not apologize, nor even mention the event. The patient simply said that she could not stand this kind of behaviour. She wondered: how can you go to somebody's house, find something beautiful, and break it without even admitting it?

Given that she wanted to preserve her self-idealization, at this time the patient was really unable to accept interpretations of the projective identification, against which she reacted with a sense of persecution. Though it was likely that her appraisal of this friend's character was correct, I knew that she was using this experience to project and deny the destructive and envious feelings she felt towards me. These feelings had clearly appeared in analysis after the transference psychosis, in which she had felt envy at the analytic context and had dreamed of violently throwing a plate on a boat, puncturing its hull. During this period of analysis, she asserted that she had finally found a self she liked, and that she felt I literally wanted to strip away this good self with my interpretations to make her feel uncertain and useless. Around this time, she constantly offered me associations on destructive character traits she noticed in other people. At the same time, she categorically asserted that she did not believe in the validity of projection. It was no reflection on her if she was so concerned with other people's problems. This loss of insight lasted only a few weeks. I pointed out to her that she was provoking me by hardly saying anything about herself, apart from the fact that she felt fine and wanted to continue believing that things would stay that way. On the other hand, she constantly sought my interpretations of the projective aspects of her self, given that she continued to focus almost exclusively on the destructive character traits of others. I realized that sooner or later I might well witness another paranoid explosion.

After quite some time, I very carefully advanced an interpretation on this issue, after it emerged with particular clarity when the patient had talked for a number of days about her brother-in-law's envious and nasty character traits. She remained convinced that I was adducing character traits to her that were not her own. Given that she construed this as a vicious attack on her personality, she had no intention of continuing to put up with such analytic ridiculousness. For the next few days, she was angry and closed, arousing fear in me that I had provoked a second transference psychosis with my cautious interpretation of her projective identification. She was annoyed because there was still a small doubt that my interpretations could contain some truth. She complained that this made the situation worse. As a result, she decided to belittle everything I said to her; but some days later, when she was visiting her depressed and obsessive older sister, she decided that she did not want to turn out like her and that she should therefore face her feelings. At this point she acknowledged that she was rigidly holding herself up, that she was afraid of whipping up undesirable feelings inside, because that would make her feel weak, tired, collapsed, and she did not want to feel like this. This difficulty in bringing out the destructive aspects through interpretation of the splitting process is extremely typical in patients with personalities containing split and projected depressive and paranoid destructive tendencies. It is the confusion of depressive and paranoid feelings that is hard for these patients to tolerate; often, this creates psychosomatic or hypochondriacal symptoms, or serious splitting. In this phase what was most evident was a process of splitting that appears immediately afterwards in physical form.

During the summer holidays, the patient went abroad with her husband and little girl. She told me that this was a difficult time for her. Every night she had a highly disturbing nightmare, which when she awoke left her exhausted and frightened. Sometimes she had the nightmare twice in the same night. She was often afraid of going to sleep; she felt bored and listless during the day and did not enjoy anything she did. She felt unable to understand the dreams, and she therefore realized she still was very much in need of help. The content of these nightmares was repetitive and usually involved exam dreams. For example, in most of these dreams *she had left it far to late to start studying for an exam, in a subject that wasn't even her own. Given that there wasn't much time to learn, she was sure she would fail.* Obviously, she felt that the analysis was a critical exam in which she would fail and be severely punished for her time-wasting, tactics which, during that period, had been much in evidence.

The following year the patient's blocking and evasive behaviour became more manifest. She recounted a dream in which *a two-ton lorry had got stuck on a hill and had blocked the road. The lorry's engine had packed up. There were two men, one of whom was leaning behind the lorry, trying to push it up the hill, but the lorry slipped backwards and he was somehow attached to it; in the dream, the patient feared that the man would be crushed. Extremely anxious, she raced to a hospital to get them to send an ambulance to the road where the incident had happened. She got angry because the hospital receptionist was somewhat absent-minded when handling the call, but, after she was put through to the ambulance driver, she couldn't remember the road she was on, where the lorry had pinned down the man.* The dream had a similar structure to the drowning dream, in which the man had cut the phone wires. I picked up on a split between this crushing behaviour and her desire to provide emergency help; but in this last dream, it is clear that her function as a connector is disturbed, and that this has become the most pressing problem. Not only did the receptionist pass on the phone call slowly, but she could not remember the area in which her crushing and blocking behaviour had taken place. She still needed plenty of time before managing to admit that it was extremely difficult for her to think about anything when she had to struggle against the sensation of not wanting to be disturbed, or her desire to be left alone.

A few months after this, she told me that she was certain she could become so heavy and difficult that there was no way I could help her get better; I would probably be crushed by my desire to help her, and she would not appreciate my help. During this period she had dreams in which she engaged in acrobatic exercises in space, and it was difficult to understand what she was doing; sometimes I felt and interpreted to her that she was not only aggressive, but that she rejected any clear definition of what was happening to her, particularly if it was positive or constructive. She agreed with me and told me of an episode that had taken place when she was a teenager.

When she was painting a water-colour of the sea, with a nice sky and clouds, a woman looking on from behind had admired the painting. She then took the painting, scrunched it up, and threw it away, signalling that that was the last painting she would do. I reminded her that in so doing she was not only throwing away what I and others had given her, but was also attacking her own artistic capabilities when they aroused admiration and interest, probably because she was afraid of provoking envious attacks. In the next session, she said she had nothing to talk about, just some trivia; after some delay she told me this trivia because that was all she had to say. That morning she had gone to a department store to take back some garments that were too small. The very kind and obliging shop assistant had replaced them with others that fitted much better; when she was about to leave the shop, another woman had held the door open for her, and she considered this gesture to be very kind as she had her baby with her. She had also thought about a nice man, a builder, who was doing some work at her house. There was a problem in the supply of building materials at that time, so the man had had to wait for a few days before he could get hold of enough bricks and cement. She felt touched by his patience, and stressed how lucky she was to have such a nice workman doing the building work for her.

The only upsetting event of the morning had been in the street, when she walked past a woman, a psychologist, who looked straight ahead as if she hadn't even noticed her. This had puzzled her a great deal. I replied that the details about which she had talked (which she thought were a waste of time and bereft of meaning) could easily be brought together in a model that told the following story. There once was a mother-analyst who was helping her to modify her feelings of being forced into the position of a little girl, and who was offering her the chance to grow and develop. The patient also felt that this attentive mother-analyst did not possessively keep her in the same position, but allowed her to develop by making it easier to go out into the world. Like a father-analyst, she felt that I was patiently bringing together the details of her associations to build the structure of her personality, and she felt grateful and fortunate to have me; nevertheless, she still feared the persecutory figure, which represented not just the envious and destructive mother, but also her own invidious and destructive self, which restricted itself simply to watching what went on between us, judging it to be completely worthless and throwing it away.

She was very thoughtful after this interpretation, and over the next few weeks it became evident that her omnipotent attitude was beginning to collapse. She dreamed that a balloon burst and fell right on top of her. It was made of very thin material, and it did not hurt her. She began to develop serious headaches and feel physically ill. One day, she had such a bad headache that she did not come to the session; when she tried to work, she felt so poorly she had to go to bed. The following day, she told me the story of *several people who were going for a ride in a balloon. Initially, they did not know where they wanted to go; then one of them said they wanted to go to India rather than to a desert because, flying in a balloon, they preferred landing somewhere where there were people who could help them, so that they would not be so isolated.* This association seemed to suggest that her omnipotent desire to fly was changing into the desire to move away from her omnipotent, destructive self, from her emptiness and isolation, to reach a point where she would be more able to establish contact and receive help. The following day she came with two dreams. The first was again a typical exam dream *in which she was not sufficiently well prepared and was unable to find the room the exam was being held in. As a result, she became extremely worried and anxious.* In the second dream, *the washing she was doing in the machine rolled up into a ball and pushed its way out through the lid; clearly something had not been properly fastened. She tried to see if she could close the lid, but she saw that this was not possible and that she should have closed the washing-machine cylinder properly— that was why the dirty linen rolled up into a ball.*

While she was making these associations, she complained that the blinding headache of the day before had come back, connected clearly with the rolling-up of the washing in her dream. This dream revealed her increasing consciousness that she could not drag her thoughts away into nothing, into space, but that she had to think clearly and use her head as a stable container in which to think through her "thinking problems". In other words, her headache was associated with the impulse to go back to her destructive way of dispersing her thoughts by thinking of nothing and letting herself be carried away. Now, though, this experience was causing her serious pain and she was beginning to understand that she was harming herself through this attitude; this demonstrated that progress had been achieved, the ego had strengthened, and better links had been established.

Despite the negative summer, the following year saw slow progress, as she suffered serious headaches, tiredness, and even exhaustion. The following summer holidays went better. At the first session after the holidays, she told me a dream: *she was climbing a spiral staircase that became narrower and narrower, until she had to cling on to the iron railings*; at a certain point, she realized she was getting into trouble and said, "Out of a quirk of fate, it was obvious that I would have got into trouble in a sort of structure that was very much breast-shaped." This brought to mind an unpleasant story. *A man who had been robbed when he was far from home had decided to wait until the thieves came back for another robbery. He built a metal contraption onto his house and waited until the thieves returned. Then he closed up the metal structure around his house, and left the thieves trapped inside on their own to die of hunger.*

During the holidays I had moved house; the patient denied any interest or intrusiveness. She thought that my old house had been interesting, and she was rather critical about the new one; she believed that she was very knowledgeable on this topic and therefore could not understand why she should have been excited or interested by it. I felt that here the patient was communicating the strength and reality of her fantasies, because she was showing me the extent to which she had felt intrusive with me, stealing from me everything good I possessed. Indeed, she knew everything about my home and how it was decorated, but she also knew that she had consumed and emptied and depressed me, so she felt persecuted by the guilt and forced to identify herself with me, an empty breast; she also felt that I was setting a trap to punish and imprison her. Her sensation of exhaustion and collapse was connected with this depression.

The following day, the patient unexpectedly mentioned the cover of a large book on architecture that was in the consultation-room. For a long time, she said, she had viewed the cover as completely battered, but now she had seen it properly she was mistaken. It was not damaged at all, on the contrary it was full of colour and looked brand-new; she was very much surprised that the wear and tear of the cover was a completely mistaken perception. And yet her attitude of not moving on with the insight continued to prevail. At the end of the session she expressed the sensation of not really being depressed, but rather indifferent; and yet she realized that this attitude of hers was dangerous because it was heavy enough and tedious enough to damage my interest in her. She admitted that she was not only afraid of being criticized, but that she was also conscious of imposing or projecting upon me her sensation of boredom, and that this was reducing the analysis into something empty and prosaic, which in the end would have put me off. She also said that she knew I could not be interested in her and would get bored if she was not sufficiently interesting when she came and talked, bringing me the material I required in order to make progress with the analytic work. At issue was not that she was afraid I had become fed up, but that she was convinced that I was fed up with her. In other words, she was saying that she was perfectly correct in the perception she had of me, of my transforming into a bored, worn-out, and colourless analyst.

The following Monday, the patient told me an unpleasant dream she had had. *It was like a picture, in a strange place full of damp and fog, and it was rather dark. There were bits of rock sticking out, isolated from one another, so that there was no continuity or bridge between them. She also knew that it was extremely cold. It was like walking over a precipice and she felt a kind of out of body sensation.* She thought that this dream had something to do with her inability to communicate, which increased her feeling of isolation; the consciousness and unpleasantness of this condition had not been lost in the dream. It had become clear that the patient was seeking a connection, the bridge, and that she had connected with her self-consciousness; it was precisely her ability to understand herself and see herself which she had cut off and lost, with the consequence of feeling isolated and unable to find out where she was or who she was. In the dream, the patient's difficulties in staying at one isolated point, with a resulting sensation of falling, was typical of the fear of collapsing that clearly appears at certain times, usually connected with a complete inability to think and use one's mind. She had admitted that her serious attacks on me were borne out of the fear of the real harm that her envy could have done to me, after having realized that the condition of depression was inside her and that I was full of life and could help her. Instead of feeling relieved by this discovery, she had felt bored and envious and had attempted to quash my satisfaction at having understood.

Thereafter, her dreams cast further light on her attitude towards me. For example, she recounted a dream *in which she was leaning against a filing cabinet and talking with Mr B, who seemed to her to be a very nice man. They were at a party, for there were other people around, and she would have liked to have had a much more private chat with him rather than talk with all those other people. While she was talking to him, she had some notes in her hand which, rather casually, she was slipping into the filing cabinet, without paying too much attention where they ended up. She admitted that she felt rather casual, that she was filing them at random; later, while she was descending a hill, a little way off she saw a group of people in a semicircle, listening to a man who was talking animatedly. Opposite her was a tramp who was walking rather quickly towards the group. Suddenly, he took out a rifle and aimed it at the man, with the evident intention of killing him. When she saw this she leapt towards him and screamed: "Don't do it!" He turned towards her and pointed the gun at her, at which point she shouted, "Don't shoot me!" Apparently he did not, but the whole group, which was on a raised platform, all seemed to fall down as if it was a cartoon.* In her associations she talked about a game that her daughter played in which she had made a giant rather similar to the tramp in the dream. Her daughter had become very worried about the giant and had given him a nice hairstyle.

I pointed out to the patient that in the dream she had clearly expressed consciousness of talking in analysis in a rather casual and vague way, with the consequence of making connections between thoughts more difficult. Projecting and constantly distributing her thoughts onto other people and situations, she felt as if her analysis were becoming public, something that in the dream was experienced as rather dissatisfying because it did not make it possible to find the connections and links she needed in order to establish a good contact with the analysis as a valuable experience. This mechanism became clearer after reconstituting the links, when she could see that I was full of life and interested in others and in herself; and yet she had also been forced to acknowledge the persistence of an omnipotence in this feeling towards me and had had to put up with the fact of having homicidal impulses towards me when she saw me clearly and when she had to face herself. It was evident in the dream that this attack was also against me and against the part of her that esteemed me, that attempted to protect me. In the dream, she had found a good expression of the way she handled these destructive attacks. And now, gradually, the pieces of the self were coming together, and the attacks against seeing, connecting, or linking were rendered clear and meaningful.

It is interesting to note that it was not just the feeling of being persecuted, associated with her depression, that caused the patient's enormous apprehension; it was the rocks dream and her inability to think that made her feel so desperately dispirited and isolated, and this state was principally responsible for her fear of caving in. Attacks on the connection and denials of reality are, obviously, important aspects of the psychotic part of a patient's personality, as posited by Bion (1954, 1957).

Repeated attacks on the connections between good and bad feelings—combined significantly with the confusional envious attacks of significant external relationships, further aggravated by attacks on the ability to see and think, had produced the fear of serious permanent damage to the patient's self and to her ability to think—as well as anxiety of being mad. A psychotic state has many ramifications, but one of the most disturbing of these is connected with the fact that patients find themselves enclosed within a mental state that imprisons them, from which they cannot find an escape on their own. It is this type of "psychotic island" that the patient found herself having to tackle in analysis when the deadly monster was gradually brought into the light. It requires very patient work to handle patients of this type, like the carpenter in the dream who gradually helps her to piece together her self and her thoughts, patiently waiting until there is sufficient tangible proof to comprehend the entire personality structure. Only at this point could detailed connection interpretations be made; these have a considerable therapeutic influence inasmuch as they allow such patients gradually to integrate their psychotic problems with the healthier parts of the personality.

The analyst must guard against idealizing this type of patient, who often manifests considerable perception and creativity in his or her ability to cooperate in analysis. The analyst must also be conscious of the risk of being pushed into perceiving such patients as underdeveloped, as opposed to acknowledging the great potential for creativity and development that such patients tend to lose when they lose consciousness of the destructive parts of their personality. This painful process must be continually tackled until permanent progress is established.

Conclusions

In this seminar, I have sought to illustrate the existence of a psychotic part encapsulated within the self, which we refer to as a "psychotic island", and which is present in many people who suffer neurotic disorders but nevertheless do not seem to be seriously ill. When these "psychotic islands" are completely split and projected, or walled up and excluded from the psychic self, they often take root in certain bodily organs—the chest, gastrointestinal area, uterus, skin, or other parts of the body. I believe that these psychotic islands are often the cause of what we know as "psychosomatic illness".

What is contained within the "psychotic island" can vary greatly, but it is usual that what prevails within its structure are uncontrollable destructive impulses, anxieties, and associated defences. Also, positive and creative parts of the self (which has become confused with the destructive self and therefore may no longer be differentiated) may also lodge within the "psychotic island". This obviously means that the whole personality may appear weakened or not completely developed, though this is masked by self-idealization and denial. Certain traumatic experiences in early infancy, and later on, are frequently recounted by the patient or revealed during the course of analysis. Often they are related to maternal difficulties in relating appropriately with the newborn child. In other words, one may discover that the maternal ability to keep and contain has been seriously damaged or is completely absent. Sometimes both parents have problems that they heaped onto their child, or children, and hence are not capable of listening to and heeding their real needs. Sometimes the pressure exerted by this environment is so strong that the child gives in and adapts completely to it, a process that Winnicott refers to as "false self". Bion describes a process—he calls this the "alpha function"—which is necessary for developing a normal ability to think and function. He describes how the newborn baby projects and evacuates to the mother impulses and mental content that he is not capable of dealing with, and, through the maternal intuitive function (Bion calls this *reverie*), these incomprehensible impulses can become comprehensible for the child if, in some way, he/she begins to feel accepted and acceptable. This situation creates a space in the external object in which the child can feel safe, held together. The introjection of this space creates an internal space in which the infant can begin to think and watch and, in consequence, build his mental system. As the child gradually learns to accept his good and bad impulses, he develops a self capable of dealing with internal and external conflicts.

If this space, which is necessary for development, is denied by the external environment, it can set off an intense and rampant rage in the newborn baby, and later in the child, as he/she feels continually forced to evacuate his/her mental contents without there being a possible solution to his/her mental problems. All that remains is to tackle these problems through splitting and denial. Another closely associated and interrelated problem also exists. The genetic endowment of positive and destructive parts of the self varies greatly from one individual to the next. The stronger the infant's destructive endowment, the greater the need for an environment capable of helping him face and accept his positive and, more importantly, his negative self, in order to be able gradually to face and overcome deep anxieties of being invaded and destroyed by his destructive impulses. If these genetically assigned destructive impulses are not accepted by the environment and by the self, they are then split and projected at a very early age, and they remain damaging and invasive monsters. Often it is the interaction of precociously split and projected impulses of unmodified violent content, reinforced by later rampant frustrating experiences, that frequently form the core of an encapsulated "psychotic island".

I have drawn clinical material from a patient in whom the "psychotic island" was rooted in her uterus. Under analysis, breaching of the psychotic island determined a temporary transference psychosis, in which the patient was invaded by the destructive feelings that had been suppressed, split, and projected throughout her life.

From the very first session, the patient seemed to feel at home in analysis; she felt accepted and contained, an experience that I believe made it possible for her to produce the dream in which she was in bed, making her mother-in-law so tired that it provoked her to leave the patient alone for a holiday. It was this dream that became concretely real in the transference psychosis and, probably, that at an unconscious level has always been a real situation.

It took a few days for her to overcome the shock resulting from the belief that I had transformed into her angry mother-in-law, but immediately after this the "psychotic island" was dislodged from the bodily organs, and the psychosomatic condition could be treated. Subsequently, it was necessary to tackle and work through the construction of this "psychotic island" by examining the transference situation, using a slow process of elucidating all the details. It became evident that the precocious splitting and projection of envious and destructive feelings was an important aspect of the "psychotic island", described as a horrid green monster nesting in the uterus.

Attacks by envious, split, and projected parts were expressed for a number of years in the patient's dreams and actions. It was gradually possible to sort out the envious attacks against her creativity and the attacks that devalued and wiped out the analyst's function (which were mixed with admiration and a protective attitude towards him). Lastly, it became clear that the destructive attacks on her linking functions had made comprehension and reparation impossible. This discovery gradually enabled her to integrate the horrid monster and the caring self; as a consequence, the patient became aware of her ability to love and protect her love objects, and of her ability to be creative.

THREE

Communication problems between patient and analyst in psychotic and borderline patients

The analyst's ability to support the analytic role greatly depends on understanding patient communications. During the course of his analytic training, the analyst gradually learns to observe the way in which the vast majority of neurotic patients communicate, the way they speak, and their emotional tones of voice, in order to grasp the patient's emotions and relative defences; narrative style and non-verbal communication also offer precious pointers.

Psychotic and borderline patients require a particularly attentive study of forms of communication. Here, I shall attempt to illustrate some of the phenomena that often considerably impede progress of analysis and can cause its failure. For example, it is likely that manifestations of transference psychosis, which so often hinders the treatment of borderline patients, are due not just to a lack of comprehension, but also to a growing misunderstanding between patient and analyst. One of the most significant causes of incomprehension lies in the difficulty of picking up on non-verbal communication contemporaneous with verbal communication: the two may contradict or complement one another. In parallel, the patient may pick up on non-verbal features of the analyst's communicative style, which can actually alter or twist what the analyst consciously intends to communicate. A number of insufficient communication issues between patient and analyst have been studied and described in detail by Robert Langs and others.

My observations refer to two patients who communicate in a non-verbal manner. Both patients may be described as borderline; however, while the first tends more towards the neurotic, the second is frankly a borderline psychotic (diagnosed as schizophrenic by a number of psychiatrists who had the patient under observation for a period).

To begin with, I would like to state that it is essential to study carefully the patient's case history as a guide for the therapist in the treatment of patients with communication problems. If the patient under examination has been in treatment with another therapist who has encountered serious difficulties, the therapist's relationship must be studied with special attention to contradictory elements and omissions regarding significant data. In such cases, the omission almost always contains the problem's resolution.

The first case I present by way of example is that of a 30-year-old married woman without children, who underwent two years of analysis with a male analyst. During a seminar he presented a short and precise case history. The patient is a teacher who has an intellectual interest in analysis. She is the eldest of four children. The most significant element of her childhood was being weaned at the age of 2 years when a younger sister was born. At this time, she was sent away from home to stay with an aunt. Since then she has lived some of the time with her aunt, some of the time with her grandmother, and some of the time with her parents. In his account of the case, the analyst makes no mention of her father. It is not clear, either, what prompted the patient to begin analysis. The analyst answered my question by saying that after two years of analysis, he is not yet certain what brought the patient to commence treatment, and he says that her father is not important in her life. In describing how the analysis proceeded, the therapist says that to begin with the patient talked a little about her life, but in a way that sounded artificial and that had not yielded results. Little by little it becomes clear that none of the things that were touched upon in analysis can be worked through. As the analysis proceeds, the patient becomes increasingly silent, and many elements that initially seemed important appear to tail off into long silences. In his description of this silence, the analyst notes that the patient seems to be very calm, almost pleased with these long and empty silences. Every session begins with a long silence, broken only by the analyst or the patient expressing the feeling that the analyst cannot stand the silence. Sometimes the patient skips one or two sessions in a row; though initially she attempts to justify her absence, she quickly acknowledges that the reason for not coming is that she doesn't want to come to the session, or she doesn't get up in time. The analyst expresses increasing concern about the situation.

From listening to this account it, becomes evident that the patient was particularly close to her mother during her first two years of life, and that, later on, this close bond was suddenly broken. Two questions spring to mind: how did the patient manage to handle the situation, and what was the father's attitude towards the mother and daughter during this process?

One may also wonder about the analyst's silence regarding the father's role. I express my opinions to the analyst and ask him specifically what he feels during the patient's long silences. He answers that he acutely senses increasing worry and anxiety; once or twice he has interpreted this situation to the patient, telling her that she seems so calm and anxiety-free precisely because she has transferred all her guilt and anxiety, including her worry at not seeing any progress in the analysis, onto the analyst and therefore expects the analyst to shoulder all her problems. To his great surprise, the patient warmly agreed with this interpretation, but then immediately fell back into silence.

The analyst's reaction to the patient's positive reception of the interpretation—though the patient was not in a position to work this through, and was plunged back into silence—would seem to contain an important pointer for comprehending the transference and countertransference issues raised by this case. The analyst obviously felt discouraged and depressed and, in turn, falls silent. Indeed, after interpreting the patient's projection, the analyst evidently expected not just the confirming reply, but also a magical change in the patient's attitude. Discussing his silence with me, the analyst acknowledges that he felt useless and impotent. At this point, I wonder if the therapist's situation has been communicated to the patient. Even before any clinical material was illustrated during the seminar, a preliminary model began to form in my mind in which the patient has an intense need of very active support from an analyst-father, as well as a need of a depressed and in fact ineffectual analyst-father, incapable of handling the patient's demands. The creation of this kind of temporary model in the analyst's mind must not be fixed, but it is useful particularly when comments or dreams arise that illustrate the problem metaphorically.

* * *

I will now present some of the actual clinical material brought along by the therapist. The patient, who had failed to come to the Wednesday and Thursday sessions, arrived ten minutes late and said she was worried because she realized she wanted to wreck everything. She had not come on Wednesday out of idleness; when it was time to leave for the session, she began to ask herself, "Shall I go or not? If I call up, what will I say? That I'm ill?" The analyst interpreted that the patient seemed worried about not telling the truth; he interpreted the silence and the failure to come to the session as a way of not telling the truth. The patient responded that she was conscious of concealing some of the material, but she hadn't worried about it before; now, however, it was becoming persecutory.

If we listen attentively to this clinical material, it is clear that the patient twice acknowledges the truth that was previously concealed: her increasing worry and the sense of persecution she cannot cope with make her feel a need for an analyst to understand the meaning. She subsequently relates a dream: "*My father says that one of his molars is loose. I start to check my teeth with my tongue and it feels like my tooth is loose, but not a molar. It falls out and I can feel it in my mouth. But now it is much larger than a normal tooth, it is a molar and I am surprised. I am even more surprised when I look in the mirror. I expect to see a hole where the tooth had been, but what I see is another even larger tooth, and a small hole. It looks horrible.*" The analyst simply interprets the teeth in the dream as a larger lie concealing

another, smaller lie. The patient reacts with confusion to this interpretation, saying: "Everything is confused and chaotic. What do
you want to know? Don't you think that I am the one who wants to
know?"

From this response, it is clear that the analyst has not touched
upon the problems communicated in the dream; now we want to
check to see if our model holds the key to the dream, which could
be a symbolic representation of the problem. I find it interesting
and significant that the dream reveals the analyst in the father's
position. When the father says that his tooth is loose, the patient
immediately identifies with him and feels as if it is one of her
teeth that has come loose and is about to fall out. At this point, the
dream presents an interesting situation: the patient looks at herself
in the mirror without seeing any missing tooth (which would be
identification with the analyst)—and thus attempts to establish
a difference between what has happened to her and what has
happened to the analyst-father—but seeing another tooth with a
hole in it, which is ugly but does not hurt. As she had previously
indicated, it seems to me that in this dream the patient expresses
a sense of being worried and persecuted, of being bad, ugly, or
guilty; all this is expressed via the hole in the tooth, which could be
expected to provoke a great deal of pain. It is obvious that in the
dream the patient is not hiding anything from herself, given that
she looks very closely in the mirror at what is happening to her,
and she naturally obtains clarification and rectifies the confusion
(the same confusion that caused considerable difficulties for her). It
is interesting that in this dream the father, who obviously stands
for the analyst, says that his tooth is loose: he therefore admits that
something is wrong with him. He cannot speak properly or describe in sufficiently clear terms what is going on. The loose tooth
can easily become a tooth that falls out. It is the analyst, therefore,
who has to work on the hole in the analysis: the session is falling
flat because the tooth is falling out. The father's molar actually
presents itself in the patient's mouth as a molar that has fallen out.
It would appear that our initial model of an ineffective analyst-
father is portrayed vividly in the dream. The analyst's silence has
become a verbal communication with which he admits that something in him is not right. This communication has considerable and

immediate repercussions on the patient's emotions, which consist of identification with the analyst-father. Comprehension of this problem may require a certain degree of phantasy and a certain degree of introspection by the analyst-father; he could, for example, think to himself: "How am I rejecting you, the patient? Where are the holes, where are the gaps in my understanding that are creating holes, silences, and skipped sessions in the analytic situation, about which I am very concerned?" We are already glimpsing that the dream indicates the patient's considerable abilities of observation and communication. Though this is a short and condensed dream, it is highly expressive and also contains great reparatory potential. The patient has not yet lost the tooth, and the ugly hole can be repaired by a good analyst-father-dentist. But the analyst is not in a position to grasp this representation and return it to the patient. The patient is already very worried about the analyst, who is not working properly, and who now, instead of acknowledging the veracity of many elements in the dream, accuses her of concealment and lying. She is despairing and confused after the interpretation, so she says that everything is confused and chaotic: "What do you want to know?" It is almost as if she is begging him, "Please, analyst-father, I have told you everything I know, but in reality there is a comprehension gap." One wonders how the patient will mould and cope with this great gap in the analyst, given that during this phase of the analysis, all the anxieties expressed in the dream have become even stronger. We might imagine that there could be two teeth that are wobbly and fall out, and that the patient then skips two sessions to bear out the dream's logic and symbolism. One may also expect the patient to feel even more anxious and worried about the therapist. This is now the atmosphere of the analysis. In fact, the patient misses not one but two sessions at the beginning of the following week; she does not come on either Tuesday or Wednesday. And when she turns up on Thursday, she sits motionless and silent. She then says she does not know why she didn't show up on Tuesday; on Wednesday, however, she came and stood in the street outside, uncertain whether or not to go up to the analyst's rooms. She could not make up her mind what to do and felt a great deal of suffering. In the end, the pain was so great in her mind that she went home. This is followed by another long silence on the patient's part, who then mentions that at school the doctors are wondering if one of the girls is cardiopathic or myopathic because she cannot climb the stairs. The analyst interprets that she is the one thinking of myopathy, of an organic cause, instead of considering the emotions she felt on Wednesday, when she herself could not manage to climb the stairs to get to him.

To begin with, let's consider what the patient communicates, through both her silence and her words. We were expecting two skipped two sessions in order to communicate the increasing gap in incomprehension between herself and the therapist. The intolerable anxiety and pain, previously expressed and illustrated in the dream, now seem to be completely conscious. After her frank admission of the mental pain that had prevented her from climbing the stairs, to which the analyst responds with silence, she addresses more open criticisms to him: she tells him that he is not succeeding in diagnosing her state of mind. The analyst's interpretation—saying that she is seeking concrete medical reasons rather than the emotions that prevented her from coming up the stairs—rings like a wholly unjustified accusation.

The gap persists, understood as a lack of comprehension of the patient's communications, so she skips another two sessions the following week. What I wish to show you is the immense effort that this "silent" patient is undertaking in her attempt to communicate with the analyst. With this type of patient, however, it is very common for therapists to have difficulty in following the material. The more the analyst consciously and subconsciously insists on clear verbal communication, the more the analyst loses grip on comprehension of the patient's silent and symbolic communication. These patients are often considered to be unanalysable, but I believe that we are not doing them justice by classifying them in this manner.

I would now like to turn to a different case and a different problem. Rosemary may be described as a borderline patient who, placed in difficult situations, develops serious psychotic anxieties: she becomes silent or continually breaks off her sentences, in such a fashion as to make incomprehensible what she is verbally communicating. Sometimes, she resorts to metaphorical language, which requires a great leap of imagination to grasp the hidden meaning. Years ago, Rosemary wrote to me from another country, imploring me urgently to take her into analysis. She had been in analysis for eight years, once a week, but this was suddenly interrupted when the therapist had rejected her, threatening to go to the police if she insisted on seeing him or calling him up.

This development left her completely lost and despairing, and prey to serious panic. For more than a year, she unsuccessfully tried to get into therapy with someone else in her country, until one of the doctors she had gone to advised her to write to me. I could not, from her letter, establish whether she was schizophrenic or if what she said in the letter was true; nevertheless, assuming that it was true, I decided to see her. I wrote to her that I could not make any decisions about her treatment, but that I would see her for two weeks, to throw some light on her problems and decide on the feasibility or otherwise of future treatment with myself or with one of my colleagues. From her letter I had the impression that she was in an acute psychotic state, but also that the external situation had an influence in determining the gravity of her anxieties.

The decision to ask her to come may seem risky, but over the last few years I have used a long consultation method to help patients in desperate situations. The patient accepted my proposal and came to see me alone. To begin with, communication with her was extremely difficult because, though she spoke English, she often remained mute and behaved as if she were in a terrifying situation. She could not bring herself to look me in the eye and, sitting opposite me, she looked very remote. Sometimes she hid herself far away, in one corner of the room, and covered her face; at other times she attempted to crawl under the couch. When she spoke, she spoke so softly that I couldn't hear what she was saying. I decided to ask her some questions to establish if the psychotic condition and panic she was experiencing was caused solely by the traumatic end to her therapy, or if she had experienced similar problems and anxieties previously, before beginning any treatment. I thought that this would have helped me manage to formulate a diagnosis that, at that moment, was rather obscure. I felt that she wanted to talk to me about her previous therapy, but the mere thought petrified her. She could not stand even mentioning the name of the doctor who had treated her.

During our first three or four meetings she behaved like a patient in an acute psychotic state, incapable of answering questions or even talking. When I told her my hypothesis that she was too frightened to speak, and that I was ready to accept that she didn't speak because of this anxiety, the situation improved slightly. I interpreted to her that she wanted me to know and feel how frightened she was, and how much she needed my help. I added that I had the impression that her difficulties had something to do with her previous treatment; perhaps it was this that enabled her to say something about what had happened. To begin with, she could not speak about it, but then she managed by using metaphor. She told me that she thought she was trying to stay upstairs, where there was a party going on, but had on the contrary been dragged down to the kitchen. She felt that this description could explain what had happened to her. I had to work through these communications to translate them into more intelligible thoughts and sensations; first of all, I had to understand her metaphorical language, and only after this would she be capable of working things through herself. At a certain point, I commented that it seemed to me that at the party on the top floor she felt grown-up and could consider herself to be somebody's partner. Nodding, she added that her father was upstairs. Now I could tell her that being dragged down to the kitchen was being forced to go back to being the little girl who is with her mother, a mother who nourishes and looks after her. After I said this, she said that she hated being treated like a little girl. Later on, she told me that for her being pushed down into the kitchen was a serious persecution, like somebody going schizophrenic. So, the persecution depended almost entirely on the doctor who had treated her and had ultimately sent her away. Every time she decided to utter his name to me, she became terribly afraid. Initially, I did not understand if this terror in my room referred to me, or if she was hallucinating the doctor in my room, and was frightened and terrified by him. There were times when she apologized for behaving so stupidly, preventing me from really seeing how intelligent she was. Naturally, this comment was apt, and I could add that she also felt frightened and humiliated, as well as stupid, because she could not handle the terror that was oppressing her. These comments came to confirm my opinion that her behaviour constituted a highly significant form of communication: the patient wanted to show me how she had been completely overcome by her terror and fear of this doctor and, moreover, she wanted to show me what she felt she had been through with him.

After this session, she managed to tell me his name, and she wrote me a long letter, which she put in my letterbox, in which she recounted many details of her life. She admitted that, the first time she wrote to me, she had also contacted another doctor in the United States, a doctor who was very well known for his treatment of schizophrenic patients. She said that she had been afraid I wasn't intelligent enough to treat her, because when she was 12 she began studying psychology, and this had brought her to full understanding of herself; now she was so shrewd that nobody could understand her. She therefore could confess to me her fear of having made her previous doctor stupid, and that out of revenge he had got rid of her. She was afraid that this might happen with me. During this first batch of meetings, I saw her twenty times. The last time, before she returned to her home country, she managed to speak more freely to me; she succeeding in saying that what I had understood of her had given her more room to think and feel more clearly. She was not, however, able to answer some of the questions that it was indispensable she answered in order for me to decide upon the analytic treatment for a patient in such a serious condition. I was, however, reasonably satisfied with the results achieved, for I hoped that I had at least partially reduced the oppressive persecution associated with the previous therapist. During her journey home, she wrote me a letter in which she thanked me and said that now she could use her mind better; she had even managed to visit the British Museum.

What followed was a tempestuous period in which she flooded me with letters, up to three a day, most of which were sent by recorded delivery. Some of these letters were full of information. In one, for example, she recounted a shocking event: a doctor had suddenly asked to meet her father and had informed both of them that he didn't want to see the patient again. She wrote: "Now I feel that there is chaos in my mind. It is as if in three-quarters of an hour my mind had been torn apart: you can well understand, my little Herbert Rosenfeld, that it is like knowing the difference between heaven and hell, experiencing a psychosis together with a doctor in analysis, a doctor you like and a psychosis made up of emotions between you and the doctor, and having to live it alone. Moreover, I am humiliated by almost everyone and by the situation itself, by all those who do not help me."

I think that this communication is wonderful, capable of arousing deep emotion; further similar communications, which I do not have time to go into here, are included in this and other letters. Rosemary explained how great was her need that I analyse her. Over the next year and a half, it was necessary to undertake a number of brief visits before being able to persuade her father that she needed to undergo analysis with me. I find it interesting to note that the initial prolonged period of twenty meetings had enabled her to achieve sufficient vitality to cope with the infinite frustrations and struggles of reaching out to me.

I shall now look at the clinical material in order to illustrate how the patient was communicating a few months after the start of analysis. In one session she begins by suggesting I play a little game with her: "Think of all the people I have talked about since I met you, and name one in particular." Unfortunately, this is a riddle to which I could not reply; I told her that for some reason she had set me a riddle that was too difficult for me to respond to. Initially, she spoke of a wild-blackthorn plum, before recalling a nurse who had looked after her at the nursery many years earlier: this was the person she had wanted me to guess. At a certain point, the patient quickly mentioned the name of a young analyst in her own country, whom I had named in our first interview, thinking that he might be able to treat her, and she burst into desperate tears. Then, with sadness, she said, "You don't want me." She repeated this again and again, ten times over. Then she kept saying, "Don't speak, your voice is hard and angry. You must not speak." She said this most emphatically. After waiting for ten minutes, I wanted very calmly to tell her something about the power of projection, but she stopped me immediately. In a whisper, I told her I understood that she was irritated with me because I had not been able to take her into analysis immediately, and I had deeply hurt her when I suggested somebody else. She answered that it was all right if I spoke in a whisper; the following day she was capable of coping with normal speech.

As well as the emotional moment of great anxiety of being rejected, the "wild plum" experience also seemed to contain another meaning that was hard to communicate. Indeed, the patient spends a lot of time thinking that something has an extraordinary yet dangerous meaning; her silence, together with her subsequent use of symbolic language, leads me to believe that she is requesting me to be in a mental state of engrossed meditation and intense introspection, united with what for her is equally intense concentration and interest, without giving me any concrete clue as to what has happened or about my participation in what is to be intimated. What she was feeling was obviously connected to a profound sense of rejection that Rosemary experienced when she wanted to be received and taken into analysis by me without waiting, without my gleaning information about the real nature of the situation before deciding whether treatment was possible or not. Given that in her own country the cost of analysis would be covered by the health service, I had initially asked her if she would be happy to accept an analyst or therapist in her own country, partly because the difficulties of organizing therapy in England had appeared insurmountable. Nevertheless, this question provoked great pain in her; indeed, she expressed herself poetically by referring to a black thorn in our relationships, though she preferred not to speak about this. In spite of this, she managed to establish an atmosphere between us that allowed us to come round to the black thorn. It is interesting to note that after a period of rather anxious waiting, I succeeded in getting close to the issues she had not initially wanted to reveal to me. Subsequently, Rosemary managed to tell me that she could talk for hours about episodes full of meaning, just scratching the surface, while assessing the right moment for us to go deeper. To make this cooperation possible, not just the right interpretation but the right degree of mental openness was required of me. What gradually emerged was an acute consciousness of her need for a meaningful object relationship, one that would contain something essential for her ability to exist—something, however, that she herself was not capable of naming. She conveyed the impression that something had been missing in the basic relationship with her parents, something that made it impossible for her to enter into a relationship with anybody, and that she was striving to fill this vacuum by seeking my help.

I would now like to examine some further clinical material referring to the two weeks leading up to the summer holidays.

Rosemary had become interested in a stray cat that was in the garden of the house she was staying in. The patient said to me: "She's a stray, I'd like to adopt her. I stroked her today, but I won't again." She repeated this three times. I interpreted that she was afraid of becoming too involved with the cat and then leaving. A few days later she noted: "I have something else to tell you. The cat can get into another garden, and it will be a big garden with wild flowers." Then she changed the subject and said: "There will be big white fields and a sweet fragrance of honeysuckle, bees will fly around, it will be hot, and there will be the sound of bells. It will be peaceful, and calm." She repeated some of these words with great tranquillity. As I listened to her, I noticed that I felt tired, and I told her that she was making me feel sleepy. She liked this very much, and she added: "You can lie down, remove yourself far from everything you know and hide; we could go to the garden together." She giggled, just a little excited now. "Your arms and hands become much smaller, I will take you by the hand, your body is now like a very light stick, I can easily throw it into the nearby garden, you are so light you can fly." I told her that in these conditions I would be completely in her power and would not have my own will and mind. Then she told me to help her, there was a black witch around; she was the witch. Her being a witch seemed to be connected with anger, her anger with her previous analyst, with her love for him that turned into hate, and her fear that the same thing would happen with me. At the end of the session she stated that she felt understood, and she explained what she wanted from analysis. I do not wish to give the impression that from now on everything went smoothly, as some very difficult periods lay ahead.

With this session I have attempted to highlight the fact that seriously psychotic patients manage to communicate using a great variety of methods. The use of metaphorical language has always taken me into delicate and important areas. Sometimes this type of language obviously serves defensive purposes, protecting delicate areas from intrusive or wounding observations made by the therapist. However, metaphorical language is also very intimate and forces one in very close to the patient; it forces one to closely follow their emotional tone in order to comprehend the emotions that they are experiencing. Also, metaphorical language must be considered a special language destined only for the very few specially privileged people who are capable of following and understanding it. The analyst needs to be able to fuse intimately with the patient and, at the same time, withdraw; he must temporarily abandon his own way of thinking in order to follow the journeys of the patient's mind.

Discussion

QUESTION: *What information is necessary to undertake treatment of a psychotic patient? In this case it is not clear if Dr Rosenfeld was in possession of this information before deciding to commence therapy with the patient.*

When one takes into analysis a psychotic patient who must travel from another nation, practical problems arise which must be taken into consideration. To begin with, the patient must demonstrate that there is somebody who can guarantee the analyst not only payment for the analysis, but also upkeep for the period during which the patient must live abroad. In this specific case, I did not know what the circumstances were, particularly as the patient was not initially granted admission into the country because her father had vouched for payment of the treatment but not for her stay. Subsequently, this problem with Immigration was resolved. By this time the patient's perseverance had led to the analysis at least being partially funded by the health system of her country of origin. One must also ascertain how serious the condition is, and if an acute psychosis might develop requiring hospitalization. Should this occur, there must be somebody who can look after the patient. Her mother was dead; her father, who was living with a young woman, had exchanged letters with me before I took his daughter on for analysis. Though there were analysts in her country who could have treated her, the patient insisted on coming to England to be treated by me. She had threatened to kill herself outside my front door if I refused to treat her. She said this to her father too. One day he called me up, extremely concerned because his daughter had run away and left a mysterious message with a probably suicidal meaning. He hoped she had not killed herself but would come to England to see me. He begged me to get in touch with the police to track her down. Because he was so concerned, I insisted that his daughter commence analysis right away.

QUESTION: *How useful is metaphorical language for communication, and how much does it serve to protect an isolated and private part of the patient?*

When the patient talks about her head, saying that it falls in the kitchen, she is referring to her illness and breakdown. She wants to communicate what the disaster and breakdown really felt like. This is an example of communication, but the way in which the communication takes place is equally important. The patient hides behind her thoughts and fends the analyst off in this manner. The function of these types of communication is defensive; communication takes place while pushing the analyst away, and the analyst has to do all the running to understand. The therapist must allow this type of communication to remain in contact with the patient, otherwise the patient becomes even more remote.

QUESTION: *Given that "Rosenfeld" means "field of roses", how should the patient's concrete communication be handled?*

The garden contained other flowers, not just roses. What struck me about the communication was the romantic, sweet atmosphere in the garden, the atmosphere of honeysuckle. The patient always described herself as a stray cat sitting outside the door, or on a windowsill of the house. She was fascinated with this she-cat right from the beginning of analysis. She was the one who had come to be adopted, the stray cat looking for a master and a home. She had told me she would kill herself if I did not take her in. The message was that I was the one who had to take her in, take her into my protection. Obviously, this aroused a certain amount of anxiety in me. I did give the patient this type of interpretation, but she did not want to take it on board. The problem was getting close to her, getting her to understand all this. During my work, I write that the patient at a certain point says she touches the cat, adding emphatically three times, "I'm not going to do it ever again." What was that all about? Was it first affection, followed by prohibition? As though everything she had done up to then had to be cancelled out? There were times when I had to confront the patient with the fact that she had to provide me with more information, that only she could help me to understand. Sometimes the analyst can have the impression of being right and of understanding even though there is not much information to go on. On other occasions, though, the analyst may have the impression that he has got everything wrong. One must distinguish between situations in which one must seek to understand and situations when there is not sufficient material to understand.

Rosemary communicates with me in two ways. First, a superficial way, a way so superficial that she feels that there is no point in going on. This was how she conveyed information to me: she would speak and then say, "It doesn't matter, I didn't say anything." And there was another deeper way, when she moved beyond this way I just referred to. If one puts oneself in the position of such a primitive patient, it is easier to understand what they want to communicate. For instance, with the cat episode we might think that she has something to mother—the cat—something that interests her or something she likes. But if one interprets it to her in this manner, emphasizing the presence of something positive, this could be a wrong move because she tends to cancel out the areas that do not work. What the patient wants is that the analyst understands to what extent she is a desperate stray cat, totally dependent on the analyst, and that she would feel lost or dead if the analyst failed to understand her total dependence.

A further complication arises here as well: these patients are not capable of keeping more than one object in their minds at any one time. When a secondary object emerges, the primary object may well be lost. The patient needs the primary object to survive. I would like to remind you that in the previous analysis the patient had manifested a characteristic symptom: she had to wear a black dress to feel she was holding things together, and she couldn't pick up books that had fallen to the floor because of her fear that something might leak out of her. Through these symptoms the patient conveys the idea of how much she has to maintain herself in a position of protection and containment. Rosemary's object-relation disturbance lies in the fact that all there can be is a fusional relationship (the term "fusional" is not completely appropriate, but it best conveys the concept). In this relationship there is no difference between herself and the object. This is the relationship she enters into with the cat, a hypnotic type of relationship in which all is one. In such a mental state the patient fears not just loss of the object, but loss of parts of herself. When the object moves away it becomes impossible for her to think and function. This is what happened with the previous therapy. The patient says that in these cases her brain swells to become as tall as a tree, she loses herself and the borders of her mind. When Rosemary is in this mental state and uses this kind of metaphorical language, she does not move, she sits still; she does not establish contact with the analyst. It is the analyst who must move towards her; he has to make this effort both emotionally and intellectually. If the analyst fails to do so, the analysis does not move forward. This attitude derives partly from her fear of being wounded or invaded: this is the "black thorn" issue expressed through concrete communication. The analyst's opening up towards her failed in the previous analysis because the therapist could not handle the "weight" of this type of communication.

QUESTION: *The impression is that this patient developed an idealized transference. If it is true that the patient moves towards the patient, it is also true that the patient moves towards the idealized analyst. It would be interesting to know if, subsequently, a negative persecutory transference also emerged. If this was not the case, it would be worth finding out if this is the result of a special technique adopted by Dr Rosenfeld.*

Negative transference emerged on a number of occasions. During the course of analysis, situations arose in which the patient thought that I hated her. She often employed blackmailing tactics: she said that if I didn't see things the way she saw them, she would not come back for analysis. She recounted in great detail how things had gone with the previous analyst, in this way highlighting that the same things must not occur with me. She told me that in her previous analysis, the analyst accused her of telling lies, and she was afraid that I would take her communications as lies. When she was scared or anxious of me, she described her fear in concrete language, as with the black thorn. The negative transference and persecutory fear issue, however, is more complex. For instance, when Rosemary arrived in England she had a great deal of difficulty with accommodation. There was no heating at the place she was staying, but because she had already paid several months' rent in advance, she did not have the courage to say she was going to leave. Her father was so worried about the situation that he wrote to me. I had felt partially responsible and, with great caution, suggested in session that perhaps she might find somewhere better to live, and perhaps she could ask a social worker for some help. I thought I had done a good thing, but the patient jumped up angrily, saying, "How dare you treat me like a little girl! If you carry on like this I'm going to stop the analysis." The social services in her own country had contributed to her upkeep in England, but she had let her father know she was completely against this. It was difficult to handle communications like this in the sessions. This is an area in which the patient feels terribly humiliated and small, belittled by the analyst. It is not so much an issue of dependency as one of humiliation.

QUESTION: *Taking up Dr Rosenfeld's suggestion of moving towards the patient and the patient's desires, one wonders if this does not lead to a dependency that is difficult to resolve, in turn leading on to an interminability issue. The experience of the questioner is that it is hard to avoid the total, definitive dependency of psychotic patients.*

Dependency is not avoidable; on the contrary, it must be sought. If we were treating an autistic child, what could be done if, trying to get close to him or her, the child fled? What can one do—react by moving further and further away? Dependency is an important part of the therapy; indeed, independence develops through a phase of intense dependency. It is the ability to assess the importance of an intimate relationship that makes it possible to create other relationships. The ability to have relationships does not arise out of deprivation.

QUESTION: *I would like to know more about the fact that the patient's psychotic space is occupied by concrete parents, and not by representations of parental objects.*

The patient has a confused picture of internal parents, and a highly disturbed relationship with her parents. I have never understood what kind of relationship she had with her mother, whom the patient had partially experienced as intrusive, partially as somebody with whom she could communicate better than with her father. I have not yet managed to see how her real parents were in order to be able to differentiate between the internal and external image. I think that this is largely to do with the patient's concreteness and her confused language.

FOUR

The analyst's use of phantasy

On the issue of the analyst's use of phantasy in the treatment of narcissistic, borderline, or psychotic patients, I would like to refer firstly to the work of Pierce Clark, then subsequently to the work of Donald Meltzer. Twenty-five years ago, Pierce Clark (1933) described the way he treats these particularly serious cases. The analyst actively encouraged patients to express not just free association, but their fantasies, and in this way almost succeeded in stimulating their imaginative activities. This therapeutic procedure was subsequently abandoned because the analyst did not consider it to be of use. In fact, it should be noted that even when encouraged or prompted to verbalize their fantasies, patients did not succeed in doing so, precisely because their ability to fantasize was inhibited. The problem, indeed, is not so much understanding the patient's fantasies, but rather why their fantasies are not florid and vivid, why they are so inhibited. What emerged from the collusion of these two people who agreed to produce fantasies was of dubious worth because the problem was the greater or less degree of inhibition of fantastical activity. In parallel with this later, abandoned therapeutic approach, Clark developed his own theory of psychotic disturbances, a theory that took for granted faults in primary mothering, a deficit of availability by the original maternal object. It was therefore a matter of giving the patient everything he/she wanted, to counter the lack of affection during the earliest period of life, with the consequence that an artificial and false environment was created in which the patient was treated like a spoilt, little baby. The hope was that by compensating in this manner, the initial painful frustration would disappear. This approach was also abandoned because it did not prove to be effective; Clark's attempts did not meet with success, and a number of psychotic patients treated this way did not demonstrate any changes at all.

It was more a matter of coming to terms with the analyst's phantasy with regard to the patient. It was the analyst's phantasy about the patient that created this vision—a vision that was not a theory but rather a veritable phantasy lacking in therapeutic insight. I would also like briefly to mention the work of Donald Meltzer, who has pursued a therapeutic style based upon interpreting dreams in a particularly vivid and imaginative way, drawing upon a base of great personal richness. The ability to use his phantasy to such a degree in order to succeed in getting to the heart of matters, to extract resonance from the patient's material whether it be a dream or association, is without doubt a particular talent of this analyst. Meltzer (1983) believed that this contribution was sufficient to stimulate the therapeutic process. He shows that patients are exalted, exhilarated, by the brilliant way in which the analyst takes part; but what happens is that true resistances are ignored—in other words, they are not analysed. Despite the evidently great fluidity of this process, in the end it turns out that with this system the incipient egoistic functions and incipient contact functions with reality—specifically, the examination of reality—are left completely untouched.

I now wish to examine other therapeutic approaches that can be linked with the use and abuse of phantasy in the treatment of serious cases. Many people, to varying degrees, use countertransference. How can it be used? It can be used very spontaneously, very freely, reaching into the patient's confusion, backing up the confusion and pathology of the other. Here too it should be said that one's own internal resonances should indeed be used, though never in an unaware or spontaneous way.

In the treatment of serious cases, the problem is how to work through and arrive at a constructive use of countertransference. What this means is carefully monitoring one's own emotional life as it emerges, and using those tell-tale elements that can help us understand what is happening in the patient, something we would not have been able to understand if not through our own internal resonances. This applies to patients who make substantial use of projective identification, using non-verbal language, and when the patient tends more towards deeds than words. As a final note, I wish to add that the analyst's phantasy can be usefully used only in relation to what is actually occurring; the use of phantasy must be associated with something that has actually emerged, something that is contained in the material. It should be used to illuminate what appears to be a blockage, a blockage that cannot be unblocked in any other way.

I am now going to illustrate a further use of phantasy in the treatment of serious patients, as outlined by Bion during the last years of his life. Unfortunately, I did not have the opportunity to question Bion specifically about this theory; I was only able to listen to what he had to say; I couldn't even point out other factors and episodes about which I would have liked to hear his views. Nevertheless, on the basis of what he had to say regarding treatment of a number of patients, Bion noticed that a phantasy sprung to his mind which was completely unassociated, detached, not pertinent to the material the patient was expressing. I recall one phantasy in particular from Bion's clinical material: a thought occurred to him that he could not get out of his head—the image of a beautiful staircase, which was a very unusual colour. As this image kept coming back to him, nine months into the treatment Bion said to the patient, "Listen, I keep thinking about a staircase that's a really unusual colour." At this point the patient exclaimed in a sorrowful and concerned way, "Why didn't you mention this earlier?", as if this revelation held some enormous significance that explained things. As to what this great significance was, I cannot say whether Bion described and explained it, or if I simply do not recall what it was. In any event, independent of the existence of these major explanatory meanings deriving from an insistent image or thought in the analyst's mind, we may legitimately infer that Bion wanted to show that we should loosen up a little, that analysis should not be petrified by method or technique, and that it is appropriate to make use of one's own phantasy.

Of course, Bion could do this, as he was an extremely sensitive and creative person who would have wanted other analysts to be able to follow his approach to drawing upon one's own internal resonances. But this method has been abused and distorted by analysts who are none too discriminating, leading to abnormal and scandalous situations in which if the analyst thinks "elephant", he says it to the patient as if it should have who knows what degree of emotional resonance. All this leaves me truly horrified and disgusted. There are some patients who in such situations have left treatment altogether, convinced that the analyst was crazy. So, what is required is a great deal of care, caution, and discrimination in the use of one's own imagination. If a thought or image keeps coming back, it may be a thought or emotion that is in some way telepathic, that is to say relational; if one wishes, one may question the patient, but with great tact, and without thinking that this is something that should be taken for granted, imposed because it must contain a meaning. The essential thing is to look for a meaningful link; one must not take for granted that such a link exists.

I would now like to share with you an attempt to work through what I myself have achieved thought a cautious use of phantasy, especially in cases where patients have a blockage in their feelings and phantasy, and particularly in their thinking process—a blockage so large that they can block us too. These are situations in which we are sat in session, behind the patient, and we feel empty, sleepy, emotionally numb. I can think of a case a few years ago, during supervision of a young colleague who was treating borderline cases, and who was ready to take on a psychotic patient. I referred to him a patient whom I thought was curable through psychoanalysis. Without going into too much detail, the fundamental characteristic of this patient was his association with a certain sect, which used the practice of influencing members' thoughts and identity (they had regular meetings at which participants thought that the strength of the group could be used for the good of one of them). Everything seemed to be going reasonably well until the situation took a psychotic turn; the patient began to feel that this sect was always on his back, as if he could not get away from the psychic influence exerted by the sect. We believed at the time that this was the beginning of a psychosis; indeed, the patient would say: "There, I can feel the force coming." The force he referred to was the force of the sect, which he felt even when he wasn't at a meeting. He did odd things, unusual things, as he could no longer resist the influence of the sect's strength. The patient engaged in both heterosexual and homosexual relationships and apparently experienced both of these without excessive anxiety; only during the course of analysis did it emerge that he suffered anxiety regarding the compatibility of these two sexual practices.

These are just some outlines to provide you with a sketch of the clinical background. The main point is this: when the patient was either lying on the couch or sitting opposite the analyst, the analyst felt so tired that he had actively to struggle to keep sleep at bay. Many of us will certainly have experienced the feeling of tiredness, drowsiness, and sleepiness that takes hold, and that often occurs when we do not know how to intervene, when we do not know what to do and do not fully understand what is going on. Generally, this condition diminishes when we have an opportunity to talk thoroughly through the situation with a colleague; a more experienced colleague may have a better grasp. In the case I am referring to, this person had regular supervision, was still in analysis, and yet these attacks of sleepiness and drowsiness persisted. He was so obsessed with the problem of staying awake that he was incapable of examining the countertransference, because his biggest problem was struggling to stay awake. I continued to insist that I wanted him to focus not just on his fight against sleep, but, above all, on himself in order to understand the phantasy that was generating in his mind, to see what it was about; otherwise, we would have remained in a mysterious situation. With a great deal of effort, the following emerged: as the analyst began to be able to observe himself, he realized that the beginning of this state, which later developed into a state of sleepiness, was a feeling of being comfortable, of being at ease, at peace. This was a way in to what was otherwise an incomprehensible situation. "There is nothing to be worried about, so why should I be occupied and preoccupied?"

Immediately, his mind diverted onto any other thought, with nothing to do with the patient, as if the patient didn't even exist. It should be noted that to create this situation, the patient resorted to levels of consciousness in order to provoke this initial situation of peace in the analyst, as if there were no problem, to put him at ease. The patient would say: "Listen, there is no problem. Yes, the sect is influencing me, this is what the sect is trying to do, but that's okay, we are aware of that, let's focus on the analysis and not worry about the sect." The effect on the analyst was so strong and he was plunged so far into this state that he could not even verbalize to his supervisor what was happening in analysis. This is a condition created by the patient; the analyst was incapable even of conceptualizing or expressing the relationship in which he was— sharing the patient's stupefying situation. Developments were tragic, as by the time the analyst realized what was happening and was capable of thinking through and verbalizing the situation, even partially resolving matters, the patient had suspended treatment and subsequently took his own life.

Aside from this particularly tragic outcome, we must note that what happens to the analyst effectively has something to do with what is going on in the patient's mind. This transmission is worthy of our closest attention, and not just for the gratuitous manifestation of the analyst's fantasies.

I would now like to talk to you about how I employ the analyst's imagination in the analytic process. This is no more than an attempt to illustrate how one *may* use phantasy; it is not how one *should* use phantasy. It is one of the ways that phantasy may be used. I am illustrating my own experience of how it is possible to influence the patient using one's own imaginative resonances. This can become necessary especially when we are faced with a situation in which we do not know what is happening. For example, we can look at the clinical material we examined earlier. We are dealing with a patient who says that, after leaving the session, he did not know where he had parked his car, and then, after finding it, said to himself: "Ah, perhaps I was the one who that man was talking about when he said, 'I saw a man park it there'. I'll also have to be very careful how I drive, or else I'll have an accident like I did when I started analysis." When we were talking about this session, somebody asked something I would like to know myself: "This is the Monday session, is it possible to know what happened on the Friday session?" But the answer was that the analyst didn't remember: "It's a pity, I don't have my notes, I left them at home." Initially a professorial approach is taken: "Well, yes, it is important to know what happened previously," as a session may unfold in reaction to what happened the time before, meaning that if we do not know what happened, we don't understand very much. Then one says to oneself: "Is it really true that we cannot use what has happened before, is it possible that somebody asks her what happened prior to this and she doesn't have the notes and doesn't remember?" This is exactly what is happening when the patient says: "Look, I am so mixed up, so involved and so preoccupied with thoughts from the session that when I leave I cannot remember where I parked my car and I have to deliberately drive very carefully." What is happening inside the patient that makes him forget the car? In order to attempt to understand this, to make a connection between the facts, what I do is put myself in the patient's shoes, as he is so erotically taken, as we have seen, with the content of the analysis, and the stimulation of the analysis that when he goes back outside it is as if he is in an ongoing dream—in other words, contact with reality is not established right away but only at a later stage, and even then with considerable difficulty. What does this tell us? My imagination tells me that the patient's relationship with his analyst is extremely intense, as we see him so totally involved with the analyst that he forgets reality, and even runs the risk of repeating the tragic situation of the beginning, when the thought of dealing with a woman's breast prompted him to crash into a military vehicle. If we bring together some elements with listening to one's own phantasy surrounding these two episodes, though a full explanation is not forthcoming the situation does begin to become a little clearer.

Phantasy can also be used in other situations—for instance, in a difficult and unpleasant situation when one feels that one's mind is empty. "Not a single thought comes to mind, I don't know what to tell him or her. . . ." This often happens with patients who persistently stay silent. In such situations, an initial twin-pronged approach may be followed. In the first case, we sit there, not knowing what to think or say, so other thoughts spring to mind, the classic distractions; what one may do is say to oneself: "Well, I may as well think about something else that is pleasant, because here there is something that is so unpleasant I prefer not to linger, not to think about it." Then, on the other hand, something may come to mind that we believe may be associated with what the patient has told us thus far, but the connection is not visible. It is not my intention to give active suggestions about using phantasy in the most difficult situations of emptiness, silence, and deadlock, but one thing that may be tried is the following: try to examine as much as possible at the start of analysis the elements of the patient's history, as this may be particularly useful in moments when the material is producing a complete blank. If something springs to mind during such almost despairing moments, when one knows neither what to say nor what to think, this something that comes to mind can be used significantly; it can be and in fact should be coupled with a reference model we have sought to build up from the beginning. What do we use to build up this reference model, what should we initially use to build this up? Well, attempt to understand more about the patient's object relations, understand what are the difficulties and focal problems that provoke anxiety in the patient, the difficult situations the patient has had to face and overcome, as well as details of the family environment and mothering. If something happens during analysis, we have a reference framework to fall back on. We have access to elements to help us try to recover from a silence, to build momentum up again, make things more fluid and less stationary. This may be enacted if we have an opportunity to orient ourselves by drawing upon some previously gleaned information; if we do not have this, we can find ourselves with gaps at times when it is not appropriate to ask the patient for further information.

At such times of emptiness, we may also turn to theory—psychoanalytic theory—in an attempt to understand. This morning's patient, for example: what kind of homosexuality is it, why is he homosexual, what is this eroticized transference that can be a carrier of any single thing? Drawing upon what we know, we can direct ourselves with greater certainty towards a review of his relationship with his mother, which should provide a solution. Here we see that we no longer have given such free rein to our phantasy as in the extremely deplorable case where the analyst thinks of and says "elephant", but rather we come up with a thought that is actually associated with indications given to us by the patient. We become more certain of what we are saying, more encouraged.

What I am trying to put across is a fundamental point that we should not use unchecked phantasy; what we need is phantasy controlled by data, confirmed by actual facts. The essential question we must ask ourselves is the following: does what I am thinking at this moment make sense when compared to everything that is known about this patient? If it does not contradict any other element, then it may be used. If it clashes, if it is based upon a scotoma or is built upon a contradiction, then it may not be used. Indeed, in this kind of work with patients whose thoughts are particularly seriously disrupted, phantasy and thought must be used in a united—never disconnected—way. Phantasy is never used alone, always in conjunction with thought. The entire reference model of the patient's inner world may be transformed—indeed, it must be transformed—only with regard to all the other elements that are out in the open. The other elements out in the open come from the egotistical function of thought, and not from phantasy, even though phantasy is indispensable for understanding moments of stasis and enigma. What we are trying to do in analysis is mobilize the patient to bring back together elements that have split within himself, as if we were facing a puzzle in which we have to return the missing pieces so that the whole picture begins to become visible and make sense. If we have a sufficient number of connections, it is possible to piece them back together with thought and with the other elements that are already in the open in a non-disconnected way, allowing the patient to be made capable of functioning. But if the patient is paralysed by too many missing connections in his inner world, it cannot function. There are some sorts of split that we attempt to repair by calling not just upon thought but on phantasy too. This is what can be used to treat so-called thinking disturbances. When an analyst is working efficiently, patients feel capable of thinking and helping the analyst create these missing connections. This is what the patient needs in order to be able to function and feel well. What is particularly important for the patient is to understand one of the most disturbing things: the repetitive nature of certain disorders. When we have found the connection, the patient will most certainly feel relieved. Obviously, we have not dealt here with patient phantasy, as what is important here, right now, is to consider the analyst's phantasy in relation to the situation of the patient with whom we must come to terms.

PART II

CLINICAL SEMINARS

FIVE

Traumatic infancy

In this supervision, Rosenfeld highlights how the past can mould the present, how it may be deformed by memory or, on the contrary, how it may manifest itself in order to be understood.

Infantile traumatic experiences may in reality be used victimistically as a defence against insight, or they may be communicated and relived in the analytic relationship in order to be transformed. The analyst's taking on of the patient's past, when it is manifestly traumatic, helps to configure the developmental blockage, the distortion of development, and the patient's difficulties, which will certainly make the analytic relationship difficult and distressful. The presentation of traumatic infancy described in this seminar is something that Rosenfeld takes very seriously.

The session material here certainly sheds light on the analyst, but it also tells the story of the past. This emerges in part in the content and atmosphere of the first dream; the present and the analytic relationship are the locus in which the basic supportive objects and emotional experiences lacking in infancy emerge only to rapidly decay, giving the analyst a perception of a frustrating and tantalizing working situation.

The reappearance of the traumatic situation in the current analytic relationship clearly emerges at the weekend breaks. Rosenfeld analyses the transference in terms of a total situation that, though drawing on the past, contains new elements of the relationship, including the analyst's lack of receptivity and understanding of the level of suffering experienced during separation. Two final enlightening dreams cast light on the complexity of this relationship.

ROSENFELD: Many years ago, we sometimes used to work on cases without an outline, allowing the material that emerged in session to develop on its own in order to begin working from the material, in the hope that something would come up. Some analysts even began analysis without any details concerning the patient they were about to meet.

In this particular case, it may clearly be seen that some patients are highly involved with what happens in their everyday life, and they connect everything with certain past events or situations. In a rather conscious fashion they want the analyst to bear in mind the fact that they have truly suffered in certain situations. It is not always easy for the analyst listening to these patients to understand whether they are exaggerating, nor gauge the degree of veracity of the way these situations are presented.

It is also evident that we may ascribe too much significance to the presentation of history as it is told, thereby failing to recognize the importance of other things and failing to realize that the patient has defended him/herself from problems of a different origin, attributing them entirely to external events.

That said, I suggest that as work proceeds, it might be useful to retain an idea of the patient's history as a model to be kept in the background; one should also be prepared to revise this model completely if this proves necessary. This model is extremely useful if one comes up against situations that are not understood and where one does not know what to do.

Often the model supplies an understanding of a situation that the patient is otherwise not capable of conveying.

The working method is critical in cases that have been particularly difficult, on which one may have worked for five-to-ten years without the patient showing an improvement. One suddenly realizes that it is not sufficient to focus on all aspects of the patient during analysis. It is far too easy to break off such situations; what is necessary, on the contrary, is to help the person to understand. This is why I always proceed in this manner, which I have found to be a generally effective approach.

Given that it is usually efficient, I shall proceed in this manner here.

First we shall hear the patient's story. When I have something to say, I will interrupt.

ANALYST: I am keen on dwelling on this patient's history precisely because it has been extremely important and extremely tough, during the course of an analysis that has been filled with her history. While Dr Rosenfeld was talking, I was pleased to think that I might get some help from this approach. The history I intend to present in summary was told over a number of years, during which time I had the constant and anxious preoccupation that I would never get to know enough in order truly to understand the real reasons behind her suffering and the reasons for her lack of confidence in life.

The patient is an only child of Jewish origin. At the age of 2 years, her family fled their home country to a new continent in order to shelter from Nazi persecution. The only merit she fleetingly ascribed to her parents was that in this manner they saved her from certain death and then worked hard to regain the economic security they had lost.

She spoke very little about her mother, referring to little more than her humble origins compared to her father and that she had abandoned her before her sixth birthday. Her mother ran off with another man to a distant Atlantic island, no longer capable of tolerating her husband's terrible character. The patient never felt sufficiently strong to protect her from the divine paternal rage, and she felt completely at his mercy after her mother ran off.

Only two vague and isolated memories of this relationship with her mother emerged, which were related to fill things in. One regarded a lovely big rag doll that her mother had made with her own hands and given her as a gift, but that the patient did not like. The other concerned the long stories her mother used to tell her to get her to eat. The image was of a mother with a spoon in her hand, telling story after story as the patient listened raptly, keeping her mouth clamped firmly shut, often with the last mouthful still not yet swallowed.

On the other hand, the patient spoke about her father at great length, time and time again. When she started analysis, she was still terrified he might catch up with her and renew his hold over her. At great length she told me episodes in order to describe how tough he was, his puritanical moralism, and above all the absolutism of his ideas and rules for life which he imposed on her as her sole criteria in life. She knew he had forced her mother to go on long so-called healthful walks in the woods while she was pregnant, almost bringing on a miscarriage. She knew and stated that she had her legs bound until past her third birthday, in an attempt to make sure that she grew up with beautiful straight legs. She remembered a haunting and terrifying interrogation, when she was accused of allowing herself to have impure thoughts and desires, accused of engaging in masturbatory practices.

She remembered that on one occasion to make her confess he hit her, made her strip off, and inspected her, looking for who knows what signs of manipulation of her genitals in a gynaecological inspection. Still naked, he then tied her to a tree in the countryside, where he left her for several hours.

Her father even strictly regulated her sleeping habits. An afternoon nap was obligatory, even after she had passed puberty. She remembers being woken up in terror by the shouts of her father, who accused her of pretending to be asleep, or else he would suddenly throw off the covers to try to catch her masturbating.

What she most laments in her father is that he did not allow her to enjoy the pleasures of family life for long. Indeed, when her mother left, his father placed her with a foster-family of farmers, because he spent a lot of time travelling on business. The patient has a very good memory of that family. She arrived weak, suffering from eczema, and unsteady on her feet, and she found affectionate care that quickly helped her to recover and regain strength.

The only obscure and ambiguous part of this experience was the fact that she was a sort of plaything for the man who should have acted as father. In reality, he was very good to her; she remembers he taught her to read and how to recognize plants. But sometimes this man enjoyed himself by terrorizing her. For example, she was highly disgusted by animal faeces, particularly cow-pats, which she had never seen before. He apparently had fun hoisting her up, holding her upside down by her ankles just inches above the animal shit, and listening to her scream.

There was also a suspicion that he had made her play with his penis, telling her it was his fingers when they were having an afternoon lie-down.

She was highly distressed when her father took her away, accusing the family of not looking after her well enough. She did not ever make any connection, when she spoke with me, of the possibility that her father had heard something about the man's behaviour towards her. It does not seem that she spoke about this, but this wasn't clear.

In any event, from that moment the patient was shuttled from one family to another. It was the same story every time: as soon as she began to become fond of the new family, her father turned up and said he was unhappy, for reasons that the patient did not understand. The same thing happened with the housekeepers he hired after bringing her back to live with him: they were dismissed one after the other for the oddest reasons. One of them was even accused of wanting to poison him. Nobody ever had the strength to stand up to him.

I would summarize her history prior to entering analysis as follows: after getting a degree to fulfil the father's wishes, she then entered a marriage that was subsequently annulled because of her husband's impotence.

I know very little about this episode. My patient mentioned it after analysis had been ongoing for some time. She decided to move away from her father after winning a scholarship. It seems she came to this decision after her father told her that if she wanted to continue with her studies, she would have to start work. This was another piece of information that she gave me at a later moment, keeping it concealed for a long time.

After arriving in Europe, she began analysis following major depressions during which she would spend days on end in bed, in complete darkness. She fantasized about hanging herself, dressed in a long black dress. She recovered before long, met a young physicist, and married him, attracted by his promises of devotion and absolute protection. She left analysis when her husband had to move to Italy. She told me that her analyst at the time also believed that this marriage could be a sign of greater maturity in her. She had been in analysis for two years.

At the beginning of her analysis with me, she had been living just outside Milan for a number of years, in reasonably comfortable socio-economic conditions. But this second husband proved to be impotent as well. She wanted to go into analysis because she had been feeling bad for some time, overwhelmed by nameless anxieties. She later told me that she also had serious sleeping problems. Unconquerable tiredness made her sleep in the afternoons, but in the evenings anxiety about not being able to sleep kept her wake. She slept with the assistance of sleeping pills and alcohol.

ANALYST: I wish to say that I have presented this case because it has been weighing on me enormously. I was quick to seize the opportunity extended by Dr Rosenfeld because I want to see if somebody could help me to contain this person—something that I am finding to be extremely difficult at present.

ROSENFELD: How long has the analysis been going on?

ANALYST: Seven years.

ROSENFELD: Do you feel that during this time you have helped her, or do you see the case as stationary?

ANALYST: What happens is that in the sessions she seems to be stationary when it comes to the complaints she makes, but in her life she is much more independent. It is precisely now, when she is working and active, that her protests against me and against life have worsened. As far as she is concerned, nothing is any good.

ROSENFELD: That's very interesting. Let's try and have a look at the facts as they have been presented. Is her history something that was told immediately at the beginning, after meeting the patient, or did it take time to come out?

ANALYST: I would say bit by bit, but without any great difficulty as she really loves talking about what has happened to her, so within a few months I knew quite a lot about her.

ROSENFELD: Let's try to understand the analyst's feelings and what the patient is repeatedly trying to get across to her. It is very important to establish what she is so persistently complaining about to you, what the patient feels she is not managing to communicate. There is something she would like to tell you, which is why everything becomes so repetitive. There are feelings that obviously you have not considered sufficiently, so she must communicate them to you continuously.

Listening to this case history, one has an image of a very sadistic father, a father who torments and constantly imprisons the patient with his possessiveness. Every time she created bonds with somebody, he destroyed the situation and took her back to do whatever he wanted with her. This is a sadistic situation, but it is also to some degree a masochistic one which in the past has dominated the patient within her family, and continues to do so to the present day. She now seems to be more distant from her father, to whom she was completely subordinate in the past. From the way this is presented, however, it seems as if this story keeps on repeating itself. Indeed, even when the father does not seem to have such power and no longer takes her away to make her do what he wants, it seems that this pattern is still being repeated. This is true not only of the past, it is still happening in the present.

What is missing in this case history, an element that links to all of this patient's problems, is that nothing has been said about her relationship with the maternal object. There is a sensation that she was deprived of maternal affection when her mother walked out; however, we also know that while the mother was there, she used to tell her stories, there were eating problems, and her mother tried to help her in this situation. What we do not know, though, is whether there was a normal nutritional relationship during the patient's earliest days. To some extent, if one wants to find out what is missing, this is a very big gap.

Later, as the story moves on, feelings regarding her relationship with her mother—of being protected and nourished, as well as feelings concerning the presence of somebody who offers sustenance and security—give way to a sadistic father who is responsible for her inability to enter into contact with any maternal object offering love and nutrition.

Even in the family where she ends up, it is above all the father who seems to look after her, including in a sexual sense, and the feeling of a maternal object is missing. It is important to realize this and to keep it in mind.

Another interesting point concerns the fact that the patient complains of not having an object who protected her in her infancy; her father, who should have looked after her, butted in every time she seemed to find an object to which she could form an attachment. As soon as the patient found an object, her father whisked her away. Therefore, her father is described not as an object that "didn't look after her", but as an object that blocked any chance she had of finding an object with which to form a bond.

It is as if there is an area in which the maternal object and her inability to find it is attributed to the father's sadistic feelings, from which her mother succeeded in engineering an escape. Deep down, she must feel strong resentment that her mother managed to get out. One assumes that the mother spent time with the patient and told her beautiful stories. One has the impression that there is something in the relationship with the mother, and one wonders why, afterwards, the patient felt completely lost.

It is as if the father suddenly appeared and said: "So, that's how it is—you want to be close to your mother, the two of you together!" One has the impression he might think: "But of course, you are masturbating together," so he butts in and takes her away.

What emerges is an image of her father as the one who interferes in her close relationship with her mother, which is not just a nourishing link, it is also an exciting masturbatory relationship.

It is as if the patient was thinking of a relationship of homosexual proximity, with the constant fear that someone would appear and say, "Oh, so that's what you're up to again!"

ROSENFELD: Was the patient originally in therapy with a male analyst or with a female analyst?

ANALYST: The patient's original analyst was a man.

ROSENFELD: Was it the patient's choice to have a woman analyst this time around?

ANALYST: Ah, that I don't know. I know she needed to enter analysis, but I don't know if she thought about whether it should be with a man or a woman. She made an attempt at analysis before coming to me, a year earlier, I think. She had tried to begin analysis with a man, but stopped after six months. There were some things that I have not written down, because she already seemed to be so prolix. It is such a trying case that I would have weighed you down if I had told you everything. There was, for instance, an episode, an attempt at getting in touch with a female analyst whom she mentions every now and then. She was very unhappy because she says she felt cheated, constantly put off, and was then accused of not remembering the appointments she had been given. In the end, she didn't start this analysis either. That's her version of things.

ROSENFELD: How many times a week does she come?

ANALYST: Four times a week. She only wanted to have two sessions when she began. She said she couldn't do it, though she was in too poorly a state to come four times, that two times would be enough, and that she didn't have enough money. I insisted on four sessions, and she agreed, protesting a great deal.

ROSENFELD: All very interesting stuff. Moving on with the story, we will see if what has been said will be useful to us or not. This image is, however, extremely interesting. But something completely different may also emerge. In cases such as this, in which situations are continually repeated, we must bear in mind that there is something important being overlooked. It is a very significant problem to resolve, and we will have to understand what has not yet been tackled in this situation.

QUESTION: *You say that the patient finally moved away from her father. But to separate, she had to leave; in other words, she is here and her father lives in another country.*

ANALYST: Yes, her father is still in the country they fled to. She went to live in another country precisely to physically distance herself. However, the first version was that she had won a scholar-ship and left because she couldn't stand her father any more. At a later date, in an off-hand way, she told me that she was deeply offended because her father had agreed she should continue with her studies, but he then said, "Study if you want to, but you'll have to support yourself." I was greatly struck by this.

ROSENFELD: Has she ever asked herself why her mother didn't take her with her when she ran away?

ANALYST: She knows that her mother ran off with another man; she says, "She completely lost interest in me."

I have drawn up a summary of the first session. At the time I felt it was her calling card, like the programme she set out for our relationship, and it worried me not inconsiderably.

> Before lying down on the couch, she took out a print from the briefcase she brought along and showed it to me with a little smile, midway between possessiveness and an excuse. It was a Goya print, perhaps the Colossus, in which a huge monstrous figure made up of shadow itself seemed to be emerging from the shadows, a menacing thing. The patient told me that she wanted to give me an idea of the anxiety she had hinted at during our initial interview; the feeling of being oppressed by the sensation that "obscure and worrying forces" could destroy any good that came to her. Her smile seemed more terrible to me than the monster.

> On the couch, she reiterated her lack of faith in life. She also said that beautiful things can conceal ugly things. For example, swans were beautiful animals as long as you did not see their feet; when you did, they became ugly and awkward. They could also be very aggressive.

> Somebody had told her about a swan that laid an egg outside a woman's house. When the woman tried to go out, with a baby in her arms, the swan attacked her, pecking at her legs, grabbing her clothes, and forcing her to go back inside.

> As the analysis went on, I have found myself with a patient who only wants me to listen to her and who, by the next session, has completely forgotten what went on the time before. Only in her dreams have there been responses to what I have said to her. There

seems to be a secret, isolated part of her that answers me. Sometimes I have been able to readjust through what she has told me in
her dreams. But beyond this, there does not seem to be any progres-
sion.

She soon began to protest against my comments. Any time I said
something, she took it as an interruption: she had not yet said
everything she wanted to say. At one point I felt the physical
sensation that she was dripping all over me like thick molasses. I
told her this, that something was happening.

When I talked to her, she really must have felt cut off from me. It
seems that she used words as a sort of glue to stick closely to me,
and it must have been truly terrible when I interrupted her. This was
the first time that she told me she had listened to me, that she had
felt a certain relief. Following this, she was able to remember some
things, and things began to go a little better.

Two years ago her husband decided to go into analysis. I was right
in thinking that she had helped him to re-conquer a certain dimen-
sion of his maleness. As soon as the husband began analysis, she
was overwhelmed by a terrible loathing for him. She accused him of
tricking her, he had promised her so much, but he was just a poor
little man. Their life became hellish. She slept on the floor while he
slept in their double bed. Then she kicked him out of the room, until
he left, in despair.

The group of sessions I am now presenting take place about a year
after her *de facto* separation from her husband, around the time of
their legal separation. During this year her life moved forwards on
two levels. On one hand, she allowed a glimpse of certain impulses
on a cultural and social level as well as greater commitment to her
work, which had expanded and become more involving. She had
been complimented for her work.

She met a man with whom she succeeded in having not just an
intellectual understanding, but also her first sexual experience.
There were moments when she felt a little happier, a little more a
woman. But this happens to be a man who does not want commitment of any sort; this makes her suffer, but it is also a useful thing for
showing me how unlucky she is. A pall of desperation hangs over
everything, nothing goes right for her. Too many things are missing

in her life, and the things she has now amount to nothing. She is around 40 years old.

ROSENFELD: In this part of the case history, we can see that the analyst has seized upon a number of important elements such as this desire for closeness. It is highly interesting that words are always the things that interrupt the relationship. We note here a strong desire for the analyst not to speak, that his should be a solely physical presence, that this is what the patient craves; this desire is well described and well picked up on by the therapist. This is naturally only the beginning—the patient would feel very frightened if they went deeper.

Did the husband go to a male analyst or a female analyst?

ANALYST: A female analyst. This is the Monday session:

[Patient arrives on time. Begins to talk to me in her usual complaining little voice, perhaps in a more restrained tone than normal.]

P: "I spent the weekend struggling not to neglect anything that might help me. I did many things to feel alive, but I sense that they are superficial . . . although in reality I was interested in doing them. This morning I would have liked to be the Eternal Father, so I could stop it ever becoming day. I feel that this need to be self-sufficient is irrational . . . [Goes quiet for a little]

"I am also terrorized at the thought that I may get pregnant: recently I haven't been taking precautions, such as washing, etc. . . .

"Perhaps my dream is more important . . . I get excited just thinking about it! I had the dream after waking up this morning at 6 o'clock; I took a little Valium and warm milk . . . I needed to sleep reassured. The dream was about my home: I was at home and it was getting dark. Somebody had come in: I could tell because there were heaps of newspapers and magazines in the corridor. I was not afraid, I was excited. It was Mr E. I saw him sitting in the corridor and he looked tired, as if he had been on a long journey. I sat on his knees, happy and a little bewildered. I did not understand why he was there. I cuddled him, it was partly erotic, partly tender-fraternal-friendly.

"Then comes the distressing part. *A class of unruly kids burst in, breaking down the door: they turned everything upside down, fighting among themselves. There must be fifty of them. The adult who was meant to be looking after them didn't lift a finger. All those children made a great mess . . . and I care so much about tidiness! I go into the bedroom and find that the children have taken the bed apart. On the ground was a mattress and a mat, on which Mr E was lying, as if he was ill. I was so worried by the situation; I was angry and distressed.*

"*There were moments when the children calmed down, but then it all went off again . . . and the teacher didn't do a thing! On the contrary, he was enjoying himself with the children.* That's how the dream ends."

ANALYST: I would like to say one quick thing . . . that here I only made my comment at the end, because this was one of the few times that she communicated in an almost serious voice. It seems that she truly does wish to convey something to me, and I am also extremely curious to hear what she has to say. Not the usual whining voice, though there is a little of that.

ROSENFELD: Is it is unusual for her to use this serious tone?

ANALYST: Quite rare. Usually she speaks in a tone that seems to be infuriating, complaining, infantile. This is a more serious tone.

ROSENFELD: Do you know anything about Mr E? When she mentioned him in the dream, did you already know of him?

ANALYST: No, no—perhaps I did have some vague and distant recollection, but I did not really know.

ROSENFELD: A dream like this in such a context is interesting because it describes a situation that strikes the patient in an oppressive manner. The patient is completely distressed and overpowered; there is so much action compared to the sessions, and the patient doesn't want anybody to interrupt her. The dream shows the danger of interrupting a calm session. It is very important to look into the emotions in the setting and in the dream. It is as if the patient were thinking: "I would like you to hold me here in your lap, I would like you to talk to me in a way that cannot be confused with all that racket coming from the children."

The important thing one must always keep in mind is that when we encounter a dream like this one, we must ask ourselves: what is the atmosphere of the dream? In what way is this atmosphere referring to me? The interesting thing is that you were capable of picking up the feeling in the patient's voice, the fact that this was not a complaint but a serious feeling that the patient rarely felt.

In this situation, Mr E has truly succeeded in containing her a little, and this is a highly interesting and important aspect—a male figure who appears in a slightly but not overly erotic form.

ANALYST: When she begins to comment upon a dream, associations are very rare; it is very rare that she makes the effort to come up with associations.

> P: "At the moment anxiety is invading me, it is overpowering me. I don't even feel ok when I'm with my friends. I relive the pain of seeing my front door broken down; in the dream it was a lovely country-style door, not like the real one. I would like to understand this dream because I recall so few dreams. It brings up so many things.
>
> "For example, that fact that I knew someone had come into my home but I wasn't afraid. I have noticed that for some time now I have been less afraid of burglars. Perhaps it's because I have a security door . . . but I'm not so worried any more. . . . Initially, I thought it must have been C, my husband. But it was Mr E.
>
> "Mr E was an important figure in historical studies. Highly intellectual but also very human. He taught me how to think. Many of my tastes come from him, though I have developed things myself.
>
> "He once came to Europe and looked me up. I was very surprised he came alone, because I knew he had married; but he told me that this did not prevent him from keeping up friendships. This struck me as strange, because at that time my idea of being in a couple was of an exclusive union.
>
> "As far as the children in the dream are concerned, they make me think that that evening there was a book about canaries on

the bed. I bought a male canary at Christmas, I wanted to hear it sing, spread a little life around the house. Then I added a female. To begin with they fought terribly, and I even thought that somebody had made a mistake and given me another male."

ANALYST: Here I immediately thought of the fights she and I had over talking. She really feels it's a fight with me.

P: "I was always scared I would come home one day and find one of them dead. But then they produced four eggs and have been sitting on them. Everything changed, everything is idyllic. They are so sweet. But then my friends told me they would lay more eggs and I would have a house full of canaries. The book says you have to keep a close eye on them all day long, but I don't want to be enslaved by then, so I think I'll give away the female and the babies, and just keep the male so he can sing. The rest of it is all too much of a commitment. I was happy that at last there was a little life in my house, at last there was love between me and the canaries. . . . I already had a guinea pig . . . but since I got the canaries I can't help thinking of it as a stupid little animal. The canary is perfect; it sings and is no trouble. It coincided with Alfredo [her lover] coming to visit, and we made love; but now I am frightened of getting pregnant, and of being overwhelmed by the canary offspring. But I feel so lonely. I feel impotent in the face of the anxiety of depression, which is always lurking.

"For example, I used to like Carnival, which makes me think of unruly children . . . a healthy joy. But two of my girlfriends saw acts of vandalism in the street and told me about them. It is impossible to find true happiness in Milan. All this violence, apples with razor blades in them . . . and I feel so exposed without a man to protect me. Ah! I cannot allow myself to collapse . . ."

[As she says this she turns on to her side and huddles up with a disconsolate sob, telling me in an infantile tone [it starts up again] of self-commiseration: "Ah! . . . I'm so useless . . . So pathetic! . . ."]

This seemed to me to be the moment to intervene. I observe that in telling me her dream, she said she wanted to understand it; but now, curled up behind the security door of her tears, it is unlikely that she will be able to hear me. Anything I say would remain sterile, external.

With a sigh the patient, who has stopped crying, lies out again on the couch in a relaxed position, with one arm over her head.

At this point I remind her of her early morning wake up and her desire to be the Eternal Father and stop the day from proceeding. This is why she takes the Valium and warm milk: to withdraw back into her dream where everything is fine, where the warmth and calm of the world are safe inside her, not outside, in reality, in the time that passes. The patient sighs softly, but she does not move and she says nothing. . . . A moment later, I tell her that she complains of the violence of real life, but her dream tells us that the violence she is so frightened of is also a place of vital impulses: she feels invaded by a host of vibrant emotions clashing like rowdy children, continually proliferating like her canaries . . .

At this point I stay rather silent. I am afraid of talking at length but she says nothing and I decide to tell her everything that is on my mind.

After a while, she says: "I am so scared," then silence once more. She still has her arm behind her head, and she is now facing in my direction.

The session is coming to an end and I keep on hoping that something gets through to her and stays with her.

I recall Mr E. I remind her that perhaps I, like him, have felt like a person who has helped her to think. But she is afraid that I do not want to make a fixed and indissoluble couple with her, much like her impotent husband. She shuts me up in the cage of her sighs, of her "don't knows" and "don't remembers", so I have to keep on singing on and on for her. Now a suspicion seems to be creeping up on her that to keep on feeding this illusion, she has to fashion herself into something terrible: to reduce herself to mental darkness, without resources enough to live her own life. This is real slavery.

When I make notes on the session, I am struck by an association I did not make during the session. Her mother had run away to the Canary Islands. I had forgotten that.

ROSENFELD: To begin with, I think that the session contains something different from what you describe as usually occurring—namely, her continual complaining. This session seems to have a different "flavour". It is clear to see that the analyst is in no way hasty, she is not in a hurry to get at anything. On the contrary, she seems to have allowed herself to be highly involved in the dream setting. Indeed, the setting is that of an opening door, with this unexpected Mr E whom the patient allows to come in. She also allows him to enter into intimacy with her even though he is married—in other words, a person who could cause worries for her. In the dream, as long as it lasts this contact with him seems to make it possible for her to sit down.

Let's move on now to the next point we can use to get our bearings. While I was listening to the case history, I was thinking about the model we had previously constructed. With relation to the feelings we were talking about earlier, I was thinking that the patient is seeking a female object. But where is this object? There must be some kind of maternal object inside her, and it is probably this that she is seeking.

So, when Mr E appears, my first thought was: he has many characteristics of a maternal object that contains her, that helps her to think. This is exactly what we may believe the patient might find in a maternal object, but here it is Mr E. The question that now arises, and this really is interesting: where is the female object?

The analyst says: "Ah, I did not realize that hiding behind the canaries was the mother issue and its associated issues." As soon as the mother model emerges, something happens, a disturbance, that makes it very difficult for the patient to carry on and continue with the feeling that seems to be emerging in the session. This strikes me as extremely significant.

Her description is of a violent interruption by these noisy children; it is an interruption that constantly happens in the patient's life and in her analysis.

As soon as the canaries are introduced, what naturally emerges is the whole sexuality issue, the matter of children and the whole arena of things that the patient is unable to face.

Remember her first husband going into analysis, lying on a couch belonging to a woman analyst? Initially, the patient was extremely angry.

When the canaries are introduced into the discourse, and the canaries begin to show an interest in one another, the patient says that they "row", that they make love, that she can't cope with it, that she feels she can't take it any more.

This appears clearly: even when she merely begins to imagine any idea of a couple making love and making babies, of a maternal object in relation to a man, the patient simply takes leave of her senses. This is what she acknowledges in the session.

ANALYST: When the mother is represented, and a man comes on the scene, she goes mad with rage.

ROSENFELD: Listening to this account, like myself you may have thought of those beautiful stories that the mother used to tell the patient. The problem is as follows: if we listen closely to this dream, it should be recognized that the moment the man enters, the mother enters too, and we do not know how she arrives and appears. I think that the bringing together of this male and female figure in this situation creates a certain tension and confusion in the mind, as, "She is my mother and my father, a male but also a female."

In this situation we do not know who her father is; somebody who arrives and interrupts represents a serious danger. The difficulty lies in the fact that the appearance of the maternal object takes place in a masked man; this is a peculiar way, not an easy thing to treat. We must remember this. When she says what she has picked up on, that's another issue. One must feel that both have emerged in the session.

The analyst feels that if she makes connections in her mind, it frightens the patient because what emerges is the idea of a couple, the idea of having children. Speaking and making connections is like bringing a mother and a new life into analysis, something that immediately frightens and upsets the patient.

There is something the analyst has already experienced often: one must recognize that simply making a connection automatically signifies creating a couple, a female object and a male object, which are immediately broken up by the patient.

What I would like you to bear in mind is the atmosphere of the session, and also what the analyst feels capable of transmitting within the session. I believe that one of the problems lies in the fact that until now the analyst has not been able to give an interpretation she felt to be of value: the patient actually experiences this as an interruption and she is immediately aggressive, and this experience makes her feel confused and anxious. What is conveyed is the experience of these seven years in which it has not been possible for her to communicate all this. Seven years is a long time.

The question that arises is as follows: how is it possible to communicate this to the patient during the session, in such a way that she can cope with the tension associated with the fact that the analyst is saying something? Indeed, we must acknowledge that it is not just a matter of saying something: the attempt to make a connection is attacked and immediately sends the patient into a state of confusion. Session after session, both of them are dominated by feelings of anger. Five, one hundred, two hundred, four hundred, five hundred sessions have been interrupted in this way. This is a situation in which one must acknowledge the flood of noises in the patient's laments, and one must acknowledge that the children represent this constant interruption which has gone on within analysis for the last seven years. One must not underestimate interruption and noise; they have been a constant in this analysis, they have interrupted every attempt to make any connections. I believe that this has priority over everything else.

We do not know what would have happened if the analyst had intervened in a slightly different way. What the analyst was aware of, and I believe this to be very important, is that during this session she did nothing that could provoke these noisy complaints typical of this patient during the seven years of analysis. The patient has always complained, and it is an important thing if the analyst tells us: "She complains, she complains over and over again, then she shouts and gets angry"—this is the image we have.

The analyst wanted to do something that would allow the patient to experience the session without this continual interference, and without her being irritated by something that the analyst might have told her and that would have made her scream "You don't understand me, you don't understand me!"

The analyst succeeded in this, and I think this is very important: she has been very sensitive, and this has enabled her to focus on the sentiments she has described to us. I agree that if the analyst had introduced herself as being represented by Mr E, or as the mother, this connection at this precise moment would have probably made the patient scream.

The patient must be made ready in an extremely careful way; telling her that in this situation it is not just Mr E who has helped her to feel calmer would make a connection with the mother-who-tells-the-lovely-stories, which would immediately bring out the whole canary business.

One would then have to monitor what happens next. If the patient said, "Yes, you are right, I will not protest", then the connection will successfully have been made. The analyst felt it after the session and therefore got very close to all this. Sometimes one does not make all the connections, but it is also true that the analyst did not make any mistakes and has set the scene for the next session.

It is interesting to note that when the patient wakes up and wants to calm down in order to carry on sleeping, she needs to do this in order to make contact with this extremely interesting dream.

Her succeeding in calming herself down and feeling that an unexpected person arrives represent an attempt to achieve a satisfying relationship with the analyst—something that seems to her to be elusive. We know that after the patient had taken Valium and milk to get into the right mood, the analyst could connect the fact that instead of getting upset and constantly complaining during the session with all these children who burst onto the scene shouting, the patient would like some respite from all this complaining, she would like to feel that she may comfortably sit on the analyst's knee as in the dream. I believe this to be of absolutely fundamental importance in understanding this communication.

The practical difficulty in this dream lies in the fact that when the patient becomes very frightened and upset, she opens up to the conflict of analytic experience. In the dream, she has a satisfying experience which is interrupted by screaming children. This seems to be something destined to repeat itself; in the dream, this is clearly shown to happen. This is why the dream offers a new model of this constant, repetitive experience.

Will this complaining still be going on fifty sessions after the patient has received a little relief from the analyst? It is highly likely. Is it a problem if this happens? No. It is necessary to experience and understand the persistence of this complaining. Does the patient realize that she is complaining once more after having a good experience, even though she is upset by her own complaints? Or is she unaware that she is complaining once more? And so on.

All this would help to create order in this highly confused state of affairs; it would also help to pinpoint what the patient is complaining about.

What the analyst offers as an alternative to milk and Valium is the content regarding the canaries and her mother, which are connections. The analyst uses her mind and offers interpretations about which the patient must think. Mr E is a representation: he is the intellectual who helps the patient think.

Generally, the analyst makes the connections that the patient has trouble handling. Despite this, in her dream the patient appears to attribute value to them, even though one may see how difficult it is for her to cope with an interpretation that helps her to understand something, so much so that the screams begin right away.

ANALYST: I have to say that there were fifty sessions just like that. This patient finds it difficult to have stable sessions, one after another, so I thought I would present the whole Thursday session, which is her fourth session, providing some information on the Tuesday and Wednesday's sessions as well.

> The following two sessions are very tormented and tiring, not just for the patient but also for me; I find myself submerged by her complaints about her miserable life, just like in the early days of her analysis.

> I feel as if I am injected with a feeling of discomfort and impotence so strong that it feels physical, like some kind of ailment. What comes to mind is Mr E, tired after his long journey, whom the patient attempted to seduce in her dream, and who represented for her a point of reference in the use and development of her mental faculties and thought.

It is true that at these moments I really do feel tired, certainly no more comfortable than Mr E, stretched out on a mattress on the floor—sometimes without even the mattress. But this image of Mr E helped me not to give up the attempt to understand more, or at least, to tackle the feeling of allowing myself to lose all faith.

ROSENFELD: I find it very important and interesting that this image of Mr E offered you solace. The dream contained a very important communication, and the analyst grasped it correctly. Just as there is liking for Mr E, there is liking for the analyst who has to cope with this situation.

One very important aspect of the dream is that the children who arrive and complain are not controlled by the patient's adult self. In her dream, the patient admits that her adult self isn't doing anything at all to control these complaining children. She is aware that an adult self might be there, and, when she wants to complain, she knows that she could also restrain herself.

There are some elements in the dream in which the patient has insights, but this does not transfer into reality. One may note how the dream situation may be of help; using its atmosphere has helped the analyst to tackle the situation through countertransference.

If one understands the atmosphere of the dream, it may be used as a point of contact, and also for interpretation purposes.

Wednesday session

The patient explicitly tells me that she wants to recount an episode and that she hopes I will allow her to "get to the end" because, she says, I never let her talk. This is what it is about::

Her lawyer has met her husband regarding the separation case and afterwards told her: "He seems to be really envious of what you have . . . and that you can survive without him." She thought this was true: now that she is no longer a "crumb in his pocket" he hates her. He adopted this sentimental phrase: it was, he said, because he loved her. And she was taken in . . . she tells me she remembers the tone he used to use when he told her, "You are so beautiful!" or "You choose your words so well!" The tone reflected displeasure, anger, almost disgust. She knows that there is nothing to be done any more, that not having him as an enemy is already something. The split between them is getting wider and wider.

When I asked her why she wanted me to listen "to the end", she replies that she was afraid I would tell her she was talking about her husband in order not to talk to me about herself. In the end, the lawyer proves that what she says about her husband is true.

I tell her that if we give credence to the idea that she is also talking to me about herself, there would be an important thing for us to take on board: that she may find a similar aspect of herself odious and unpleasant, and fear that, seeing such a thing here, there is no possible solution for her other than to be sent away forever.

ROSENFELD: This Wednesday session is a difficult and interesting intervention, one that I believe it is difficult for the analyst to manage.

The patient says: "If you allow me to speak, I can get to the bottom" because what she wants to assert clearly, and what she wishes there to be an agreement about with the analyst, is that not only is she a noisy and destructive child, but her husband in reality also possesses destructive characteristics, harbours envious attacks within his character, which she has correctly perceived in him and wishes to see acknowledged. It is not a figment of her imagination, but a given fact that must be acknowledged.

I believe it important for the analyst to be capable of highlighting that the patient was talking about herself as well. The patient has a real difficulty in recognizing that both she and the analyst are ready to accept the destructive aspects of somebody on the outside, such as the husband, for example. These are aspects that the patient is capable of correctly perceiving when another person interrupts, as has occurred so many times in the past.

This fact is important because the patient might allow herself to also correctly perceive the part of herself that complains in an infantile manner, the part of her that launches attacks and, in the sessions, interrupts the feeling of comfort and comprehension every time the analyst succeeds in establishing contact with her, in containing her like Mr E. Almost immediately this is interrupted by what she refers to as noisy children.

It is necessary to recognize that inside the patient there is con-fusion between the self that interrupts and the analyst as an inter-rupting voice; she is unsure whether this is potentially helpful or destructive. This is an element of confusion in this analysis. Note the sense of danger aroused by the analyst talking, which immedi-ately brings on the complaining children. This happens time and time again in the analysis.

We have the dreaming session, the complaining session, and this material regarding the husband: now we must bring them together. If we fail to do so, the importance of the communication is lost.

It clearly appears that the patient requires the analyst to be capable of helping her recognize attacks against her from the outside and to acknowledge her clear perception of this. This is what the patient is afraid of in the dream. Here, it clearly appears that Mr E is an object that contains and helps her; the patient can sit on his knee and feel comforted, without feeling attacked and wounded.

While Mr E is doing something comforting, an attack comes from the children and the adult who does nothing to protect the analysis from them. In this situation, the patient feels that it is the analyst who interrupts. In the other situation, she has a constant fear of experiencing the analyst interrupting and attacking her.

The patient wishes to clarify this in the session: "Please, don't interrupt me—acknowledge that this is not a projection of my hostility towards him, but an attempt to correctly perceive my husband as an envious and destructive figure who wants to harm me. Please, keep all of this from me, and help me to differentiate."

If one manages to clearly differentiate the material available, one may help the patient recognize when the attack comes from outside, and when it comes from within herself.

Thursday session

[*The patient arrives about ten minutes late.*]

P: "I'm so scared . . . I don't know what I'm scared of any more. . . . Perhaps of being alone: I cannot manage to see anything posi-tive in it . . ."

A: "Who told you that being alone is positive?"

P: "Well, I think people say it . . . you, others . . ."

A: "In what way?"

P: "Not depending on people, and not making others depend on you . . . I'm so scared of separation . . ." [Falls silent]

A: "Which separation?"

P: "Separation from my husband. Perhaps it's my pathology, but my external condition is that I am alone in this world and this is important for me. Yesterday I saw Alfredo; I think he comes to see me on Wednesdays and Thursdays. I wanted to say no, but I just can't seem to. . . . He is so nice! It's as if he cultivates solitude in order to have the pleasure of meeting up again, like Italians who cultivate their appetite only to satisfy their hunger. It seems inconceivable . . . He says to me, 'Through solitude you have earned the pleasure of having somebody who comes to see you.'"

[As far as Alfredo is concerned, for the last year or perhaps a little longer she has been having a relationship with a man who is not interested in a stable relationship. At this point the patient stops. She remains silent for a moment, and then, when she starts talking again, her voice, until this moment querulous and infantile in tone, suddenly sounds serious.]

P: "No, the truth is that I'm afraid of facing life on my own. For example, I can't stand the idea of my husband sending me a monthly amount that I have to look after myself, with all the catastrophic ideas that my sick phantasy rolls out in front of me."

ANALYST: I would like to underline that these ideas and this definition of "sick phantasy" is her own, I have not used these terms with her.

I tell her that this is the way things are, and she can see it when she thinks seriously. There is a sick phantasy that presents what she really wants as catastrophic: to have a mental storehouse of experiences and knowledge that enable her to run her own life.

P: [She writhes on the couch and says with a grimace of pain and anguish in her voice] "But I can't . . . I'm not ready . . . [Then in a less anxious voice] Perhaps I am ready, but I'm afraid. . . .

It's important that everybody looks after their own affairs on their own: everything I'm hearing, from all sides, seems to say this."

I hear the swing between the querulous and the serious voice, and I am also a little bewildered regarding what she seriously thinks and what there may be of this sick phantasy. I tell her that we can look into how this stimulus to cope on her own and her fantasies are experienced. Not by chance, she takes the example of Alfredo.

What does this man tell her? That it is wonderful to suffer solitude, that the more she misses him, the more she is capable of enjoying his return. She also attributes an idea of this kind to me: feeling lonely is a good thing. I think that for her the proof that this is how I consider her situation is represented by weekends, vacations, perhaps even the interval between one session and the next. It is a system inconceivable in its cruelty, but one that I employ so that she suffers the fact I am not there, and then gratifies me with her enthusiasm and gratitude for my return.

P: "Ah! . . . [sighs] I never used to feel this lack! Now I do, though."

A: "You didn't used to feel it because you had a husband on whom you could hang the weight of an intolerable sense of useless-ness, the anxiety of being left alone and rejected for your inabil-ity to make him happy. But this did not, of course, stop you from suffering yourself. Do you recall how you noticed how bad these tensions became on the weekend?"

P: "It's true [she murmurs in a sad voice], it's true . . ."

A: "Don't you think it possible that when you desire the return of your husband it is also an attempt to re-establish precisely this kind of relationship?"

P: "I'm frightened. [In a serious voice] It's been over a year since C left and, all things considered, it's been a good year, I have had good experiences with friendships and at work. Yet they just fall away. You are right when you tell me that I do not pick up on the good experiences. A friend of mine tells me the same thing: how can I be so anxious? Despite the bad things, I have been lucky as well: I have my home, a job that seems to be going very well. . . . But it's as if I didn't consider this worth a thing! I am so terrified. I was doing weird things yesterday! . . . I lost my head.

". . . But then I can get hold of myself again: I stop thinking about any of it. I am so struck that C doesn't want to look after me in the specific sense of the term, he just wants to send me a sum of money."

A: "You have to think that it is better not to have anything of your own: when you stop thinking, you live in mental poverty and you don't have anything to draw upon to look after yourself. In this way, I'm supposed to look after you time after time, forever."

P: "I know how bad C was for me. I know I could have died. I know that I have to grow. But I'm frightened. This year, only good things have happened to me. For example, I haven't used this time badly, yet I still don't have faith."

A: "There's also the time spent on analysis that you think you have used well to get to know yourself and fulfil yourself. But it seems as if you have been afraid of realizing this because it is closely connected with the idea that if this is so, I will leave you to get on with things on your own."

P: "About my fear of becoming pregnant—these last few days I have been trying to get in touch with my gynaecologist, but I haven't been able to track him down. A girlfriend of mine reassured me, though, and told me that if I know what I want, it won't be traumatic . . ." [she falls silent].

A: "In what sense?"

P: "If I decided to have an abortion, she knows the right person, somebody who uses the least dangerous method, aspiration. I think that in the end, I've got friends who help me out when I need a hand."

I tell her that she brings me a singular example of help: help to have an abortion. Does she want this or is she being forced? I ask myself whether, now that the session is finishing and we are coming up to the days when I am not around for her, whether all this has not really felt like much help.

I take everything away from her; I leave her alone, bereft of her own resources, like a little foetus pushed out into the open. If in her deepest recesses there is this sensation of anxiety, what I am doing must really seem to be inconceivably cruel.

She falls silent. A few minutes later, the session is over.

ROSENFELD: It is very interesting that the patient seems to be beginning to accept interpretations regarding her relationship with her
analyst. She is still very confused about relations in outside life,
with her husband and with others, the lover and the analyst, but in
this session patient and analyst come close in a way that the preceding material would not have led us to expect.

It is truly gratifying to see that after the dream the patient
manages to bring material in a form that is no longer one that
makes it so difficult to offer interpretations. I would say that this
session is much less confused than the ones that preceded it.

It all starts at the beginning of the session, when the analyst
helps the patient to draw a distinction in among the confusion. The
patient says, "I cannot imagine being alone as a positive thing",
and the analyst replies, "Who tells you it is a positive thing?" The
patient states, "I think it's you and other people who say it."

In what way does the analyst say it's a good thing? In that she
goes away on her own at the weekend. "It's good for her that she
goes away, otherwise she can't handle it" is what the patient thinks.

Many patients—patients we see, whose feelings about the
weekend we often interpret—feel that we think that it does them
good, and this is something the analyst enjoys. Analysts often talk
about it and consider it to be important, though in a different way
to the patient.

In this dream we see an important admission. The patient complains that the analyst thinks the weekend is good, she complains
that it hurts her. It seems very clear to me.

Then there's the situation with Alfredo, who represents the
seducing analyst, who is very kind to begin with but then doesn't
want to stay with the patient. This is an extremely disturbing
aspect of the analysis for our patients: we make ourselves very
pleasant and agreeable and then we go off for the weekend, and
patients think that we don't care a thing about them.

One may acknowledge that certain complaints emerge clearly:
these are the ones referring to the weekend, and they must be
analysed in detail, for they reveal themselves to be of great help.

The patient hates talking about the weekend, she really doesn't
like it at all. When the analyst asks her to explain these complaints
in a clearer fashion, the patient describes her so-called sick fanta-

sies, her catastrophic ideas. She really can no longer stand coming to the sessions, being treated well, and then being left to her own devices. It is as if she is saying, "Go to hell!", a thought followed by catastrophic ideas of being left on her own.

When one comes into contact with a patient who has a strong transference, when the weekend arrives one turns into a sadistic analyst, an analyst who first is kind and then goes away. On Saturdays, patients are consumed by furious rage, they feel they could kill the analyst; they become so adamant they don't want to see the analyst that they can develop a destructive type of anxiety.

A good relationship and then being left on one's own is really typical of such catastrophic anxiety.

I would like you to bear in mind that the patient has supplied details of a catastrophic separation. Naturally, you should return to this material and interpret it further: it is extremely important as far as the patient's complaints are concerned, and one must understand the different ways it is used.

All of this brings us to the issue not just of a relationship with Mr E, but also a female relationship, a mother who excites her by telling her lovely stories and makes her feel comforted. It is as if the patient was thinking, "It is so nice to be with this mother, I want to sleep in her arms," and in reply she hears, "No, you cannot sleep in my arms, you have to go away."

Not just a male analyst, it is a seductive mother who tells her beautiful stories and then goes away again. One must remember that all this is connected with something that is very hard to differentiate between at this stage: the transference relationship with Mr E and with the mother.

Our model thus becomes important: it is highly unlikely that this patient will fail to interpret this seductive maternal transference as part of a relationship in which the mother subsequently leaves.

It is also important to ask oneself a question of help in understanding later material: what is the real transference situation?

The maternal transference may be described thus: "Let me sit on your knee, inside your belly, let me be a baby in your tummy from which I never wish to be separated. Can I be inside your tummy so that I never have to go away? You don't want to have an abortion during the weekend, do you? Let me stay here, please, I want to stay in your tummy." The reply is: "No, no, you have to go."

If one imagines this maternal transference, one can acknowledge what it means. If one confirms what is happening behind this proximity, one discovers that it is frightening; it also entails the fear of being suddenly expelled, like an abortion.

"I have nothing and I am left with nothing."

What can happen with an abortion is: "She is expelling me during the weekend only because she wants to go away. How can she do this to me?" This might be the representation of a dialogue on what is happening with the analyst and with the mother.

If the patient has this sick image of being the analyst's foetus, of being a child inside her, and if the analyst does not want all this, it is as if she is saying to the patient, "You can look after the baby, I don't want to." The patient thinks: "I should be pregnant by myself, and look after myself on my own." The analyst replies: "Look after yourself, because I don't want to."

In this sense, the weekend means that the patient must be pregnant with herself. The analyst wants to have an abortion, and it is the patient who has the baby. How can this problem be resolved? The patient says: "Are we going to have an abortion or not?"

If one interprets this as erotic transference, it is the male analyst who has seduced his patient. If one interprets the maternal transference, a completely different meaning emerges concerning the desire to be the patient's foetus, a baby inside her which cannot be separated: and what we find underlying this is a completely different atmosphere to what we had before. This is interesting, because it is part of the model we referred to at the beginning, the framework model that helps us to stay in contact with what has been said up to now.

I have mentioned that this model can sometimes be helpful, at other times less helpful, but in a situation like this it brings us back to the question: where is the mother? Where is this mother? It is important to return to this question, as the patient does not allow it to be readily visible; Mr E appears as a man. One must therefore recognize that there is a female object behind him.

What we must think about is that we must imagine using the material in the various forms of transference: it is a separation, it is a male figure, it is an early relationship with the mother.

We should take note of the patient's feelings, of the fact that she cannot stand being left alone, and that, in the end, she feels like a little baby girl. This is very primitive material. How grown-up does the patient feel? Has she been born? Is she returning into a state of absolute non-separateness? She asks: "Do you think it will be good for me to be separated? Do you want to have an abortion?"

If the analyst replies, "Being separated is a good thing," this means that it is good for a foetus to be born. Because the patient still feels like a foetus inside the analyst, being born is a bad thing.

It requires a great deal of imagination to compare what the patient is saying with the various situations and stages of her development, with the entire range that the analyst must stay in touch with.

We should be in a position to recognize if this is a very primitive thing, in order to be able to contain the patient. If, on the other hand, one attributes it to an overly advanced stage of development, this means not taking up and rejecting the patient.

The patient returns to her husband. She is afraid: "I can't do it, I can't do it." She goes back and forth, from the analyst to her husband, with this enormous fear of separation. We should recognize what this separation is. "I am terrified, I am terrified," and suddenly the patient goes away.

If one does not bear in mind the full horror of separation, one cannot recognize that it is connected with the feeling of the child inside the analyst-mother.

The analyst has been in very close contact with the patient, but suddenly she has become passive. She has been able to follow through the patient's terror of being left alone, but not the weekend experience, which is felt as an abortion.

If one connects the right phantasy, one arrives at the feeling of an abortion, which is a different thing: the patient is a child inside the analyst, so how could she stand this? She can't. I would interpret this in a different way, emphasizing that the patient might be incapable of living outside the tummy, and this is why the weekend fills her with terror.

This situation is truly catastrophic: the sense of being expelled is, naturally, of a psychotic nature. The patient cannot survive, she will die. Her complaints in this situation are justified.

The analyst can only help her to understand and put her in touch with this material, to contain the child for her. The patient needs to sense that the analyst has understood all this, that she has space for this phantasy.

What the analyst can do is avoid telling her, "Stay with me over the weekend," but, "You can stay here with this phantasy and with all these feelings." If one overlooks the fact that the weekend provokes psychotic feelings, it is as if one is saying to the patient: "No, you cannot have fantasies like this, leave me alone, I want to feel free, I have room for other babies but not for you."

It is important to remember how the last session finished, as this will naturally have a great deal of bearing on the following week's sessions and, in general, how analysis proceeds. The material, especially the "pregnancy" material, is of enormous significance.

In this situation, I have attempted to show the analyst's rejection of the patient's most infantile level. What has been analysed is the male object in the oedipal relationship. There is a great difference if one analyses the mother–baby relationship. The implications are as follows: analysing the oedipal transference situation, one is accepting the oedipal relationship with the patient, her desires for proximity, and her need of a male object; at the same time, however, one violently rejects the patient at a very infantile level.

It is important to understand this, for when one makes a mistake—and we all make mistakes—we must ask ourselves what we are doing for the patient, and what we are doing against them. Working at a very infantile level can be devastating for the patient; but on some occasions, it can work very well. From this material, it is possible to create an image and have the opportunity to understand what has gone wrong.

If one works at a highly infantile level, there is a chance that as well as the patient feeling bad, physical disturbances may appear; the whole body may seem disorganized, above and beyond feelings of anxiety and depression.

Let us now turn our attention to the next session, recapping how the previous session finished.

ANALYST: This session takes place a week after the last session I read out. I have here a very brief summary of the intervening week: sessions that take place in the usual atmosphere, complaints alternating with spontaneous comments on how strangely opposite her ways of experiencing her life are: freer and calmer, yet also desperation and total disinterest in the very things that just a moment earlier had been giving her pleasure.

> In one session she comes out with something completely unexpected: "You have given me life," she says. But the next day, when I remind her of this, she turns against me, denying it and crying: "But what kind of life do you call this? What life?"

> The next Friday, her fourth session, she calls in the late afternoon. In a weak, lost little voice, she tells me she feels so "lost", anxious, and alone. She cannot explain.

> I tell her that there is not a lot I can do over the phone, and I ask her if she thinks she can make it through to Monday. She says she thinks so, pauses, and then thanks me before saying goodbye.

ANALYST: The two following sessions are from the week after this. Even though I did not make notes, I recall that I mentioned the last session, specifically, that, if she really thought about it, she wouldn't feel so alone. Unfortunately I do not remember exactly what I said to her. I am referring to the last session of the week which I've just summarized.

ROSENFELD: What's interesting is the fact that she has often hinted at being abandoned by her husband and analyst. The patient does not just feel left alone on the weekend, the fact is that she feels aborted by the analyst for the duration of the weekend.

ANALYST: I provided an interpretation on the abortion on Thursday, but the end of the session she was referring to in this phone call was not actually that session.

ROSENFELD: But the interpretation does not go right to the heart of the issue. There is a fundamental difference between being a child left alone, capable of waiting until its next feed, and a foetus that is aborted and left to die. It is much more cruel. Separation is one thing; leaving somebody to die is another.

It is also important to note the analyst's countertransference, for this recalls to the patient a previous session, and she tells her that it will be fine. If the patient was able to remember, everything would be okay. If she had simply forgotten the interpretation, the analyst would have been able to remind her over the phone. The patient would have replied: "Thanks, I just forgot." I doubt that the analyst went sufficiently deeply into the patient's catastrophic situation, that she understood it profoundly.

Monday session

P: "I felt really terrible on Friday. I wanted to give it all up. I wanted to call work and tell them I wasn't going to come in, but I didn't; that's not how I want to behave.

"I have never felt such deep depression. A great desire to get into bed. This was all right when my husband was around: it made him feel useful and important. When he was around, he took me to emergency if there was nothing more he could do at home. But I was alone, and if I had let myself go, it would really have meant dying.

"To begin with I thought: it's great to be alone. Alfredo is quite right. You don't piss anyone off, and there's nobody around to piss you off.

"I can do what I want: eat, not eat, get up, not get up.

"But I have realized that I think like this when I'm feeling bad. On Friday evening I called Alfredo [*this is the day she called me, too*]. I was afraid because sometimes he can be very brusque. But he came over and stayed for four hours. He's nicer and nicer to me, it seems like we are changing roles. Then I went to see my friend Lucia. The idea of not being able to stay in bed all day frightened me a lot. But it went all right. Last night I had a dream.

"*I was in an institutional school, but it was a place for adults. It was a bit like an old people's home, but it was full of young girls. It was a nice place, decorated in a simple but elegant country style.*

"*It seemed that the people there did different jobs, depending on their interests. There was nice rustic pottery . . . and elegant stuff as well. . . . I had my work tools with me . . . but I didn't need them because everyone could use what they wanted, and that was fine with me. I could have used my own things, but there was no need. There was a dining-room too, very big, but it was split up. It was split up into groups of tables.*

"Lucia's lunch comes to mind. It was for her mother's birthday; she's got a real archetype of a mother: fat, spread. She is straightforward and direct: if she doesn't like something, she lets you know. Then she gives you the leftovers, wrapped up, to take home and eat. There is no need to try to be something you are not, like my mother-in-law, who always has to show how good she is, how clever. With Lucia's mother, there's much less hatred that needs to be hidden behind a mask of niceness. After my experience with my husband's family, I was under the impression that this was how all Italians behaved. But it's not so. Alfredo is different. The way he talks is pretty much free association."

ANALYST: The interpretation I gave here was something I took from very brief notes I wrote up after the session. I had the impression that I did not understand the dream very well, which is one of the reasons why I decided to present these sessions here today.

I tell her that she really did feel the weekend was a desire to let herself die . . . I thought that the call she made to me really was a call for help because she had understood what dying was, and she had been afraid. This was different from pushing the urgency of helping herself onto others, without realizing what danger she was really in.

It follows that in the dream, analysis is no longer a place to let herself receive my treatment like an old woman waiting for death, but a place where she may exercise her own abilities, draw on her own resources, and, if needed, draw on mine too. In other words, a place to find the time and space to go back and work-through her own experiences.

ROSENFELD: There is something ridiculous about this dream. If one thinks that the patient called the analyst saying she was dying, it is ridiculous to note that this dream is in such an ideal place where adults are busy and happy.

Considered as the realization of a desire, the dream presents some highly complex features. Indeed, this dream may only be understood by drawing upon the entire transference relationship, as well as on interpretations given during previous sessions.

What I feel is that the analyst has told the patient that she is an adult or young lady, perhaps in love with the paternal figure: this is her problem.

This interpretation is at an overly adult level. The only problem is that the patient does not feel grown-up; she does, however, feel that she will die.

The dream has not helped her to feel better: there is something missing here, something towards which the patient has attempted to draw attention. She is not grown-up like in the dream, she feels very different.

I think that the patient has attempted to use an instrument with the analyst, but the analyst has not used the patient's instruments. She has not taken on board the material that has been offered to her. The analyst has rejected the instrument. This dream may only be understood on the basis of the transference relationship, this is the only way it takes on a meaning. But that's the point: the patient has given the analyst instruments that have not been used.

It is as if the patient said, "I could have used my own instruments, but there was neither any need nor opportunity." This is the reason why the patient felt lost.

Interestingly, patients who are at such an infantile level can give highly detailed information which is more adult than it was regarding the transference. If one does not grasp this information, the patient feels useless. Such patients are not capable of using the information; it only comes alive in the transference situation. They are completely dependent upon the analyst's comprehension.

The analyst must ask him/herself: "What happened to me with this dream?" It is as if the patient is saying, "Thanks, you have made me into an adult, now you can leave me alone, I'm fine." But the complete opposite is happening.

I would venture that a dream in analysis is always entirely a communication by the patient to the analyst. It does not imply any detail at unconscious-material level. If one does not attempt to use the dream from this viewpoint, one gets nothing out of it: we must consider the communication to be 100 per cent important, or else the dream cannot be used.

Dreams are the instruments that the patient uses to enter into contact with the analyst. If the analyst does not grasp the dream, he/she does not grasp the instrument. If it is not used as an instrument, what happens is what happened in this patient's dream, which includes a dining-room split into many areas but where there is nothing to eat. These dreams are used by the patient to enter into contact with the analyst.

Why does the patient offer an image of two mothers? Though seemingly preoccupied with her mother's attitudes, at the same time she leaves out the analyst-mother. The patient seems to talk about a mother, another mother, and a third one—the analyst-mother—who always says: "You have to grow up, you have to grow up, that's the only way everything will be okay."

I do, however, think that this is an exceptional case, given that very few patients are capable of communicating something like this.

There is more, too: this type of patient teaches us a whole mode of communication. I think that we do not sufficiently realize the different ways patients use dreams.

A dream like this, after a situation in which the patient feels that she is almost dying, has something of the fantastic about it. We have a dying child on the telephone, and in this dream a nice adult in a beautiful house. This is the point. If one unconsciously interprets not at the infantile level but at the adult level, it is as if one were saying to the patient: "I don't want you to be a child who is on the point of dying; I want you to be an adult, I want you to understand what it is like to be grown-up."

The patient responds, "Yes ma'am, I will try to be this nice adult, and of course the child will die, because you do not want a child who cries all the time on weekends. I will be a good grown-up, you don't want to know that I am dying, so I will bring you a nice dream."

ANALYST: This is the Tuesday session.

[*She lies down on the couch with a long, weary sigh. She says she is over the major crisis, but what is left is weariness, a nuance different from depression. She would like to know what has happened, but she doesn't. . . .]*

A: "What are your thoughts about the last session?"

P: "I don't know ... I was left with the impression that it was interrupted before it was made clear.

"I had a dream. *I'm at home, and it's invaded with friends. There is somebody who has not eaten, and I feel very irritated that I have to look after this. How can this be? How can somebody act like this? Visit somebody's house and then scrounge a meal? I thought I had nothing at home to eat, but in a compartment in the refrigerator I find a tin of pineapple which I did not know I had. I think this will sort things out, no problem. "*

I point out the similarity to the dream of the children bursting in, I tell her this. She immediately tells me that she had thought of this herself. I try to show her the contrast between the vitality of the dream and the tired sigh she produced at the beginning of the session, and I tell her that vitality gets on her nerves, irritates her, makes her tired: friends, children, emotions, feelings that require care and nourishment.

P: "Yes, it was precisely the idea of having to do things that irritated me."

I point out to her that this is something we already know.

P: "But I do do things. [*She counters, whining a little*] I obsessively make myself do everything I have to."

I point out to her that she defines her activity as obsessive, but does not see her inertia as obsessive, the monotony of her life, the impetus to go to bed and not do anything else.

Perhaps what is missing is a complaint from her about feeling pushed to go to bed, she doesn't want to, she feels it's like an impulse.

P: "It's true, I really do feel it as a coercion, an oppression I can do nothing about, like my father who used to come and check to see if I was sleeping, and I had to pretend I was or there was trouble."

I also ask her what I am supposed to do, if she tells me she doesn't know what has happened, and doesn't remember what we said? "Nothing", as if she were a little girl faced with her father. It's exactly as if she were saying what her father used to say to her: "Quiet, it's getting dark, it's time to sleep."

P: "Ah, yes, that's true. I do feel this. [*She falls silent for a moment. Then she starts complaining about her life again and, at a certain point, a rare event this, she mentions her mother. This is one of the very few times during the analysis that she has brought up her mother*] Perhaps I am like her. Nothing ever went right for her. In the end, her life was a failure. But I haven't heard anything about her for a long time."

I point out to her that she recalls a mother who left her. She wants to show me the damage that has been done to her, she has nothing, no energy.

But the dream says that she has found something she did not know she possessed. She enjoys finding resources, but she does not want to allow herself to know this, so she has frozen them, put them in the fridge. Irritation pushes out the friendly, affectionate friends/feelings.

I notice that she starts rubbing her tummy, her face contorting, and then she says in a complaining voice:

P: "It must be that I feel I'm owed something."

I tell her that this is partly the case because there is something cruel preventing her from acknowledging the good resources, something good that she found in the mother who left; pineapple, which comes from the warmth of the tropics, from maternal warmth, which she freezes. She is so angry that she has trouble handling this.

The patient suddenly doubles up in a spasm, clutching her belly.

P: "Ah! my stomach, you must excuse me, I have to go to the bathroom."

She leaps up from the couch, and, as the session is over, I say goodbye.

ROSENFELD: This is another highly significant session, closely connected to the preceding one. Both the patient and the analyst want to know what is happening.

When the analyst asks the patient her thoughts on the previous session, she answers that she does not know. We have the impression that this is a very genuine reply, that the patient is truly not in a position to cope with and understand the session.

I think it is interesting to note that the communication and instruments are very powerful. If the analyst does not grasp them, the patient feels useless, that no value is attributed to her instruments.

Even in cases where a child is highly talented and very communicative, it can happen during infancy that parents fail to pick up on what the child is bringing them. In this case, the child may feel useless, bad, and stupid, despite the large amount of valuable material there is. This is material that must be reflected and mirrored back. It is absolutely essential for the mother or the analyst to mirror this.

Together we have seen how the analyst is very angry and dissatisfied with this situation. The patient, on the other hand, is concerned; the analyst is expecting her to be nourished. It is the patient who is hungry and, given that she is not receiving sustenance, her preoccupations are justified.

She does not consciously say that she can no longer stand the analyst, but in the dream she openly expresses criticism of her. In the dream, a number of people go to somebody's house to eat, and this is related to the issue of not having anything to eat. But the patient keeps a tin of food in the fridge; this is an important admission on her part.

What continues to crop up between the analyst and patient is the image of an analyst who keeps on asking, while the patient has already supplied good material. It is clear that the patient cannot stand this any longer. I believe that the difficulty lies in the fact that once some significant elements are lost, there is a tendency to lose more and more such elements.

The only thing that can be done is to ask oneself what in this material is completely different, what in this dream is completely new compared to previous manifestations. We must force ourselves to rethink the situation and find a different approach, inasmuch as one may clearly perceive another complaint in this dream.

I would say to myself, "Good heavens, this patient is furious with me, and I don't know why." In a concealed way, this is a transference dream, and I would feel chastened by this patient. I think I would be able to recapture what I had lost, and, with the patient's help, perhaps I would subsequently understand even the preceding dream. What has happened? Why is she so furious? She must have given me instruments that I have not used. This is the point: it is a matter of interpreting the transference disturbance. If this is understood, the patient feels comforted, she feels that the analyst has recognized something significant. Patient and analyst can move back together again.

I would like to thank the analyst for this fantastic material, which has enabled us to meticulously work through this issue. The material presented has been particularly interesting in many ways, including how we have worked through it together.

The fact that something may have been forgotten in the telling is less important than the desire to learn, and the clarity with which this has been expressed. This should be a shining example to us all.

Even though it can be tiring at times, I hope that this work has been useful; there is something for all of us to learn here.

SIX

Transference in psychosis

The following case was presented to Herbert Rosenfeld in Milan by a psychoanalyst in 1982 and again in 1983. We have chosen to publish the 1983 seminar because it is so full of comment illustrating Rosenfeld's contribution to the psychoanalytic theory of psychosis and the theory of technique.

The case history regards a young woman who has her first psychotic breakdown during the consultation interviews, at the end of which her analysis begins.

Rosenfeld comments on the evolution of the analytic relationship. He focuses on the patient's changing perception of the analyst, and he distinguishes between various types of projective identification.

He highlights the importance of showing the patient healthy aspects and areas of functioning, which can contribute to the analytic process, and counsels against an all-absorbing concentration on transference: the analyst must distinguish the transference relationship from other relationships that exist in the patient's inner world. This is all the more important with psychotic patients, who might misunderstand transference-related interpretations.

As far as interpretation of negative transference is concerned, the crucial point for the analyst is to reach the patient. Rosenfeld draws upon the clinical case material to show how, by monitoring responses to interpretation, one may gauge whether the patient manages to accept and tolerate it.

It is also fundamental to pick up on the initial appearance of depressive anxieties, remembering that the patient is terrorized by them, but without letting oneself be swept up by this same terror.

Finally, Rosenfeld is particularly persuasive in demonstrating that the patient's "mute" communications are precisely the ones that let us in on what is most important in the patient's mental life. It is the analyst's duty to provide the words that the patient is not yet able to find.

A NALYST: Francesca is a 31-year-old woman, of a pleasant appearance, with a detached and rather impersonal attitude. A little over two years ago, she asked me to take her into analysis because she felt shy and insecure in relationships with others, especially men, with whom she believes she has never succeeded in establishing satisfying relationships, at either a romantic or an erotic level.

An only child, after the death of her father and mother (respectively seven and four years previously) she has lived very much alone, absorbed in her daily work which she undertakes with a measure of success, even though she is continually tormented by doubts of not being sufficiently good at her job. Her father, who worked in the same field and was particularly well known, is remembered as a cold person who scorned feelings and emotions, and who was continually seeking success and renown in his professional life.

He always pushed his daughter to undertake a rapid, brilliant career, first in school, then in work, and to give precedence to a "sense of duty" as an essential value of life. From before the time of her marriage, her mother suffered from a serious psychotic condition characterized by hallucinations and a quantity of delirious raving.

Francesca says she has always felt oppressed and controlled by her mother; she often felt upset by the bizarre nature of her mother's words and behaviour; her "illness" also appeared to her to be something about which the family should be profoundly ashamed. Indeed, as far as possible, her father avoided going out with his wife or inviting acquaintances home, because he did not want to "look bad".

From what I have been able to reconstruct, he continually denied his wife's psychic suffering; he was profoundly disturbed by it himself.

Francesca remembers a very unhappy childhood and adolescence, spent in great loneliness: like her family, she was isolated, closed, withdrawn. She often had to take care of her mother, reassure her, and calm her down.

After a couple of preliminary meetings (she hardly opened her mouth at all at the first interview), around three weeks later, after the Christmas holidays, I see Francesca again.

The patient has just returned from a long trip to the Far East. She is upset as she tells me that she has been sadistically persecuted by her travel companions, who floated highly threatening "rumours" that she was homosexual, and as a result she was derided and ridiculed.

As far as I have been able to ascertain, this is the first time that Francesca has suffered a psychotic breakdown.

Though evidently convinced of the "reality" of this experience as a whole, she nonetheless decides to commence analysis.

I would also like to mention that at that time her psychic condition struck me as extremely worrying. I decide to give her the name of a psychiatrist she should see in parallel with the analysis. Francesca agrees, and willingly accepts.

I would now like to mention some of the difficulties that emerged during the first two years of therapy.

Some phases of treatment have been characterized by the dramatic emergence of a great deal of psychotic material. For example, in the first month of analysis the patient frankly revealed her delirious beliefs; after around nine months, back from a second long trip following the summer break, she told me that she had once more been subjected to persecution as on the previous trip. I remember fearing several times at such moments that the patient might break off treatment and suffer complete dissociation.

I was sensing a desperate call for help from Francesca and, at the same time, feeling fear that I could not grasp and cope with her psychic suffering, the "weight" of her emotional problems, just like her father could not cope with his wife's troubles and, at least for a period, seemed not to have been able to heed his small daughter's more infantile and needy demands—just like her parent, she has a tendency to deny any critical consciousness of her own delirium. Living in her own phantasy world, her mother most likely did not have any "space" to take on board the demands of the patient as a little girl.

She defensively turns to a particular mode of behaviour. Avoiding any dependency or emotional involvement and rendering the relationship cold and impersonal, she subjects me to insistent, monotonous requests as to "what to do" and "how to act" to solve her problems. She expects rapid, practical, and concrete solutions.

In a countertransference sense, at times I recall feeling frustration at being some kind of inanimate servant at her service. She speaks very rarely and extremely superficially about her relationship with her mother, as if she had to keep a distance, even in transference, from a very disquieting object she fears has "infected" her. I have the impression that she herself must in some way keep me under control (like her mother in the past), keeping at a "safe" distance, as if in a persecutory sense she was afraid of establishing a closer, more intimate bond.

During some interminably silent sessions, I recall a frankly intrusive and overwhelming desire to delve into Francesca's thoughts, which she seems so provocatively to have kept from me.

At such times I perhaps come to represent the mother, by whom she felt inquisitorially controlled and invaded, and who had to be strictly kept in the dark about her own thoughts.

At other times, on the contrary, in these silent pauses (sessions of this type are very common) I have felt that Francesca was simply asking me to be with her, not push her but patiently await her communications. In such cases, the atmosphere in the session is very calm; from a countertransference point of view, I felt that a relationship had, in any case, been established, and that I could communicate to her my willingness to look after her even through my silence, my ability to wait.

Despite the above difficulties, Francesca has almost always turned up on time to her sessions and has hardly ever skipped analysis. I must also point out the amount of attention that she gives not just to my interpretations, but above all to the very sound of my voice, to the least variations in my tone of voice.

Before moving on to the most recent material, I feel that it is important to comment briefly on several elements that have emerged in the last few months.

For a while now, at certain times the patient seems to be better disposed towards communicating more personal, infantile aspects about which she had never previously spoken.

For instance, I recall that in one session, after calling up the "fear" (her word) she felt as a girl at her mother's presence, she told me a dream (which she had when she was 5 years old, and which terrifies her to this day) in which *she recalls a woman's face, seemingly rigid and stiff like that a ghost's, which is completely missing its mouth.* On another occasion, she told me that she once felt, in her own home, like a "decorative plant", or, at other times, like a "little dog" that has to keep her mother company and obey her father-owner. She felt that her parents were highly dependent on her, needy of her presence to "fill up" (her words once again) the desolate feeling of emptiness that reigned in the family.

In her relationship with me, there have been times when I have intuited greater affectual participation compared to the past. Yet in its transference repetition, this has been held back by the constant fear of being rejected or manipulated.

Other times, Francesca generally established a more detached and ascetic relationship. I have the impression that at such times I am reduced to a loyal, motionless, and decorative yet significant presence. Through these approaches, identifying herself with her parents, she seems to want to induce in me the feelings that she once felt towards them.

This reversal of the relationship has also allowed her many times to cope, defensively and with apparent indifference, with the weekend and holiday separations. Indeed, Francesca believes that she can quite happily go away, certain of finding me always there ready and waiting on her return.

At other times, though, there is a more intense involvement in the relationship and a consequent acknowledgement of dependency as a separation becomes more imminent, leading to a frank denial of the objective link through devaluation of this link and a recourse to intellectualization and all that this entails.

ROSENFELD: I do not think that I need comment broadly about this extremely clear presentation. We will soon be seeing what the situation is in the sessions. There is just one thing I would like to say at this point. Certainly, it is always highly important to see to what degree patients have been able to find an object other than their parents in the analyst; naturally, there is always a tendency to project the persecutory object onto the analyst, but a very important aspect in psychotic patients is that of finding a different object which is not exactly like parents, but far more idealized instead.

You will recall that initially the patient showed that she felt better, and that in one of her dreams the analyst had shooed the mice away [this is a reference to a dream from the 1982 seminar]. In other words, he appeared as an omnipotent protector against internal persecutions. As a result, his powerful presence is felt as a reassuring embrace. This is the initial phase.

But there is another phase too. What is this? And is it really a phase in itself? What actually happens after this omnipotent phase?

I suspect that once the analyst ceases to be this omnipotent protector, the patient must face up to the persecution. Now, the analyst, rather than scaring the mice away, wants to put him right back in their midst, so in this particular moment the patient feels persecuted, disappointed, and highly suspicious: which one is the real analyst—the omnipotent protector or the persecutor? So, we may now consider this second phase. This phase concerns projection of the persecution anxiety onto the analyst, making all problems his; this allows the patient to feel good because she protects herself from these problems. But what arises now is the technical issue of what the analyst should do.

Indeed, if the analyst starts to mention this, there is a danger that the patient may feel it simply as an attempt to rapidly reverse the situation—namely, the anxiety she had pushed onto the analyst is being pushed back onto her. If this happens, it all becomes like a ping-pong match. Feeling the analyst's attempt as an intolerable persecution, the patient might become very upset, aggressive, and silent and send everything right back at him.

If this situation is not analysed in all its detail, there is a risk that things may go on like this for some time in a reciprocal interplay of defensive attitudes.

The situation described so well by the analyst is one in which he is considered by the patient to be an extremely curious and impatient person who wants to know more, whether she likes it or not.

Following this, there seems to be a more normal model, an atmosphere in which the patient appears much more calm, and she feels that a relationship has been established. The analyst seems less impatient, capable of accepting her and her slowness; the analyst is therefore in a position to listen to what she has to say. Another sensation is that the analyst is not a person loaded with projections and impatience, who wants quickly to free himself by forcing her to bring her things up; on the contrary, he is emotionally felt to be a subject who looks after her in a healthier way and is therefore in a position to establish a relationship.

In other words, he is not the crazy mother, nor is he the father who always proved himself to be incapable of coping with the situation as it was.

One detail of the dream which the patient recalls is interesting, when the mother is viewed as a ghost. This is a fascinating and extremely important dream.

When the patient was 5 years old, she dreamed of her mother as a kind of ghost who moved and had a human appearance, but whose mouth was completely missing. I believe this dream to be hugely significant.

The persecutory figure of the mother is inside her, and she hears voices; the persecution seems to come from an excited mother who is incapable of talking.

It follows that communication must have taken place in a non-verbal and extremely disturbed manner.

It is of the utmost importance that she mentions this to the analyst, because we do not have any information in the transference that indicates to us a model of this type.

Try to imagine what it is like to have a persecutory figure who moves around you, who does all kinds of things, but who does not speak. Imagine how one must feel; it must be terrifying. In this situation, the patient has many "things" that talk to her, but this is not the case with the most persecutory figure of all who does not speak.

It is thus essential to understand what it means when she does not talk, or when there are silences.

I would put a red circle around this point.

What we have seen now is a model that is different from the model where the patient describes herself as a plant or a little dog, because in this case it is a matter of being there, sitting there in silence, doing exactly what her mother wants, and so on; but this mother without a mouth is terrifying: why is she unable to talk? Is it perhaps the patient's job to supply her with words for speaking, for understanding what she wants to say, and therefore to express this?

This is one of the most important and interesting features of analysing psychoses: what needs to be verbalized, and the way in which it is necessary to give words to patients who don't have words. The analyst is a person who supplies the words, who understands how much the patient is persecuted by silence, and how strange this persecutory mother-figure without words truly is; you can connect all this with the hugely regressive picture she gives of herself when she says that she is just her mother's little dog, so she cannot talk, only behave like a little dog. In the situation described, what this signifies is: "Mummy wants me to go bow-wow and follow everything, and that is enough."

Behaviour of this nature is completely contradictory. It is important to strive towards an opportunity of showing this contradiction to the patient, and the way that she changes from one moment to the next. This is the art of analysis.

You never know what situation you are likely to find yourself in: does the patient expect the analyst to talk—and feel that this is absolutely necessary—or does she feel that the analyst's speech is merely an intrusive moment that turns her into a little dog? In this case, feeling that she must stay in her place and "follow", she protests a great deal; all she wants is to be silent and run away. This opens up enormous opportunities to see what happens in the transference.

There is another factor of note: after describing varying transference situations, we must now clarify the order in which these appear, how one follows the other.

We have diagnosed a particular situation in which the analyst becomes a little dog and is treated as if he should stay in his place; this is what the patient projects onto him.

We now have the problem of whether this is really a powerful reversal of the situation (as it seems from the present transference situation) for whatever reason, or whether this is a type of communication showing the analyst the possibility of a positive relationship that she has the courage to communicate through projection.

A further situation is one in which this takes place in a more aggressive way, when the reasons (for the projection) are of a vindictive nature for which, in the transference, the patient feels threatened and dominated and angrily throws everything onto the analyst. This latter scenario is completely different from cooperation through projection, where the projective identification is used to make the analyst feel what she is feeling for the purpose of communication, not to try to change or paralyse him.

The patient's feeling was to show how important this particular aspect of the relationship has been in the past and continues to be at present. This gives the analyst an opportunity to think things over, to comment, and to help the patient.

The vindictive situation is far more difficult to tackle, as a danger exists that the analyst may feel it necessary, in turn, to overturn the situation and send back to the patient what she feels. In this case, the patient might say, "Is the analyst angry, or does he understand?" It really is extremely important to distinguish between whether this is a matter of aggression or a moment of communication: the interpretation is completely different in each case.

QUESTION: *You have outlined two possibilities in this case. In one option, things are being shifted, offloaded, onto the analyst, in the other there is a form of communication. My question: is this the difference between projection and projective identification?*

ROSENFELD: In my books, I have described at least twenty different processes that have been referred to as projective identification. It has been used in reference to normal, abnormal, pathological, and so on, and therefore it is a term that gives rise to a great deal of confusion. It is used very broadly in early Kleinian literature. Sometimes Bion describes it as something to do with a container and its contents, connected with the primitive communications of the newborn baby to its mother, as a normal process of communication for the purpose of being helped by the mother to support intolerable emotions. According to this approach, the baby can cope with intolerable anxieties through an act of comprehension.

Certainly, anxiety in adult patients is diminished by a comprehensive attitude from the analyst, accompanied by language confirming that these emotions have been understood.

On the other hand, the other process simply has a different purpose. It is only for teaching purposes, for making it easier to understand, that I have split up the process of projection into two completely different situations that we must understand and sometimes combine.

In one situation, the hostility present in the projection is greater; in this case, it is felt by the analyst above all as an intrusion, inasmuch as he feels that the patient no longer allows herself to exist for what she is, but turns into something different, something much more powerful.

The analyst therefore realizes that something is intruding for a very unpleasant and dangerous purpose. As far as he is concerned, it is as if the patient were saying: "You want to talk like an analyst, but you are nothing, nothing, nothing. You sit there like a dog, without being able to speak, without being able to understand a thing. Now see how it feels! Can you stand this? . . ." and so on.

It follows that this particular situation would be a form of angry retaliation which partially derives from the past; nevertheless, the analyst must also understand if there are elements in the transference indicating that the patient has experienced the analysis not as something in which the analyst gives her words, so that she may understand, but only to show that he is the one who can talk, whereas she is nothing, she can only go "bow-wow".

There is a huge difference when the patient reacts to the analyst in this way; it can sometimes be up to the analyst whether the patient reacts in one way or the other. Nevertheless, if the analyst is sufficiently sensitive he can, to some extent, realize when fears of being subjugated emerge, in such a way as to analyse the sources of the fear that has been communicated to him.

The analyst must pick up not just on how the patient makes him feel, but also on how the patient must have experienced, perhaps even some weeks before, the feeling that she is now putting on to him. The fact that the patient may have felt persecuted and dominated by the analyst has been neglected in the analysis.

In the Wednesday material we are about to see, what is interesting is the fact that communication starts with a dream. The analyst certainly knows what has happened in the preceding sessions, on Monday and Tuesday, and during the week before. We do not know this; we are only informed through the dream.

Now the dream—and this is interesting—may signal an advance or a setback or, in some way, a portion of the work that has been done, which may be reformulated in order to show the analyst how it has worked, what has not been understood, and what still remains to be understood; it could also be a new formulation bringing forth something unexpected, a new piece of material, for some reason, and therefore the analyst might think in surprise: "Oh! She seems more relaxed . . . she is coming up with something new."

Here it seems that the Wednesday session involves the appearance of new situations.

We do not know. All we have is the dream, and it is therefore interesting to see what type of dream it is. It is also important to recognize that even if the dream leads to many associations with the past, the main communication is probably oriented towards clarifying certain elements of the transference.

Wednesday session

P: "I've had a dream. *I was in a place near an area where I once lived. Perhaps it was the offices of . . . [she names her job] . . . it was full of light . . . the house was big . . . then somebody was following me, perhaps some policemen, I had to hide, I was running away . . . maybe somebody was running away with me . . . [It seems to me that her voice has become more dramatic; at the start of her story it was somehow more detached, more impersonal]. First I hid in a wardrobe . . . but I don't remember very well, then I went into the garden where there was a cemetery. I could have hid there but it already had dead people in it. . . . Back inside I hid under a table covered with a tablecloth. Somebody, an enemy, wanted to pull the tablecloth off . . . which would have uncovered me . . . but some friends prevented the policemen from finding me. Then I had to find somewhere else to hide. I was with somebody who was driving, I was in the back, but to begin with I couldn't hide myself very well, and I was afraid they might shoot—I don't know whether it was the policemen or enemies—but then I managed to hide in the boot! I was safe at last.* This is not a new dream for me: when I was a girl I used to have running-away dreams. To start with, it was a nice dream. [*She is speaking in a more relaxed tone now*] Perhaps it's to do with work, *I thought it was going well but then I realized that things aren't right. But then the dream becomes dramatic . . . perhaps my parents were in the cemetery . . . Do I also want to go underground to follow up my links to them?* [*All the anxiety has returned to her voice*]. Somebody said: it's a good thing she didn't hide there, because an arm was poking out of the loose earth . . . just as well! [*Silence*] Who is helping me?"

A: "It seems to me to be very important that you have managed to take me into your dream. It is my belief that through this you wish to convey the anxiety you have felt, from thinking that in order for you to be understood and helped I too must feel a little of what you have felt."

P: "Yes, it's true, I was terrified . . . I didn't understand anything any more . . . What's going on? I'm going crazy . . ."

I tell her that perhaps she feels threatened by something inside her, she is afraid, she is scared she is going crazy, partly because she does not know why she is being followed, and she is disoriented because the police and enemies all seem to be mixed up; she doesn't know if she has done something bad or if she is being persecuted.

P: [*For a short while she speaks in a more relieved tone of voice*] "We can wait for another dream. . . . [*Silence*] But who are these people? These enemies? . . ."

I point out to her that inside herself are not just threatening aspects, but also good, valid parts, friends on whom it seems she may count.

A: "In the dream you feel the need to take shelter by going into or underneath something, perhaps find shelter with me or, better, with the image you have of me—'as a man who drives'—or you almost want to take refuge inside me [*in the boot*]. I think that, similarly, by communicating your anxieties to me in session, you not only want to share them, you want me to be able to "carry inside myself" the "weight " [*boot*] of your fears even when analysis is not ongoing and, on your behalf, think through something you cannot understand on your own, something which makes you go mad . . ."

P: "Perhaps it is possible to understand things . . . become lighter . . . which means I'm not completely crazy!!! [*Silence*] I had a similar dream when I was six. . . . Perhaps I was running away from my parents . . . perhaps I was running away from madness!"

A: "It seems to me that you are seeking help to clear up the relationship you once had with your parents, and continue to have with the representation you carry around of them. As a girl you may have been afraid of a negative attitude on your parents' part towards you; you didn't know whether this was because of something you did, or whether it was down to some mysterious hostility they felt towards you, something which you were unable to understand. At other times, however, you may have feared you were too closely linked with them, almost as if you were being called into an oppressive mortal embrace. All this may perhaps have confused you, made you lose your way, lose your head."

P: "In fact, I never understood what they wanted from me. One moment they would be shouting at me, the next they were sending me away . . . to my grandmother's . . . and then the next thing I knew they wouldn't let me go out . . . it was never clear what was going on at home."

[*I seem to remember that after an initial pause, the patient made some associations regarding an office she had visited a few days earlier, specifically an association with the amount of light there, which had struck her particularly. She also insisted on the change that took place in the dream, which to begin with seemed acceptable to her*].

A: "Perhaps a part of you thinks that things will become more difficult as the analysis goes on, "enlightening" and clarifying our relationship more and more. You may indeed fear that you are excessively linked to them, that you will feel anxious and guilty at my interpretations, and even now feel disoriented, just like you did with your parents."

ROSENFELD: Despite her desire to hide, the patient has been able to expose her own anxieties. This is what kind of dream this is; it is also a dream in which the dreamer is in another mode, which is why she could reveal it to the analyst. Her behaviour is different from that in the dream, where she hides (remember, she didn't use to be able to remember her dreams), attempting everything she can in order not to be recognized, without distinguishing between police and enemies.

The police may be of help, whereas the enemy is dangerous; the dream emphasizes that she is still very confused about the analyst, she does not know if he is an enemy or a policeman. This is very important.

And yet the patient discloses the dream, and in disclosure she demonstrates that she perceives the analyst much less as an enemy than she thought, otherwise she would not have revealed the dream at all. This is the point that should be emphasized.

The analyst told the patient that she wants to use the dream to communicate her own experience to him, her trust that he can feel what she has felt, so that he can understand and help her.

In this way, however, he simply interprets that the patient communicates to him her desire that he use the dream to understand her; this does not mean that he has understood—he has simply interpreted her mechanisms. Generally, it is not enough to interpret the mechanism alone; when the analyst feels in this position, he must also select certain things that are meaningfully connected.

For example, as occurs here, the analyst may say to her: "In revealing your dream, which includes the element of hiding yourself, you consider me to be less of an enemy; but in your dream the policeman who is ready to help and protect you (remember the policeman who protected her from persecution) must have been confused."

It is clearly emphasized that the patient feels confused about the analyst's role, whether he is an enemy or a policeman. But, given that she reveals the dream, this demonstrates that the analyst has become less of an enemy. This is already a significant point which the analyst can directly focus on when he picks up on the communication and dream content.

The patient responds to the analyst's interpretation by saying, "Yes, it's true, I was terrified, I couldn't understand a thing any more . . . what is happening, am I going crazy?"

It is important for the patient, via the dream, to reveal her madness, to communicate this. What does she mean by this?

What is the particular aspect of her madness that she feels is so disturbing, and that the analyst must pick up on? The analyst has shown that the patient does not know why she is being followed—this is a point that the patient subsequently confirms—and has also recognized the confusion between enemies and policemen, though this has not been highlighted. What I would like to say is that I would have stressed this more.

One of the important things about psychotic anxiety is confusing good and bad objects; this is a point that it is vital to recognize. This is where the madness lies.

One must show the patient that one has understood that this confusion drives her crazy: not being capable of realizing whether the analyst is on her side or against her; whether the analyst is the policeman who is following and wants to kill the patient, or whether it is the enemy who is doing so.

In the dream there is still somebody protecting her—the person in whose car she goes to hide. The main anxiety is associated with an inability to differentiate. It is vital that this point is not neglected. One way of showing it to the patient is by saying to her: "Listen, this is what is making you feel so crazy."

The patient does not know whether to hide or reveal her material, because she does not know whether the analyst is going to make her feel better or worse.

A little more trust has been shown at this time, which is why this material comes to light.

ANALYST: I would like to emphasize one thing. In her story of the dream it seemed to me that the policemen did not have any protective function, but rather that people were out to get her; they were very threatening and hostile.

ROSENFELD: It is most certainly significant that the therapist says that in recounting her dream the patient emphasized that the policeman felt excessively dangerous and inimical. Showing this to her could be of great comfort and use. This represents a highly painful contradiction, and the analyst must show it to her. Being able to reveal her dream to the analyst means that the patient must in fact feel a great deal of trust in him, in his ability to understand her, in his ability to make her not feel worse. Nevertheless, for some reason, she is still afraid that by drawing things out from her, analysis might make her feel worse; analysis, it follows, could be an extremely dangerous thing from which she must protect herself and hide even more, preventing the analyst from understanding what is going on.

This needs to be clearly set out to her. If not, the patient cannot understand the conflict within herself between her conscious and unconscious attitudes as revealed in the dream. The dream reveals precisely this, as does the countertransference.

It is significant that after the analyst has talked about her confusion and fear of madness, the patient says: "Let's wait for another dream." Why, precisely at this moment, should the patient say that perhaps they need another dream? Is it possible that she feels that the analyst has been confused by this dream and has not been capable of understanding her, so she believes that she has to do more to make things easier for him? Alternatively, the analyst could have understood the dream more completely, and told her something more. This would have removed the burden of having to have another dream right away.

My response would have been: "No, you have given me a great deal and I have not given you enough." It is up to the analyst to give more, rather than make the patient feel responsible for unravelling the analyst's confusion.

It is extremely important to decide who has responsibility in analysis. Is it the patient or the analyst? It is the analyst who has the greater responsibility, and this must be demonstrated through comprehension.

In this situation, the patient feels that it is her responsibility to clear up the analyst's confusion, to make things clear and easier for him. I would have thought that the analyst could have done a little more. We may examine things from this point of view: the analyst should not burden the patient with something that was his responsibility, not the patient's. "If it is my fault, I must do something more, as much as I can. If I don't do this, I am automatically pushing the guilt of responsibility for something onto my patient, who really is not in a position to handle it and feels overburdened by it." What has happened is a recreation of the situation in which the parents were confused and the little girl felt she had to do much more than she possibly could to sort out her own parents' problems. This can be seen in the discussion we are undertaking. The analyst has discovered this important element now, right now. Let's assume that the analyst picked up on all this and brought it to the patient, who therefore would not need to have another dream: this would be of great relief to her. Indeed, she might feel as a result that the analyst has understood a great deal; it would be such a relief to feel that she is not a bad little girl because she has not given up enough information, and therefore does not have to go back to sleep to have another dream merely to sweep the confusion from the analyst's mind. On the contrary, the analyst could remove this guilt from her, revealing what is going on to her, allowing her to see more; in this case, the patient might say: "Ah! Good! He has understood!" And she does not have to feel guilty for what she has hidden from the analyst.

Indeed, hiding too much, not revealing, is part of her guilt; if she says, "I have to have another dream that reveals things!", her guilt not only covers the past, it is partially engendered by this not revealing, by this confusion of things. But if the analyst understands this, he can immediately provide considerable relief from this specific type of guilt.

There is one particular moment during the session when the analyst finds that the patient also has good aspects. Now, her good aspects can be pinpointed when she says, "I should have another dream. . . ." There is also the issue of the police who may kill her. This is an extremely punitive and destructive superego which does not help her; it makes her feel guilty and could kill her. This would be the moment to make her see this.

Another issue is associated with finding out who it is who protects her. In reality, she only feels safe when she gets into the boot of the car; the analyst very clearly interprets that she wants to be completely protected and supported by him. Given that she is completely defenceless, the analyst must do all the running, must think for her because she is closed up in the analyst's mind-boot and cannot move at all. To feel protected, she puts herself into a paralysing situation, at the risk of once more becoming a little dog that can only go "bow-wow". In this manner, the actual positive element of hiding in the boot brings new anxieties to light. Pessimism brings up new anxieties. The analyst has clearly described and has interpreted well that the patient has completely stopped thinking, forcing him to think for both of them. It follows that she feels defenceless and dependent because the analyst knows everything.

I suggest interpreting this dream as a reconstruction of an event that perhaps really did happen in the patient's life.

I feel it is important for the patient to speak and make associations. She is a highly lucid patient. The analyst should therefore demonstrate his awareness that he has a healthy patient before him. Why shouldn't the analyst at this moment make her see that he considers her to be sane, capable of contributing and experiencing pleasure in contributing to the analytic process? It is also necessary to show her the contemporaneous onset of those anxieties that tend to force her back into a less clear situation.

This communication enables the patient either to continue undertaking this work alone or, if she does not succeed, to find other ways in which to represent her problem, in such a manner as to allow the analyst to make further connections. In reality, one should as an analyst attempt to do the minimum amount of work, leaving room for the greatest amount of work on the contribution provided by the patient, by her healthy side.

This healthy side, mentioned by the analyst, should be communicated in a much clearer fashion. Her abilities should be connected with the experience that the patient is going through right now with her analyst.

If this is not clearly stated, the patient might think that this part of her is not accepted, and maybe even rejected.

Thursday

P: [*Arrives a few minutes late*] "I have nothing to say. [*Silence*] I once dreamed of *visiting a beautiful house, but there was a luxurious graveyard in the cellar. I was afraid, I ran away.* Recently I had another dream . . . *there was a man I wanted to meet . . . In the dream I meet him and then tell a friend who says it's a good thing . . .*" [*She seems to be distant, detached*]

[*There is a long silence*]

A: "Perhaps these dreams make you think of something . . ."

P: "Well, the second one is clear: in my unconscious I would like to meet somebody, but I'm not capable of doing it. In the first one, I think I was in a country house, it's connected to yesterday's dream . . . the office . . . perhaps I am dead . . . or I'm afraid of dying and I run away. I have already dreamed of succeeding in meeting that person other times. I was telling my friend in the dream that I really had met that man, and that it wasn't a dream like the other times . . . but then I woke up. They are not important, though . . . these dreams aren't interesting . . .

ROSENFELD: At the end of telling her dream, the patient says that these are not interesting dreams. In fact, she expresses a certain degree of dejection.

Looking back at the interpretations I gave at the end of the last session, you will realize just how important they are.

Indeed, at this precise moment it emerges that in the very moment she reveals herself, the patient is afraid. This dream confirms exactly what was said earlier.

The patient refers this dream wonderfully; the analyst can point out to her how she connects this dream of being alive with an awareness of being threatened—in the background, an idealized death situation persists. This continues to threaten her so much that she feels anxiety thinking about it and produces this dream. Therefore the patient has made a real contribution: thinking more clearly about being alive evidently leads her to think about her dead parents.

And, given that certain aspects of her parents perhaps had not seemed so bad, she feels very bad herself, because she is alive and they are dead. How could she possibly be allowed to feel good? Poor parents! There they are, drained of life in that beautiful cemetery. This obviously does not leave her feeling good; I wouldn't feel very good either.

She feels all of this, gets much closer, but she does not fully understand the importance of her fear of her parents, who appear in different forms, while she feels so much alive. I consider it to be extremely important that, as she feels happy and alive, she starts to think of her parents as dead but perhaps happy. A highly important aspect of the sense of guilt and her worry for her own parents lies in shifting the patient towards a depressed mode of thinking, which is threatening her precisely at the moment of improvement. Her improvement is threatened by massive depressive anxiety, rather than by persecutory anxiety.

This is precisely what the patient conveys: when she is improving, she is threatened by a depressive anxiety.

One must succeed in understanding and differentiating between depression and persecution. This is something that must be clearly stated in this case.

In her second dream, the patient says: "In my unconscious I would like to meet a man, but I am incapable of doing so."

She begins by stating, "I am dead, or perhaps I'm afraid of dying and I run away." She says she is afraid, and then soon afterwards says that she would like to meet that person. In the dream, she told a friend that she really had met that person.

It seems to me that in her interpretation the patient is aware of her fear and runs away, but she is not able to understand why this is so. I think I would try to get her to understand that she is running away because if she feels better, she also feels worried about her parents in their "happy" death.

This provokes a certain type of anxiety in her: "Am I allowed to be happy? Am I allowed to meet this man? Am I allowed to enjoy life?"

In the next dream it seems that she is still alive, and not just in the dream, because she appears to suggest that there is a follow-up. She even allows herself to think she is alive, to be able to meet a man, to meet him without being criticized—indeed, on the contrary, she is encouraged by her friend. This situation is terrifically frightening because it is a matter of moving towards life, while depression hangs over her and makes her say, "Do I deserve this?"—"Can I have this? . . . no, no, I mustn't . . . my dreams are no good, they are worthless, I haven't seen a thing."

She must therefore devalue these two beautiful and very constructive dreams and speak as if she had nothing.

The analyst must tell her all this. He must explain to her that this way of behaving is a result of her depressive guilt.

There is still one more thing to consider: it seems to me in particular that the appearance of this man may very easily and consciously be relevant to the transference.

A number of feelings towards the analyst emerge during her improvement; she acknowledges him, feels attracted by him, and can entertain thoughts of this type.

I do, however, believe that the first dream, the one in which she feels better and thinks about her dead parents, shows that it would be too early to make interpretations in this direction; this would be an interpretation that she is not yet able to cope with.

If, on the other hand, the analyst does this now, he would be plunging the patient into a great deal of anxiety. In other words, the analyst must bear in mind this interpretation and be aware that he must make it soon, but first he must tackle the depressive anxiety in the first dream; he must prove to her that these dreams, which she describes as worthless and meaningless, are clearly connected to progress, understood as a movement forward compared to the time before.

He must show her that precisely because she has understood so well, she is now dealing with a particular type of anxiety that is described in the dream. In other words, the analyst must not interpret the dream by telling her that she feels driven back, but that, in moving forward, she comes across this specific anxiety and picks up on an old dream to illustrate this particular problem of hers.

This is a wonderful communication that demonstrates that the patient is still in the phase of deep insight and comprehension towards the analyst. On the other hand, there is already an attack on this comprehension when she begins to devalue what is in her dream.

The analyst's task is to read the dream and show it to the patient, to explain to her what is happening in reality and explain to her how she returns to attacking herself because of this anxiety. When her dead parents appear, the superego pushes her back and tells her that she is worthless. This could not be more clearly visible from the way she behaves.

Just one more point: a colleague once told me that it would have been interesting to examine material relevant to the issue of separation anxiety and how it is presented. It certainly would be great to examine it . . .

But what this patient demonstrates, and what we may look at here, is the difference between persecutory and depressive anxiety as they appear here, and the enormous importance of the analyst's ability to distinguish between them. Not being capable of doing so is horrible; in such a case, the persecutory anxiety is once more pushed back inside the patient, who is entirely dependent upon the analyst to tackle it. You may be able to highlight her great fear at that moment, but you would not immediately be able to pick up on the fact that the stress comes from persecutory or depressive anxiety. It is the patient who has contributed to showing that the stress comes from depressive anxiety.

This, I believe, is the point most worth remembering: if you leave the problem open without saying anything, and therefore without confusing the patient, it will be the patient herself who tells you.

You may touch the patient much more profoundly if you show how much she has contributed, instead of allowing her to diminish herself by saying that she has nothing. This is also far more important from the countertransference standpoint.

During the first part of this session, we still have a dream that is a continuation of the previous session; the patient develops the same theme in two dreams. Nevertheless, the moment the patient feels capable of developing in a more vital way, she becomes increasingly depressed and wants to discard the dreams, saying: "These dreams are not interesting." In fact, they are extremely interesting. As the patient makes progress, what appears in her dream is a lovely cemetery beneath a beautiful room; she has to face a depressive anxiety that fills her with dread and makes it impossible for her to go on living.

She feels very upset and anxious in the second dream too, the one in which she meets a nice young man and somebody encourages her to go ahead with this relationship. We return to the session with the patient helpless and depressed.

ANALYST: Before reading my interpretation I would like to say what was going through my mind. The first thing is that in the dream material she had produced I had been struck by the fact that she felt she might have been dead. The second thing I had in mind is that it was the last session of the week. Now I'll read through my interpretation.

> "Yesterday you told me we had to wait for another dream, to understand more perhaps. It seems to me that you are now communicating to me one of your fears regarding the desire to 'get more to the bottom of' your problems [visit the cellar] through analysis. It is likely that the fear you feel in the dream regards the fact that, for one part of you, undertaking analysis means establishing a very particular relationship with me. As we were saying yesterday, you can fantasize about pushing yourself almost inside me to find help and comprehension [perhaps particularly on a day like today, just before separation], but at the same time you can also, one might say, fear being trapped inside, be afraid of feeling almost as if you are suffocating and dying."

P: "Strangely enough, when I realized I was late, I thought: that way I can get a little more air before going in there. . . . I wanted to come in, but I felt better outside. . . ."

A: "Perhaps you hope to have a relationship with me that is different from what we were talking about earlier, in which you think you cannot breathe sufficiently . . . what you want is perhaps to see me, get to know me a little, as is the case with the person in your dream.

P: [*Replies in a tone that is both mysterious and a little curt*] "No, no, it wasn't you in the dream . . . it really is a man I would like to meet. . . ."

[*I sense that she is absorbed in secret thoughts, far away. . . . Silence . . . I feel rather disappointed and disoriented.*]

A: "Perhaps because we are at the end of the week and you think that it won't be possible to see me over the next couple of days, you prefer to be the one who quickly moves away from the analysis and from me—for example, by not investing any importance in your dreams, withdrawing into yourself, or thinking about your relationships outside here."

ANALYST: After a brief pause, Francesca winds up the session by talking to me about a number of very concrete topics, the details of which I cannot recall right now. Despite the content of the communication, it seems to me that she is now closer, less isolated.

ROSENFELD: It is very interesting that to begin with the patient seemed open to the interpretation; she did not feel persecuted and was expressing the sentiment of feeling accepted.

I mentioned that I thought that the man in the dream was indeed the analyst, as the analyst himself recognized, but that for another reason I would not have interpreted this in the session before helping her to understand the fear she had regarding this dream. I thought that the combination of the beautiful room upstairs and the nice, elegant cemetery might have referred to feelings—emerging in this moment of improvement—connected with her parents in a positive sense.

The patient may indeed feel persecuted by her parents if she thinks that they drove her crazy. But the cemetery was a nice cemetery and, when she feels that life is moving on, the thought comes up of her buried parents, brought to mind in a better form; this makes her feel worried and anxious, but in a different way from the persecutory relationship she had. It is an expression of the progress she is capable of making when she comes into contact with something more beautiful and luminous, something that can give her greater hope in devoting herself to life.

In connection with this dream, the patient immediately feels a fear of dying, a desire to escape, and so on. The fear that appears at this moment is consonant with the material from the preceding day, when contemporaneous with feeling better she felt the threat of her fear reappearing.

My advice would be to put to one side the problem of what type of fear it is that appears so often when the patient begins to make progress. Also, I would suggest refraining from finding out ahead of time what this is about, whether it is based on persecutory fear, and so on.

The reason for this is to allow the patient an opportunity to experience this herself, to let her come up with the existing link.

All this is connected with an explanation of the encroaching fear contained within the dream. It seems to be something that the patient is not capable of taking on, something she feels she must flee; but, from an analysis point of view, as is clearly stated in the dream, it is highly instructive and constructive because it produces an awareness of what she is afraid of. She is afraid of having to face the feeling of the death of her parents, for whom she had admiration and love, although this is happening exactly at the time she feels herself coming back to life.

This is the fear that the analyst must show the patient, the fear of feeling like this: "How can I be alive when my parents are dead, my good parents, not the crazy ones."

Let's summarize the situation, and let's recap the analyst's interpretation. We see that finding it completely impossible to work through any transference feelings in the session, the patient becomes increasingly anxious and wants to run away. I think that some of the things that the analyst is aware of are wholly correct, specifically that the patient is not capable of coping with separation and with the separation anxiety associated with depressive feelings. Coping with feelings of love for the analyst would immediately lead her to acknowledge the separation, the moving apart as well.

The phantasy interpreted by the analyst—namely, of being at one with him—would be a regressive phantasy of non-separation and, therefore, a negation of the progress that the patient is attempting to make. Moving backwards—towards fusion and feelings of this type—could make her feel closer to the analyst. But in the dream it seems that the appearance of the person she wants to meet and the courage to meet this person represent a step forward.

One has the impression that the patient has spoken to him and then somebody has encouraged her, telling her that it is a good idea, almost as if in this way she wanted to overcome her fears that all relationships with men end in failure and that, as a result, there is no reason to begin relationships.

It follows that the interpretation one may make is that she is so scared of the anxiety and depression from the loss of her parents that she thinks she would lose anybody she might love and, would therefore have to suffer depression and anxiety. In consequence, it would be pointless tackling the anxiety of which she is so afraid in the dream by turning to any man, not even the analyst. This might bring the two elements together. In this manner, the analyst may attempt to help the patient tackle the depressive anxiety; otherwise, the patient, missing this aspect, struggles unsuccessfully to put things together.

Perhaps the fear felt in the dream may be connected because the patient thinks that the entire situation is connected with the frightening experience in the dream, the fact that one part of her, especially in today's situation, fears constructing a very special relationship with the analyst—the attempt to get inside him to seek help and comprehension.

In other words, the analyst interprets the regressive phantasy bound up with the fact that the patient dreams of being in the car boot. Being in the boot, wholly dependent, paralysed, and half dead, is interpreted in the analytic situation as a hope of something good, as if to say that the patient is not in such bad shape. After this, the patient does not stay in the boot; she comes out again, speaks freely, and does not seem to be oppressed at all. The interpretation, therefore, reaches her without pushing her back into the relationship of oneness with another which had been so frightening.

Immediately after this, the analyst makes his interpretation, pushing her once more into a relationship that is too tight, which makes her suffocate and die. This aspect should be considered as we look through the later material, to ascertain to what degree the patient may take this on as a problem, and whether it changes the way she thinks.

Moving on to the next session, we should bear in mind that the patient has been left with an interpretation which we must recap. The analyst said to the patient, "You have a strong desire to be at one with me, to be with me in the boot. This feeling is too disturbing, so you free yourself from this dream and now feel that you are without hope." In other words, "If you can tolerate the desire to be at one with me, everything will be fine."

So, the situation would be: "Face this regressive feeling of being at one with me and you will feel fine when you are in the boot." This, I would say, is a highly dubious point because it is not true that she will be fine when she is in the boot. How will she use the analyst's interpretation? How will she use the material, and how will she work with it? In my opinion, the analyst has (with his interpretation) pushed her back into the situation from which she had managed to escape.

Monday session

P: "Men are only interested in me for work reasons; they only talk to me about work! I am only interesting if I talk about work. Then they treat me almost like a man. . . . Hah! . . . it must be my fault. . . . I lack femininity! [*It seems to me that I pick up a mischievous and yet bitter tone*] My parents' fault. . . . if I have to blame somebody! But in the last few years it has been my work. When my father was around, he didn't teach me anything, he did everything himself. It's obvious that my femininity was neglected . . . with my parents, with Dad, as a woman I was nothing. . . . I was nothing . . . I learned how to work, I wanted to become interesting as a woman by being good at work . . . but it's been a mistake . . . [*Silence*]

Perhaps I should resign myself to just working . . . but no, it's not fair! If other people don't treat me like a woman, I can't be a woman!"

A: [*I note that my thoughts are partly occupied by presentation of this written report, and that perhaps at this moment I am dealing with Francesca as an interesting "case"*] You are resentful towards me because you think that my interest in you, the reason I am seeing you, is only because of my work, and that therefore to me even as a man you are just a patient, as if you didn't have any feminine attractiveness. Analysis takes place during the week, when we work, but not during the weekend break, when you feel left on your own and you feel you are not appreciated and sought by me as a companion. Similarly, in the past you perhaps thought that you could only be interested in your father because of the work you both did."

[*I also attempt to emphasize the positive aspect of her need to be desired and acknowledged as a woman, and not just for her "work as a patient" by me, or for her professional life by the people she comes into contact.*]

P: [*Now she seems to me to be very engrossed. After a brief silence, this is how it goes on*] "I said to myself: at least let's get this job thing down right . . . [*Silence*] Some people are born pretty . . . others ugly . . ." [*She is very sad*]

ANALYST: It seems to me that as she does not like her looks, or perhaps out of a fear of not appealing to me or of being rejected, she forgets that she is a woman and tries, in turn, to consider the relationship between us as an impersonal, professional affair, in which there are pre-established roles as patient, analyst, and so on. Similarly, in the past, out of fear that her female wiles were not well accepted, she perhaps handled her relationship with her father in a formal and neutral fashion.

ROSENFELD: The patient wants to be at one with the analyst, and the analyst interprets her oedipal desires for him. I think that this is a big mistake, because the patient does not at all resemble this type.

The patient has not yet tackled her depressive anxieties; with a mental age of 5 or 6 months old, she has the phantasy of merging with the analyst in the boot. For the analyst, however, it is as if the patient's problem were that of expressing oedipal feelings; in consequence, he seems disappointed that the patient has not accepted his suggestion and does not say to him, "Yes, I love you" and so on. Poor Dad! The patient, on the other hand, seems a rather modest partner for him. The analyst was hoping to have a partner, but that's not the way it has turned out.

I think that this interpretation is mistimed and that it has nothing to do with what has previously been interpreted. If the analyst interprets the fusion as being the two of them in the boot, in fact he is interpreting it as a way of avoiding separation anxiety. In this case, the analyst is not a male figure but, rather, a female one.

If it is a matter of being one and the same, it can only be either a male or female one and the same. This is not a relationship in which a little girl can perceive a differentiation within herself, whether it be female or male. With a phantasy like this, there is no opportunity to recognize oneself.

In order to understand and move on from a situation like this, one must consider that there is a conflict not just in the current situation but in the past as well, where the patient is addressing her father.

At this point I would like to mention a patient of mine who tried to please her father because she did not get on with her mother. As a result, she followed her father in everything and did what he told her to do. But this did not mean that the patient became feminine. On the contrary, she became masculine; she wanted to please her father so she dressed like a boy and lost her femininity.

This is a similar situation. In the past the father wanted her to follow him, he told her what he wanted her to be; the patient tried to do the job her father suggested, in order to please him. This did not make her feel feminine but, rather, masculine. Now she wants to please the analyst by attempting to follow his interpretation, as if he had suggested to her to try to be a woman and think about making love with men and with him. For the patient, this is simply an instruction that comes from the father who tells her what she must do. In consequence, there is no possibility of feeling female identification. All she can identify with is her father's request.

Now, the analyst emphasizes that the patient wants to be acknowledged as a woman and not just as a patient with whom he works. Perhaps in this session we will see what he means.

In other words, the analyst feels that the problem at this moment lies simply in the fact that the little girl who feels feminine is turning to her father and, frustrated, does not know what to do, given that she feels like a little girl and not like an adult woman. This, however, occurs in the oedipal situation. I do not believe that this is the case, which is why I am trying to delve further into the detail.

The patient says that she has at least acquired a professional role: "My father wanted me to do something, and I had to follow him." Her father did this same job. The patient has tried to build something that her father wanted her to do. "At least I am capable of doing this," she thinks. Here we have an indicator of what the problem really is. Then she says: " Some people are born pretty, others ugly." It seems that the patient has no hope of feeling like a young woman because she feels that inside she is a long way from being able to develop as a woman. For the time being, she is forced to be a child, her daddy's little tomboy. And she feels pushed in the wrong direction.

When the analyst says that she does not feel attractive to him and that she feels rejected, the analyst approaches this almost entirely in terms of her relationship with her father, in the most formal and neutral manner. The father was very insistent that his daughter be successful, and that she aimed at this. This was part of his relationship with her: he had a high opinion of her intellectual abilities, so he encouraged her to pursue this particular direction.

And yet it seems that this relationship did not help her to tackle the extreme insecurity she felt towards both parents. She wanted to feel like an accepted human being, she wanted to see the truth, to see this beautiful picture of happiness and health. Once more, she feels she is a person who is depressed and repressed, not the person we saw before when she felt beautiful and alive in how she was facing the world. This has all disappeared. If this kind of thing happens, I feel that as an analyst all one can do is try to find out where the serious mistake was made. When the analyst becomes aware of this error, he can attempt to resolve it; however, if he does not become aware, then he will continue pushing the patient in the wrong direction, and the patient will feel increasingly unhappy.

If the patient manages to pull herself out of this, to bring dreams and get back to the feeling of freedom, then things will be going well. From the material regarding her, the patient says, "Perhaps I should decide just to throw myself into work," but then she says, "No, no, it's not like that, if other people don't treat me as a woman, I cannot be a woman." In other words, the patient feels she must acknowledge that something unfair has happened: this is an objection to the analyst, who thinks he has made her into a woman, whereas she feels that he has turned her into a man and so she is rebelling; she feels that the analyst is not treating her like a human being capable of developing as a woman. Here we have a misunderstanding between the two of them.

QUESTION: *How do you differentiate between a precocious oedipal situation and this situation?*

ROSENFELD: Well, I do not see how, in this situation, there could be anything that has anything to do with a normal oedipal situation. It has much more to do with the relationship that apparently existed with her father, to whom she is attached, who wanted certain things from her, and whom the patient attempted to satisfy in order to please him. Satisfying her father's requests is similar to her efforts to satisfy the analyst's requests. The patient may attempt to satisfy him in everything except in this.

There are problems in the course of development, there is a real situation between parents and child, so the child reacts out of this enormous insecurity.

I think that the girl feels extremely insecure about her mother and about her sense of identity, to the point that she feels like she is her father's object-toy, her father's little dog, a "thing" that belongs to her father.

A patient who came to me after experiencing great difficulties in getting married, several times in a row, told me that she had a very strong relationship with her father. The problem was that she had not found her own identity; indeed, being with her father, who looked after her in an almost stifling way, had not allowed her to discover her own identity. All this had nothing to do with her, and everything to do with her father, who seemed to need this.

My patient, who did not know what she wanted, became everything her father wanted her to be. What do you call this? It's an identity problem, it has nothing to do with the Oedipus complex. Identity problems can occur at any stage, earlier or later, and must be diagnosed as an identity disturbance in which one or other of the parents, or somebody else altogether, takes part.

There is indeed a relationship with her father, but I would say that it is wrong to call it an Oedipus complex. Perhaps this is removed. I have tried to put myself in the shoes of a girl who has something similar to an Oedipus complex. Now I am talking as if I were her, like a 3-year-old girl in an intense oedipal situation. "When I was three I often masturbated because I was jealous, because I thought a lot about Daddy, because I thought that he would prefer being with me—but he was with Mummy. I looked on at their relationship and this annoyed me, and then, when I realized that there were some problems between Daddy and Mummy, that Daddy was not satisfied, I ran in to calm him, to satisfy him, thinking that I could succeed; but then Daddy died and I am still here, a three-year-old girl with this thwarted desire, the impossibility of seeing if there was some possibility."

In my view, the problem raised by the question posed does not actually exist. This is the situation: the patient who at a certain point showed a glimmer of developing an identity is now running the risk of losing it once more. This is the problem: it is a problem that stems from an interference in growth, in development of the identity. The patient feels ugly not as a woman but as a human being; she feels she has lost her curiosity and her dreams.

I am certain that when the patient talks about those beautiful rooms, she herself feels more beautiful; then, when it all goes dark, the rooms are ugly, or she is ugly and the rooms are too.

QUESTION: *When the patient says that she feels ugly after saying, "Once again I have got it wrong by turning into a professional," it seems to me that there are signs of very early genitalization which is linked, in tone, to these depressed undertones.*

ROSENFELD: I can only talk about how this material has developed; what you say about very early genitalization might be correct.

And yet I feel that the patient is not ready to develop this aspect before tackling and working through her depressive anxiety. If she succeeds in tackling the depressive anxiety, if she succeeds in differentiating it from paranoid anxiety, then she can differentiate between positive aspects and negative aspects of her parents, between thoughts of her father and mother.

So, tackling the depressive anxiety is fundamental for development of the ego, in the sense that it allows differentiation of the personality, without which the patient runs into problems in every situation.

When depressive problems appear in a seriously psychotic patient, it is very important to make her conscious of them, even if she may be terrified by them. The important thing is not to fall into the terror alongside her. When you understand what you have to do as an analyst, it doesn't matter if the patient is terrified; you are there to help her overcome, work through, and understand the depressive anxiety, not to fall into this abyss, not to kill yourself. In this case, it means helping the patient realize development of the ego.

It is development of the ego, inside the patient, in the direction she feared to go, that brings up all these fragmented issues.

One must help the patient to find her direction, after which she will feel better accepted, more flourishing, and perhaps even more beautiful. At this moment she will succeed in drawing distinctions within herself.

Before moving on with this material, I would like to return to the question asked by one of you regarding the treatment of psychotic patients. Specifically, the question was: "How do you treat negative transference? Do you avoid it or not?"

During a seminar in London last Thursday, a colleague of mine presented a case of a psychotic patient who had been in analysis for two years. The problem was as follows: the patient often began the sessions with violent and furious attacks of anger and devaluation, saying that she was useless and so on.

When the analyst acknowledged the existence of these states in any way and attempted to interpret them, two seconds later the patient walked out of the analysis-room. After a while the analyst realized that it was necessary to modify treatment of the situation and avoid stirring up this anger at all.

What the analyst did was stay silent throughout the entire Monday session, a session full of violence and anger. The following session, the patient said to him, "Well, I'd like to hear what you are thinking; last session you didn't say a word."

The analyst says that he felt placed in difficulty because he did not want to return to that situation, but it also seemed impossible for him not to respond; he interpreted that the material had something to do with a confused, angry situation that the patient seemed completely incapable of containing.

The patient reacted the same way, shot to her feet, and walked out. She did not come to the next session, nor to the one after that.

At this point, the analyst wonders what to do: let it go, or do something.

He decides to call her up. I don't recall the details, but what I do remember is that the patient was not at all resentful, she felt that he did not want to abandon her, so she came back for the Friday session.

In the meantime, the analyst has had time to think through what to do, and decides it is a good idea to go back to the previous Friday session, to try to see what had happened once more. He is referring, therefore, to the weekend, during which the need had become so much of a torture that the patient became more and more angry, to the point that by the Monday session her mind was completely filled with anger.

I would like to point out that this interpretation was taken on by the patient. It is the interpretation that connects the positive and negative aspects.

The patient later works through this and says, "When you, the analyst, say that I am full of anger I feel worse because I am only anger and I don't know what to do. It feels like I am exploding; it is as if your words penetrated inside me." I think it's as if the analyst were saying to the patient, "You are worse, worse than a wild beast."

The escalation that follows has no therapeutic function.

It is extremely insensitive and stupid to interpret negative transference like this, because the patient is incapable of containing these feelings unless she has a relationship that is sufficiently positive to feel able to say something that otherwise is intolerable.

In the next session, the patient begins by telling the analyst about something that happened at work. A friend of hers who works at the same place, somebody whom she admires and esteems, provoked enormous feelings of envy and violent jealousy in her. She does not know what to do in the situation, and she talks about it for half an hour.

The analyst obviously thinks that this problem is connected with him, so he wonders: "Should I interpret the transference or not?"

He decides not to interpret the negative transference situation. What he does instead is to talk in detail about the friend situation, and the patient is very happy, she thinks that he has succeeded in understanding her, and so on.

Nevertheless, the analyst feels a little anxious and asks himself, "Did I do the right thing or not?"

In my opinion he could not have done anything else, because this patient has not yet reached the point of being able to face competitive feelings in the transference; after feeling admiration for the analyst, she felt envious. There is no chance for her to work this through. The patient would think of herself, "You are an aggressive and envious shit, I hate you." What would grow inside her is a sensation of not being accepted, and she would walk out of the session. Despite the sensation of always having to do something, of having to interpret in the transference in order to move on, the analyst has resisted and has done nothing, which is absolutely the right thing to do.

If the analyst interprets everything in the transference, he reduces the patient to only having relations with him. The result is that we are constantly turned back in an intense positive and negative relationship with the primary object, which does not allow relations with anybody else outside itself.

So, if the patient talks about somebody else, the patient understands it as if the analyst is saying, "Are you doing it with somebody else?" The patient feels that she should not have anything to do with anybody else.

And the analyst says: "Here she is, she wants all of me, all my love." The patient very intensely senses this situation but is unable to react or put up with this, so the result is an explosion and flight. This is the only way the patient can handle the situation.

But our colleague did not do this—he created an opening that enabled him for two sessions to have the patient there, without running away.

It is very important to acknowledge that there are some rules in psychoanalysis. However, one must use common sense, for if one forgoes common sense, one forgoes any sense at all. If the analyst makes a mistake, he must learn from this mistake, he must realize that the patient will not tolerate a certain interpretation, and he must, at that moment, employ a little common sense. The analyst should therefore say to himself: "I should dwell on this one; I don't know quite what to do, but I have to allow something to develop before I can tell the patient something that she can take on board."

The patient must be able to consider being angry, the patient must feel that she is somebody who arouses love as well as somebody who can experience extremely intense anger. The patient wants to find the reason for this anger. When this is not possible, or the patient lacks the security to do this, during sessions the patient feels that the analyst is casting her into a position in which he is able to think and analyse, but she is not.

One really must be aware that this may not be asked of the patient.

Let's look back at the patient's relationship with her colleague: what harm is done to the analytic relationship if they go into detail about the feelings of love and affection, as well as the possessiveness she feels for this woman, who can arouse such envy and jealousy? One must make explicit that not only does she hate this friend, she also cares a lot about her.

There are some analysts who might think that this approach fails to contain the patient; in fact, this approach offers the patient room to think about feelings that previously felt intolerable.

If one achieves this goal, particularly with borderline patients, one achieves a great deal.

Now let's get back to the patient.

I need to understand the analyst and the efforts he makes to help the patient.

Most recently, the patient's complaint is that she had no space. The analyst feels that he is being very kind to her, as if he were telling her that she is beautiful; but in reality she finds that she does not have space, precisely at a moment when she is beginning to win some.

There is a cemetery in a dream, above which is a beautiful set of rooms.

I believe that when it is possible to think of a nice space, or look outside and say, "Oh, how lovely it is outside!", at that moment it is possible, more or less, for the patient to feel beautiful.

The patient is saying: "I don't have a room any more, a nice room. The problem is not just that I feel ugly, it's that I don't have room. Where has it gone? Did you take it?" The analyst can help her find it again.

ANALYST: I would like to say one brief thing about the Monday session. I remember—I wrote this down—that I felt rather distant from the patient, and in a countertransference sense it occurred to me that I was not sitting opposite the little girl we had been talking about, but a neurotic patient with moderately regressive neurotic or at least narcissistic problems. At the time I thought that this pseudo-growth—if one may call it that—may have been caused by separation, in the sense of growing up very quickly because one is left alone.

Or perhaps she had wanted to start again, establishing a more superficial and immediate adult-to-adult relationship.

Another thing that came to mind was that in reality her pseudo-adult and pseudo-neurotic way of functioning is a constant, it is a precise mode in her life, for this is a patient who at some moments is truly psychotic, whereas at others she leans more towards the neurotic or neurotic-narcissistic: for instance, she holds down a job, she has a social life.

I wondered how to grasp this more neurotic side of her, which seemed so much in evidence at that moment.

I would like to ask Dr Rosenfeld if he could talk to us a little about the level on which to interpret.

ROSENFELD: One must not forget that when the patient brought the dreams of the cemetery and the meeting with a young man, the analyst interpreted anxiety of death within the transference situation created by emotion, by the patient's very intense desire to "be at one", which is not at all an adult desire.

How can the analyst think that, by interpreting the regressive infantile situation, he is helping the patient tackle the pseudo-adult level?

It is as if the analyst had pushed the patient back for making progress.

From a situation in which she had a space, a nice room somewhere up high, she has gone back to the car boot, where she is cramped and can feel nothing. One must ask oneself: is it the patient or the analyst who sees certain things?

If the suggestion comes from the analyst, then it really is he who pushes her back down and then has to face the consequences; the patient will defend herself by becoming a pseudo-patient.

There will be no progress here until we stop seeing only the situation between analyst and patient, not as if she weren't bound up with anything else.

One cannot analyse the patient by saying to her, "Ah, I thought you were grown up when we were handling the things we analysed earlier."

If the analyst initially viewed the patient at an infantile level, and then later at a neurotic level, he must ask himself if she is protecting herself from being pushed back, back into the boot.

If this is how things stand, then the analyst has made an error. He must take this into account, he must acknowledge it with the patient, bring her to a more open level and help her to understand that he did not notice what was going on. These comments will greatly help the patient to realize that the analyst is capable of reconsidering things, and that it is not true, as all patients think, that the analyst is always right. If the patient sees this, she will say: "There can be an adult space where we can reconsider things together."

Tuesday

P: "I feel stupid when others are successful and do better than me. Yesterday I looked back over a piece of work I did and I was very satisfied. Then today I heard about something my cousin did [*he also works in the same field*] and I thought I was worthless. My cousin was helped by friends after his father died, but I wasn't!

"I'm always making comparisons and wasting people's time. . . . [*Silence*]

"I had a fright the other night . . . [*She does not specify which night, but I seem to understand that she is referring to one of the weekend nights*] I can't really explain . . . first I was asleep . . .

and then [*her tone is anxious*] I felt as if there were people talking in the room. . . . I got up and after a while it stopped. I thought back to what Mummy used to feel. . . . I remember many years ago, when I was with her keeping her company and she told me she "heard things" . . . yes, I heard voices in my room, but they were not talking about anything to do with me . . . they didn't refer to anybody . . . it's not looking good for me . . . so I took the pills and that was the end of that."

I asked her what frightened her more—the situation in itself, or the fear of being seriously ill like her mother ("things are not looking good"), or both.

P: "I said to myself: I'm like Mummy, and there's nothing I can do about it! But then I managed to get away from that, I made the voices stop . . . it was like waking up. Perhaps I spend too much time alone. Am I going to get worse? I'm not finding out a thing here! . . ." [*She says the last sentence in a harsh, aggressive way*]

A: "You are angry with me because I have not told you why I leave you alone at night, on weekends, just like your father left you alone to look after your sick mother not just after he died but in the years before that, when you were little and you were not told why you had to do this. Perhaps being so close to your mother upset you, making you fear that you could feel what your mother was feeling, that you would be like her. It is as if being left alone by me now means that once more you are back with the mother inside yourself, it means you almost confuse yourself with her, and therefore you are frightened of feeling worse."

P: "So I'm feeling it all now! . . . [*She goes on in a sarcastic, bitter tone*] Daughters get their femininity from their mothers! Being crazy, for me, is the height of femininity. Is that how it is? Men run a mile . . ."

A: "The same way you think your dad had to almost run away from your mother when he left her alone with you, or the way you think that I, now, do not want to deal with you as a woman."

P: "I take refuge in my work, but I am a man there. As a woman, I'm crazy! I'm useless, . . . if you don't have the mental abilities, you don't get anywhere!

A: "It seems to me that you are talking about yourself the same way that perhaps your father talked about your mother.

"In doing this you scorn and devalue your femininity or, in other terms, as a woman you consider yourself to be ugly or crazy. This forces you to take refuge even more in your work, to try to be superior, male—like your father—but with a constant fear that you are inferior because you are a woman: this makes it extremely difficult for you to properly see the value of the good things you manage to do at work."

P: "Maybe Mummy did some good things as well . . . she used to paint . . . she drew as well . . . but she didn't have the consistency, the commitment, the same way I don't. . . ." [*Silence*]

At the end of the session I tried to show her that succeeding in telling me the upsetting night-time episode means that despite everything, she thinks that in me she has a person who is different from her father, in whom she may confide her fears, and that this approach has enabled her to no longer feel completely confused about her mother; as she has told me, it has allowed her to get a little distance.

ROSENFELD: Let's go back to the beginning. What strikes me is that the patient is perfectly capable of making comments about herself, weighing up whether she is a successful or stupid person, and sometimes she feels competitive.

The significant things come after this. She says: "Today I learned something from my cousin." But she does not say what. She adds: "I thought I was worthless. My cousin was helped after his father's death. Not me."

I think that it is true that the patient accuses herself of making comparisons, but she also focuses upon the fundamental point, the impossibility of working through the depression and anxiety surrounding her father's death. In other words, the patient needs the analyst's help to get over the depression following her father's death, given that she had no chance to do this earlier. The patient has consciously expressed that this failure to work things through lies at the source of all her problems. It is impossible to be her father, but it is possible to give her a hand to get over her father's death.

She is perfectly clear that her failure to work through this depression is the cause of all her problems.

Here, the patient not only feels that she is losing the analyst over the weekend—and this is an issue that the analyst understands—there is a specific reference to what she needs, and I repeat that one must never leave out the anxiety specific to the interpretation: she needs the analyst in order to get over her father's death.

The analyst cannot be her father. There is no point in the analyst pretending to be her father. She says that her cousin received help, but she does not feel that she has been helped.

The problem she presents is her father and her parents in the cemetery. During the session, this topic has not been taken up by the analyst, particularly the issue of her father's death. The patient goes back to this and explicitly tells the analyst that this is the problem. The analyst must listen to her. This is about her father, and one must help her cope with her father's death. Interpreting the transference only confuses the patient.

I'm sorry I'm having to make criticisms, as it does seem that the analyst is in contact with the patient and has understood a number of things, but it is important to be aware that the father is separate, that the analyst is somebody who is there to help her get over the anxieties surrounding her father's death.

The patient says once again: "I am like my mother."

The patient very clearly says that with his death she not only lost her father, she also lost the protection of her crazy mother, and she found that she had to tackle the situation alone because there was no one else around to help her. This is why the patient did not have space: she was taken over by this fear, by this anxiety, by the situation in which she was the only one who found herself in such a position. Then she says: "I'm not finding out a thing here. . . ." This is an expression of her lack of faith in being protected; she doesn't know what to do, and she asks: "Please, help me get over my father's death, try to understand what it meant to me, how defenceless I felt, how much in difficulty and anxious. . . ."

The patient is saying: "You, too, are going to leave me alone with my problems, forever."

She cannot succeed in establishing even a partially stable emotional situation.

But when the analyst offers his interpretation on her father's death and how she couldn't cope with it, she expresses the desire to have an analyst who not only understands her but feels what she has experienced in order to help her tackle the deeper meanings of these experiences.

This is why she gets angry; because the analyst does not seem to acknowledge what she had gone through. The analyst persists in emphasizing the whole negative transference when he says: "In the same way as you think that your father. . . ."

I don't have any objection to this, but first the analyst should have helped her to make the connection. The analyst is the helper, not the father; taking refuge in work is identification with the father, a non-realization that the father is dead, as well as a realization that he did not help her enough.

SEVEN

Persecutory anxiety

The patient presented in this seminar initially appears to be a mysterious geometric object. During the course of the presentation the
patient frees himself from the nebulous atmosphere in which he has
enveloped himself to reveal a way of mental functioning that may be
understood, reached, and touched. But being touched can represent
a danger, a source of persecution. Rosenfeld shows how one may
handle this delicate situation in such a way as to access the relationship. This requires great wisdom and the ability to wait: wait for the
patient to perceive the value that the analyst figure takes on for him
and, above all, wait for the patient to achieve the ability to keep
things together when he connects with his emotions and with people, moving away from his world of geometric figures.

This case presents additional interest in its illustration of the
difficulties of tackling the particular depressive anxiety that emerges
from analytic insight, associated with the painful and intolerable
perception of how much life has been wasted in the psychotic state.
Drawing upon prophetic words from Pirandello's Henry IV, the
patient describes this pervasive anxiety in a touching manner; this is
something that often appears during the course of improvement in
the analysis of psychotic cases.

An important part of this supervision is the description of complex manipulation operated by the patient, who is in danger of confusing the analyst and effecting a breakdown in progress during treatment.

Another aspect brought to light is the analyst's need to stay awake and maintain faith, emerging from the angry and impotent child position, a position towards which the analyst is drawn by the omnipotence of the patient's predictive identifications.

ANALYST: The first time I met the patient, he was 33 years old. He is now in his fifth year of analysis. The first-born child, he grew up in a small town in the provinces and moved to Milan when he was 19, after his father and his sister had been killed in a car accident.

He has another two brothers. One of his brothers attempted suicide by hanging himself in the bathroom using the dog's collar, seriously risking his life or severe disability, soon after the birth of his first child.

When he was a student at the Faculty of Law, the patient had real trouble sitting exams, and he graduated with the help of a course of psychotherapy. He works as a lawyer.

He is seeking analysis because he is unable to have relations with women, after his first experience with a prostitute ended in an episode of impotence. He communicates the fact that what he is really missing is the impossibility of having "a relationship".

I do not obtain further information about his past life because during the first two meetings he tends to tell me the most varied range of things, expressing himself as if he were already in an analytic session. The reason for this behaviour was to become clear as analysis continued.

I would like to add that my first impression was that this case was too serious for me, that he went beyond my abilities. I decided not to take him into therapy because I glimpsed something shapeless and indefinable within him that made quite an impression on me.

Even now, some of the reasons why I changed my mind are still not clear to me.

ROSENFELD: Did you expect him to be psychotic?

ANALYST: I don't know, because the psychosis aspect is not something that has been rationalized inside me. It's also true that I no longer remember the first meeting.

After this the situation changed, the patient began talking. There was a change at that point. The next meeting, a week later, the patient told me that his mother had been away from home for a few days, that it was a complete mess, and that he wasn't fixing anything to eat. I thought he had given me positive feedback on something that had happened between him and me.

ROSENFELD: It does seem as if the patient feels lost and abandoned; sometimes he knows he is lost, at other times he gets frozen in a state of feeling lost and lonely.

During the course of analysis, his mother is described as a highly religious person who has always looked after things at home and took on the leadership role in the family after his father died, "forcing" her son to study law (instead of philosophy, which is what the patient wanted) because she thought that this was a better bet for the future. The patient rarely talks about her, generally only on the infrequent occasions that his mother is away from home. It may be understood that she looks after all the patient's needs; a number of episodes allow one to perceive a peculiar relationship between them. One such episode came up a few sessions after the holidays. The patient wakes up one night with the impression of having heard noises on the other side of the front door. He thinks that someone is trying to break in. Soon after, he hears his mother padding around the house: she had the same impression. Both of them panic, frightened by the fantasy that somebody is pouring petrol beneath the front door to set the place ablaze. They open the door: there is no one there.

ROSENFELD: Both of them panicked.

ANALYST: Yes. I was very struck by this. It happened after the first summer break. Both of them waking up gave me a sense of a mother/son unit, both of them panic-stricken at the same time.

His father sometimes makes an appearance, in one form as the affectionate and understanding person who got up at night when the patient, as a baby, was woken up by nightmares, a man who took the patient around and explained things to him, who brought back books and encyclopaedias and magazines; however, he is also depicted as somebody who completely lost control of himself when he had arguments with the patient's mother, screaming at her as if he could not stop, as if he had no earthly doubt that he was right. The patient became ashamed of him because he came from a family of lower rank than his mother's, and because he had only finished high school and gone no further, unlike his brother (the patient's uncle) who was a doctor.

Rather than giving a linear account of these years of analysis, something that is almost impossible anyway, I prefer to run through the points that have formed in my mind.

The tendency to talk ceaselessly manifested in those initial meetings has been a habitual aspect of his analysis. The verbal content of sessions is a long sequence of anecdotes, thoughts, film or book reviews, episodes from his everyday life, and so on. At the beginning especially, there did not seem to be a connection between these topics, and he often made me feel either sleepy or, on the contrary, angry. It is still common for me to feel that I have grasped something during a session, only to sit down to make notes at the end of the session—this happens the more we go on—and notice that the patient's words and my interpretations are poles apart.

The greatest difficulty regarding the formulation of interpretations lies in succeeding to isolate the most significant aspects in the economy of the moment. What's more, long, detailed interpretations often provoke drowsiness in the patient.

ROSENFELD: Did you just feel drowsy, or did you actually fall asleep?

ANALYST: He made me feel sleepy, but I have never actually fallen asleep. Since sessions were in the early afternoon, initially I thought it was to do with having just had lunch.

ROSENFELD: You have something in common: the patient falls asleep when the analyst is talking, and the analyst falls asleep when the patient is talking.

ANALYST: Sleepiness was not a problem in every session, just some of them.

> The "truest" request from analysis seems to me to have been deter-
> mined by a sense of inconsistency that the patient felt, sometimes
> very dramatically. There are moments during his everyday life when
> he is seized by a sensation of panic that forces him to sit down and
> wait for it to pass, though this can all be over in a few seconds,. He
> says the same thing a number of times over, noting that as a child he
> was completely incapable of understanding "long division", or
> other mathematical problems: "Nothing in the problem gave me
> anything to get hold of so that I could get on with it." Something
> similar occurs in analysis on the rare occasions when the interpre-
> tation seems to really touch him; he immediately states: "I don't
> know how to go on from here."
>
> To overcome this sensation of panic, he has built up a rigid system
> of thinking; everything he does and all his relationships must be
> slotted into these categories. His free time is almost wholly absorbed
> in a systematic reading of oriental philosophical texts. Managing to
> do this is a success for him. He forced himself to start doing this one
> day after moving to town, after a long period when he had done
> nothing but spend all his time wandering aimlessly around town.
> That first summer, for instance, he took up his wanderings again. He
> stayed in town throughout August, walking around the place be-
> cause he had nothing to do.

ROSENFELD: That summer when he was just roaming about the place, did the patient consciously connect this behaviour with the analyst's absence?

ANALYST: No. He told me he didn't do anything; he brought me the anxiety he experienced during the first session after the holidays, when he related this episode to me.

> During his wanderings, he caught sight of a little kitten next to its mother, which had been savaged by a dog: it was covered in blood and was blind. The patient went back the next day but they weren't there, so he assumed they were dead. He added that if he decided to stop reading, he would have to sell his books, and that would leave an empty space in his bookshelf. His room would look different. He would have an empty life.

ROSENFELD: With this sensation of an empty life, the patient seems initially to be expressing his attachment to objects—books—followed by visualization of empty spaces in the bookshelf. It is very interesting that the patient cannot say that this gap is related to his analyst or his mother, he can only say it in reference to a book: this has something to do with the patient's conception of the body as a geometric form. It is quite common in this type of patient to encounter the sensation that the body alters and becomes a geometric shape. Even the analyst becomes a geometric shape, and therefore the patient does not need to think or worry about him; the analyst does not run away, books cannot run away, there is no way of moving off. He seems to be dead, but in fact the patient is very much alive. Patients like this who seem to be dead have actually invested a great deal of life in these books, in these geometric forms.

ANALYST: Years later I connected his and his mother's panic attack with the kitten episode. I made the connection in my mind, and during the summer it pushed him to re-experiencing a breakdown, with the analyst becoming a highly persecutory character who threatens to ruin his symbiotic relationship with his mother.

ROSENFELD: This would be connected with his becoming much more real and alive. It is as if you said to him, "Hey, I'm here too!"

ANALYST: The patient makes similar use of his ability to fantasize, something that seems to be boundless.

> He tells me about something that happened: as a boy, his friends tried to build little missiles and then launch them. The patient says,

"I also tried to get into this and, between one fantasy and the next, I built a real missile that was very light, and could take off and fly in space; I could see myself inside as it was rising up."

I think I can shed more light on this point by referring to a fantasy that often accompanies his masturbation: he masturbates lying on one side, imagining that there is a woman behind him who is having intercourse with him. The woman is working for an organization that wants to get hold of his semen, which is considered to be very valuable because it belongs to such a great man.

Another aspect I have encountered concerns the analyst figure. This figure is not in a state of symbiosis (or perhaps parasitism?); it makes its presence felt with interpretations which touch him very deeply, and therefore the analyst becomes a source of danger to the patient, and is sensed as a source of persecution.

Several times the patient has mentioned the anger he felt when his mother called him down to lunch when he was busy building "windmills". Another episode: he forced himself to vomit on the way to school, and the more his mother struggled to make something he could eat, the more he vomited.

Something similar happened with me: the patient told me about a bus driver who stopped during a trip to rescue a wounded bird. He must have been a sensitive person to do this. A few sessions later, however, this character reappears as a man who perhaps tried to seduce a girl who was left on the bus alone and feeling unwell.

A similar topic comes up in a dream. *In his pocket the patient carries a golden lighter [which he really does own]. Some muggers attack him and some of his relatives. While his relatives allow themselves to be mugged, he does everything he can to stop them stealing his lighter; first he hides it and gives them other objects, then he runs away but they catch up; he runs away again, they catch up and so on.*

ROSENFELD: The things he is frightened that the analyst may steal from him are the golden lighter and his sperm, and yet he talks about them. It is very important that he talks about them. Over the years the patient has been keeping the analyst interested with some of his secrets. Often psychotic and autistic children have something that they keep concealed, a phantasy that people want to steal something very precious from them. The problem with these patients is that you need to have an enormous amount of patience; you have to wait a long time, for it is not possible to simply turn the situation around by interpreting the fact that the patient believes he wants something precious from the analyst, because if this is done, there is a risk of setting off an extremely persecutory situation. Since the fear of intrusion is so enormous, one has to wait until the patient thinks that the analyst has something valuable for him. Because this anxiety of intrusion is so major, it generates fear, violence, and desire of wanting something from the analyst. Patience is the issue. For the patient who says or dreams, "I have precious sperm," or "I have a valuable lighter," an interpretation by the analyst that it is he who wants something precious would be an intrusion. It would specifically put him face to face with his greatest anxiety—namely, the violent way in which he wants to get something from the analyst, or in other words, the anxiety of being the intruder himself.

With almost perfect timing, a few days after telling him my holiday dates he bumps into an acquaintance he considers to be "crazy", who is into telepathy and things like that. The patient tells me that this man, "Is very disturbed that I am in analysis, as if some part of him was called to offer the analysis. For years now, every time we meet he has tried to persuade me to stop the analysis, as if it had something to do with him."

ROSENFELD: This episode bears some similarities to the geometrical-shapes business: the patient thinks that he can keep himself together if his relationships are with geometrical shapes. It is dangerous when things become personal, because that means that the patient is coming alive; if he comes alive he has to face his need to have something and the fear that his feelings and emotions, whether they are negative or positive, might make everything fall apart. Emotions are perceived as violent; it is therefore important that nothing moves too quickly. The patient challenges the analyst to recognize this fear and to protect him from feeling things. By telling us this, he is seeking protection from experiencing personal feelings; to some extent he is trusting the analyst not to take advantage of him, trusting that that he can understand all this.

> When he "becomes" his acquaintance C it seems impossible to engage in communication with him; it even becomes difficult to see him. The patient says: "In Pirandello's *Henry IV*, the King says, 'I can't come back to life because the others have moved on. I had to play the madman, and now all I find is leftovers.' His rival responds: 'What should they have done, should they have waited for you?' This answer cannot have satisfied the King, for he has the man killed." This matter has come up in analysis hundreds of times, so many times that the patient has said, "Enough, I'm getting too old . . . enough, I should have gone into analysis when I was a boy . . . but now I'm at the end of my life. . . ." At moments like this, he often says "there's no point any more".

ROSENFELD: This expression brings us back to the fact that "coming alive" is very frightening, because feeling means realizing that one is lost, how isolated life has been, how long he has not been taking part in life. Living in this "dead" way, which, as the patient says, is a crazy way to live, means that he has lost the meaning of life. You then say something else about the patient's fear; that others may be frightened by his violent emotions. Here, the patient has almost revealed his secret.

> In such cases, the patient often invokes sleep as his only resource. While I am talking he falls asleep, or almost falls asleep, forgetting what I have told him when he wakes up again. On one such occasion, when the patient woke up he told me the following dream: "*I was on the couch and the analyst was behind me. There was another person behind him, but it was me, bent double with my head between my legs. The analyst was watching through a crack beneath the door; because he was in the corridor; he was much bigger.*"

ANALYST: A further point I would like to make is the sensation of often being completely manipulated, but without having elements to clear up the terms of this, first to myself, and then to the patient. This often happens just before the end of sessions and, in particular, during the final weekly session. I no longer understand "who is talking" and "about whom". This feeds into my constant underlying mistrust, even during positive moments in the relationship. Indeed, it is likely that this occurs precisely after those positive moments.

ROSENFELD: In such cases the problem is that the patient employs methods to annoy the analyst, to confuse him. This does not alter the fact that the patient needs somebody who is not angry and confused, even though he himself engenders exactly the opposite situation. It is difficult to know how to handle this situation. When the analyst becomes so angry, it is as if the patient says to himself, "Oh, that's what I thought, I could have predicted that." Because he is incapable of facing up to the situation, instead of feeling this anger himself it is the analyst who is angry and confused.

The fact that he wants to take up a well-known situation and repeat it may be functional, because he is no longer at the mercy of an unknown situation that terrifies him. This kind of manipulation—putting the analyst in the patient's situation—is very irksome for the analyst, as he does not know which way to turn. Being put in the patient's situation creates a situation that is very difficult because of the manipulative state it creates inside; this way, it is the analyst who gets angry because he has not got what he wanted. At this moment the patient is in control. He also, however, has to move away from the analyst, who has not supplied him with the interpretations he needed. In the end, he finds himself back in a situation in which he does not know what to do. The patient is afraid that the analyst isn't capable of giving him anything; he is also afraid that the analyst can indeed function, but has decided not to give him anything because he feels superior; he is keeping things to himself, leaving the patient in a state of frustration.

In reality, when he puts himself in the analyst's hands, the patient establishes a relationship with him. But when he enters this state of confusion, he forgets the fact that there is somebody there to help him. From a practical point of view, it is much more important to interrupt the patient, not just to talk about his mother, and so on, but to help him find himself again: this is the only thing that the patient considers useful. It is important to wake him up, not to let him sleep, because by waking him up he can think rather than have dreams.

If this is undertaken, the patient becomes much calmer and usually adds other details because he can perceive the experience of being helped, of being saved, of no longer being alone. If you don't do this, he will carry on alone, without ever stopping. In the background one may glimpse a very close relationship between him and his mother, as if they were a single person. His mother needs this as much as he does—witness the panic episode. Neither one of them has the upper hand: it is a balanced situation.

This model represents what has always happened in the analytic situation: the analyst is somebody who may step in between the mother and patient. One may hypothesize the analyst becoming a father, or a couple, in a workable position.

QUESTION: *In his relationship with his mother the patient appears to be someone whose personality development could be characterized by the tendency to fuse with others. Thanks to the reversal he manages to achieve in his relationship with the analyst, the patient seems to be in a situation that at least is more involved, in which he may use projective identification. Things may be exchanged. Isn't this already a step in the right direction?*

ROSENFELD: What I would like to say is that the non-confused parental couple is represented by an analyst who is capable of thinking, an analyst who is not angry, who can cope, and who stays calm; this kind of analyst expresses the possibilities of parents united in a comforting way; this is the mental state that the analyst must seek to achieve and maintain in order to be able to draw upon what lies within his own mind; if on the contrary he becomes vindictive and angry, he becomes exactly the same as an intrusive situation. The analyst must recognize what is happening to himself; it is pointless to focus on mechanisms, as what is happening is a very real situation. Despite his manipulations, the patient is in fact exposed to the huge danger of losing everything he needs to live.

One must consider the fact that if omnipotence becomes concrete and interferes in a parental relationship which has worked well, in which attention has been paid to the child, the parents themselves may becoming infantile and angry. The identification may be very powerful, but the issue is to recognize what is happening to the analyst himself, and what kind of mental state must be maintained. One should not just have mechanisms in mind; one has to recognize that all this is very real indeed. One must be capable of grasping that the patient may dangerously destroy the things he needs; in particular, one must remember that he needs the analyst. In consequence one must think for him, help him, make the connections of which he is unaware, and provide the answers he does not have. Although the analyst does have some of the answers, he is behaving as if he did not have any at all; if he places himself in the child's position and allows himself to be treated this way by the patient, things can only finish badly for both of them.

It is dangerous to say that this is "projective identification" or a "representation of the penis, yes, I'm certain it's that". If this does occur, the analyst is just like a child who uses a mechanism to feel powerful. One must be very careful not to use analysis as an acting out of infantile experiences. It's like using a piece of machinery or something concrete to throw back at the patient; it's like saying, "I have this thing and you don't." One must be very careful not to use omnipotence; one must contain the desire to understand, and this takes a lot of time; one must also realize that one will not understand the patient for a long time—it is a matter of being with him and containing one's desire to understand. I do not know if this model can be of help to us here, but it is more alive to the idea of projective identification. When you thought that this was projective identification, did your mind perhaps feel clearer? One must regain calm, one must realize that the patient makes us lose what is in fact the most important thing for us: our mental clarity, our calm and space. When these are lost, we tend to grasp at definitions and use them for a predetermined purpose.

Monday

[*Most unusually, he arrives a few minutes late*]

P: "I was late because I didn't leave enough time to get here. I walked over from a court hearing that overran; the judge wanted to keep on going even later and settle proceedings. If that had happened, I would perhaps have had to skip the session altogether. This is a judge whom I feel to be hostile; I was feeling very tense, and now I feel as if I had escaped some danger. It was a case I was so anxious about that it was preventing me from relaxing, despite the fact that over the last few days I bumped into an old friend after many years."

[The patient has in mind Thursday's session, in which he recalls that we talked about drugs, even though he does not remember why we were on the subject]

"I spent the night at my friend's house, then as soon as I got home I masturbated. Being in other people's houses makes me feel impeded, and I couldn't masturbate. As soon as I got back home I did it, but not being able to do without felt like some kind of imprisonment: proof that it's impossible to change things."

[He falls silent for a moment and then, as if inwardly smiling at the thought of what he is about to say, he tells me of two thoughts that had come to mind. The first was the thought of Captain Ahab pointlessly attacking the white whale, which refused to die. In the other thought, he, as a child, is asking his grandmother if the little crab he had just caught, which had a "cross on its head", might be the baby Jesus.]

As far as the smile is concerned, I cannot see the patient, but my knowledge of him indicates that his little smile and silence mean that something has happened during the session. I have sometimes seen him laugh or smile, and it is a rather striking thing. Three or four times the patient has got to his feet, unable to contain this smile, as if he has just got one over on me, as if it were one of those situations that Dr Rosenfeld was talking about earlier. It's a smile of victory, the smile of a madman. On occasion, when I come to open the door at the beginning of the session I have seen more of a smirk. It seems to be a kind of inward smile, a little doltish, a little crazed, the smile of somebody who is laughing at what is going on in his own head.

ROSENFELD: There are elements of desperation in this material. The patient is aware of how dependent he is on masturbation to resolve his problems, he knows he is trapped in a cage and that he needs somebody else to help him get out. He cannot smile triumphantly and say, "I won!", but he does seem to acknowledge the need to do so. I cannot say if it would be useful to interpret at this stage; this we cannot know, but it is important to understand what is happening to the patient.

P: "I want to tell you a dream I had. *I was smearing ice cream onto my head as if it was hair gel, to make my hair soft and shiny.* Then I ate what was left. I had eaten an ice cream with my friend and his wife. I think it was nice, but I couldn't relax enough to really enjoy it. Thinking back, it seems I was wasting my time: I was not able to take advantage of the situation of friendship. The bar, too, was run by friends of ours."

I tell the patient he has the sensation of wasting time (not just the minutes today) because he is unable to take advantage of a situation that he has in some way perceived to be a friendly one, with an analyst friend. He is wasting the analysis situation because of a fear that I want to draw conclusions (in the sense of moving forwards), whereas there is something inside him that wants a drugged situation (referring to previous sessions), in part out of the feeling that meeting with me restricts him and prevents him from masturbating.

The patient ends up improperly using something that could be nourishing. One may say that he uses it as an ornament: more for the outside of his head than the inside.

The patient remains silent as I tell him these things; I have the impression that he is falling asleep.

P: "I feel as if half the session is already over and the second half is about to begin. It might be an advantage to have two sessions, but I wonder why I can't even manage to get through one."

[*He tells me about a film he saw with his father when he was a child, in which there was a king who was brought a pair of strongboxes completely covered in velvet and full of gold coins. The patient thought that the covering was much nicer than the contents. Then he spoke about his grandmother, the fact that the older she gets, the more she remembers childhood events; they come to her like flashbacks, but she can't remember what has happened recently. He did not consider this to be a pathological fact.*]

A: "Half the session has passed and you are suggesting that this fact, this loss of what has happened now, this focus on distant things, should be considered a symptom of ageing."

P: "It is as if I was faced with a really tough question. Time has passed . . . and there is old age. . . . Like this morning, when the judge asked me a question and I answered, it seems extraordinary to me. When he asked me another question, I asked for time to reply. Like at exams when I hadn't studied, and the question was on the only thing I knew. The examiner was then amazed that I didn't know anything else. I felt guilty. There must be three or four questions in an oral exam: if I had answered all four of them I would have got a good mark!"

So, finishing up one session and moving on to the next is like taking time. As if he knew nothing beyond this: "I have already given you everything I know."

ROSENFELD: In the ice-cream dream, the patient knows that what he needs is a couple, he knows that the couple is important and has produced something good for him, a nice ice cream; this situation has brought home to him that he is in a very bad state, as he has not been able to eat this good thing. It is important for the patient to acknowledge the model of the couple, and it is important that the analyst knows this. What the patient wants to do with good interpretations is, like Jesus Christ, to stick them away in his head. A situation in which there is some good is distorted by his omnipotent part.

What is the child's experience? When the child senses a good experience, the patient becomes jealous; this is where the aspect of infantile omnipotence, of Jesus Christ, emerges, and this makes the patient feel crazy. Instead of leaving the session thinking it has been a good session (a good feed), the patient perceives that he has had a good experience and wasted it, which pushes him into depression. I insist on the fact that the patient is now in a position to acknowledge the good experience. I would have told him that.

In the meantime, the patient must be presented with the concept of the analytic couple. I am pleased that the patient has followed the analyst in the model constructed previously, so let's return to the couple model. The important thing is that what is seen as good is subsequently wasted. One may say, for instance, that in the first interpretation put forward by the analyst he is presented as separate or divorced, outside a couple. One may tell the patient that when something good happens, something competitive and envious leaps out too, something that winds up eating away what is good and leads him into the situation of the omnipotent Jesus Christ, which makes him feel wonderful. The patient knows this and therefore takes on interpretations in a twisted way, "sticking them in his head", becoming an analyst who says: "I already knew this!" It is important to describe in detail what is happening and then add something to what the patient has said. It is important to supply clear and detailed interpretations, for they allow the patient to understand that he has not bamboozled the analyst, that he has not destroyed him; if this were the case, he would feel lost.

The analyst is right when he tells the patient he is using something incorrectly, but this fails to provide sufficient information for the patient to use. The analyst adds nothing more, when he should realize that, unable to use his own mind, the patient only has the analyst's mind to draw upon. The patient becomes confused if the analyst thinks in an overly superficial manner. If the interpretation is too limited, it is like a blow to the head, and he allows himself to fall asleep. The analyst must add something, he must augment the patient's ability to think, he must supply sufficiently extensive interpretations to be able to broaden what the patient is capable of thinking and saying. Only then will the patient wake up.

It seems to me that this experience, this account, makes it look like the analyst wants to know things about the patient that the patient himself does not know, and that what the analyst should do is allow time. One cannot interpret by asking the patient for something, one must interpret in such a manner as to give the patient something; in addition to what he has said, bringing together different elements in the material. There is a kind of blockage in the patient's mind. The patient knows about it because it has always been there; the only way he has been able to take this on has been to withdraw. The only thing that can be done in such a context is to desist from forcing the situation. If the analyst is in a position to use the material, it will become significant, and the patient will feel that nothing has been lost. If he is not in a position to use it, that's fine too. If that is the case, he has to think about it and use things differently. What is important is to be aware of this. Here, in my opinion, something has failed to work. Having given a great deal of information, the patient is required to give still more. In my opinion that's not exactly the way things are. He has given a great deal of information, and the analyst should give him much more. It is not easy to do as I advise, but you have to think over the material often and ask yourself why the patient feels that he is wasting time.

This is a situation that the patient feels with the couple and with the analyst.

If one succeeds in conveying to him how one feels in this situation, the patient can use the material. If the analyst does not understand this, there is no question of the patient understanding it. If you are working alone and do not have a supervisor or somebody to consult, you have to read back through the material, examine it, and ask yourself questions. In my opinion, this material is very clear and of such a nature as to be able to show the patient the significant elements. At this time the patient is having a depressive reaction; now, an ability to react to the situation, which he describes as a sense of loss, is already an improvement in the way his mind functions. When the analyst does not succeed in making all the connections, he becomes a judge; he becomes somebody who always wants more from the patient, somebody who is experienced as the one who "wants even more". The patient must be relieved from this superego-sourced sense of guilt, he must be alleviated of it.

I have no desire to attack or judge you, but it does seem to me that the patient cannot improve on the material—it is already so rich. The last interpretation expresses the exact opposite of how things are going: in effect, the patient has said everything that he can possibly say, and it is the analyst's turn to say more.

QUESTION: *What you say is true, but we also need time to achieve understanding. I am wondering if, in the session, the analyst could interpret that he has understood that he doesn't have enough answers, with the addition of a little technical feature, namely that of saying this to the patient.*

ROSENFELD: I agree with making the patient more aware of the fact that the analyst is human and needs time. You could say to the patient: "During the session you have given me a great deal of information I believe to be important, but it's hard for me to digest and I need time to supply you with a more complete comprehension of what's happening." In this case, the analyst relieves the patient, though it is also possible that the patient arrives at the next session thinking that he has not said enough and thereby risks sliding into a very difficult manic situation. One may also tell the patient that not everything regarding what happens between two people is pathological, as the patient himself was implying with regard to his grandmother who, as she got older, only has a certain type of memory.

Tuesday

P: "On my way in I was thinking of telling you about some things that have been happening at work. R [*who owns the company*] and S [*a young female colleague*] helped a woman in a difficult case. R very much insisted on reaching a settlement [*a payment schedule worth many thousands*], but as soon as he pocketed his handsome fee he lost all interest in the matter. The people who are meant to pay this money are unreliable, and the woman is not very bright. A few days ago, the woman called to find out if the cheque had arrived, so I asked R, who answered me very rudely, shouting at me not to disturb him. He passed the whole thing on to S, but she can't ask for a fee because the woman has already paid. I decided to get out of there, to close myself up in my own little world and carry on studying to become a magistrate. [*The patient's voice is loud and distorted*] I feel anxiety and confusion, but having told you about this, I must say that I feel I am in a situation that is slowly maturing. An image comes to mind of faeces coming out of the anal orifice and falling. It may seem disgusting, but it is a perfectly normal thing I experience everyday."

[*Then he complains that before this he used to work in a legal partnership where he was happy to practise because of the quality of human relations, but that is not the case now. It's all the same for him whether he works there or somewhere else. He feels that his situa-*

tion lacks affection, even from his mother. He does not have ideals, and all he thinks about is making money. He takes on cases that he is not very convinced about because he thinks they will be lucrative.]

I point out to him (going back to yesterday's session) how he seems to be satisfied with the possibility of stopping the sessions, and how he already considers it as being valuable; as if it had given him what he wanted. At this point he abandons the other parts of himself (the dense woman, S), and even the analyst.

P: "All true: it almost always feels like I am getting hold of something between the beginning and 4 o'clock. Being able to talk and get an interpretation seems to me to be of great importance, it goes beyond what I feel immediately, like slow-growing seeds. Yesterday, I came here from a hearing where I was getting somewhere, but then obstacles came up. The judge wanted to press on, but because I was tired, and because I was a little euphoric, I was in danger of saying something stupid."

A: "From the outside it looks like a session: you are on the couch and you are talking, I am behind, and I interpret. For you, this is a good gain, as if it was analysis, though it is not certain that this is what it actually is. So, get rid of the woman, S, who faints, etc., and bring the session to a close."

I point out that this is a drug: one hit per day, it has the effect of producing euphoria, and then it's time to break off so that he doesn't start spouting stupid things.

P: "Why can't it last for the whole hour? And why does it have to end? Can we do 'as if'? Inside me, it no longer resembles an analysis."

A: "You should take on board what I'm saying to you [not just the fact that I am speaking about it] regarding the woman who does not understand, and about S who is offloaded a job where there is no money to be made."

P: "I understand why it's over after half an hour, after the analyst speaks. First I talk, and bring up everything I was thinking about back in the waiting-room: my world. Then you talk and you take me on to other problems: that's your world, not mine. Interpretations are seeds that ripen because I can bring them to the next session as my own. You may talk about 'old age', etc., refer to the fact that, wretched as I am, I am still looking for something, but to me that's just a pleasant thought, it doesn't make anything germinate. I think it's untrue—I'm a wretch and that's all there is to it."

A: "You have the session in the waiting-room [you think over what you are going to say]. Then I speak. There is never an encounter, each of us is in his own world. And yet sowing seeds, without knowing whether or not they will germinate, is already a good payoff. And you can continue to tell me that analysis is not giving you anything, while you are getting older and older."

P: "You may tell me that there is no encounter, but this is innate, it's part of the very practice of analysis: I, the patient, am in front of you; I cannot see you. I also wonder why people are so persistent. I was thinking about a book, "Interrupted Analysis". One guy who fell asleep in analysis—I didn't like his character—said he had homosexual and narcissistic tendencies. He had broken off the analysis, but some time later the analyst called him to ask about something or other. He thought he had seduced the analyst."

I tell him what the good payoff is in breaking off analysis. Whereas before it was he who came into analysis and was seeking the analyst, from now on it becomes the analyst who is trying to get in touch with him, who is seeking him, seduced by him and seduced by his culture, and so on.

ROSENFELD: The situation has been reversed. The patient seems to clear up a certain number of things, and he confesses this. For example, he says that it is hard for him to put something of the analyst's inside himself because their worlds are completely separate from one another. He feels that all analysts show themselves to be clever and intelligent, but in actual fact they want their patient's money, so they say the first thing to come to mind, after which they pocket the money and leave. In reality, this is what the patient is doing when, for example, he talks about valuable seeds. These seeds have a meaning, but it is the patient himself who has them in his possession. It is important to show him this, because he is making a series of admissions, he is confessing secrets, and it is important to show him the way that this is happening.

This is how things seem to me to be going. The patient says: "I must have something good and interesting." The analyst talks about old age and poverty. At this point it is as if the patient picked up these scraps and said, "Oh, interesting. Old age, poverty: but what use have I for being poor? It is not a good thing or a gentle thing. I am a thing of poverty, I have nothing to give and nothing to receive either." He picks up the interpretation in bits, as if he were breaking up the words "old age" and "poverty" into fragments. The analyst must therefore be very careful to connect things together, to interpret them, for the patient tends to nibble at things, rip pieces off and take them away, and in the end all that is left are fragments of interpretations. It is also worth talking slowly, repeating yourself often. The patient considers the analyst to be intelligent inasmuch as he manages to winkle all the gold coins out of his chest—both his physical chest and his treasure chest. The patient must be very quick, peck up something here and there to get hold of anything for himself. What is needed here is to connect, talk, go slowly, repeat, and consider that this patient presents both the mother and the analyst as superior persons who are not there for him to give him something he needs, but rather to show him how intelligent they are.

EIGHT

A primitive psychic structure

What is interesting about this seminar is the attempt to put the patient's complex personality structure into focus; an attempt to understand the difficulties of handling a particular analytic relationship.

In this case, Rosenfeld refers to a psychic structure that though highly primitive must not be confused with an infantile structure, something with which we psychoanalysts are more familiar.

The patient in question is so much lacking a sense of separateness that he is almost physically interpenetrated with the analyst; for him, separations are perceived as lacerating occurrences affecting his body.

Defences against perceiving a relationship of dependency are so violent that they impede normal modes of communication and transference.

Resulting from a condition of traumatic birth, the patient nurtures a desire to return to the womb; he employs defences and communications in which projection of the self onto others predominates, here becoming a special form of intrusion into the analyst's mind and body.

The analyst's communications, all of which must be formulated neither too explicitly nor too tightly, should take into account the violent and primitive corporeal and mental sensations experienced by the patient, and channel them in such a way as to help the patient emerge from chaotic and excited mental states, denuded of any affectual significance.

Interpretations should therefore sometimes be restricted to "cleaning up" the material's crudest elements in order to facilitate access to a mental state of greater contact.

Rosenfeld specifically talks about manicality as a protection against emptiness, and how the analyst can positively establish contact with this mental state.

ANALYST: The case I'm presenting throws up considerable problems. When we first meet the patient, Mario, he is around 30 years old, and he works as a trainee doctor in a hospital laboratory near Milan. He is seeking analysis for "a series of insecurities".

He does not believe that he has any particular symptoms or problems—perhaps a little indigestion which might be psychosomatic in nature. He often feels depressed, a vague sense of dissatisfaction; he does not have much get-up-and-go, but in his life everything has happened in a straightforward manner. The only element he insists upon is insecurity, a term he uses in a generic and all-encompassing way, making one think of a desire for mathematical certainties; at times this seems close to a perception of insufficient contact with his own inner world, a sense of not belonging to himself.

I took Mario on but did not consider him to be a particularly stimulating patient. His physical appearance confirms this impression: well mannered and a little meek in his behaviour, an ordinary, almost anonymous figure who tries to give himself an air of masculinity but conceals extremely infantile traits.

He surprises me at the end of our second interview one month later, when we arrange terms between us. After a moment of uncertainty in rising from his chair, his meek manner suddenly disappears, and in an almost arrogant tone he tells me that his wife, quite rightly, accuses him of being shy. Being a much more forthright person, she would have said: "You've made me say who I am, you have put restrictions on me, but you haven't said anything about yourself. Who are you?"

This patient's history was revealed through the analytic material as well as the initial interviews.

He comes from a very affluent middle-class background. His father, a noted surgeon, is the dominant figure; he undertakes all decision-making and educational duties within the family. His mother appears to be a very fragile person, a sort of eternal child, much younger than his father.

The patient was allegedly born through his father's will, because an attempt had to be made to have a male child after two girls had been born. This appears to be the first of the patient's impossible roles: apparently surrounded by so many privileges, with hindsight Mario sees himself as a rather comic and pitiful caricature of the little man who wasn't there. The virile ideal subscribed to by his father means omitting physical displays of affection and communication of difficulties; the boy must be able to look on without so much as a peep as his father administers first aid, and so on. His relationship with his father has always been a source of unease: embarrassment, not knowing what to say, difficulties in tolerating his physical proximity. Left to his own devices, he does not know what to do and where to go; he is incapable of having a communicative relationship. When he is not busy practising some hobby or engaged in manual activities, which he does in an obsessive manner, he goes to sleep: everything weighs on him—work and family life.

He completed his studies without failure and without shining. His wife is his one and only romantic attachment. They work together at the hospital. He does not know what kind of bond he has with her; he has never felt great passion. He now considers her to be the pillar of the family, a very active person whose interests are exclusively practical.

Mario does not feel greatly driven by sexual appetites. He does not want shows of affection, and he generally succeeds in having quick and rather brutal relations (for example, pushing his wife onto the bed and being violent); he has a degree of disgust for the genitals and for physical contact in general. He did not have full sexual relations prior to marriage; as a fiancé, he sometimes felt it was his duty to provide some proof of virility, which did not go beyond clumsy and violent groping and ripped underwear.

He has two daughters, both young. He thinks he loves them, but he is afraid he doesn't know how to deal with them or enjoy their company, because they disturb his desire for almost catatonic peace and quiet. He enjoys their physical contact: he likes taking a bath with them, he likes cuddling them when watching television together, and at such times he feels overcome with tenderness. From certain remarks he has made, it seems that the first-born girl has serious problems, but Mario does not seem to be aware of this.

ROSENFELD: The analyst's thoughts concern the patient's identity problems; he must use any variety of methods to pin back his own insecurity. Patients like this, who constantly depend on the analyst's ideas, are in danger of undergoing a false analysis: the patient asks, "Who are you?", as if he has to fit in with the analyst by trying to control him, while meanwhile the real patient has vanished into thin air. It is as if he is presenting a series of images or sketches of people, making it impossible to understand which one is him.

ANALYST: The start of analysis was put back by two weeks because I had to urgently go into hospital. I could only inform him of this delay a few days beforehand.

In the first session, Mario told me that he reacted to this news with a violent attack of colitis, accompanied by unusual haemorrhagic phenomena.

After this episode, he seemed to fit perfectly into the analytic situation: collaborative, productive, controlled, sufficiently satisfied with the decision made—in brief, practically an ideal patient.

Only as time passed did I begin to form an impression that the patient had very little contact with me; his polite manners were stereotyped (after he once witnessed me saying goodbye to a patient at the door with a handshake, he begins to do this himself, only on the way out, accompanying the gesture with a little smile). His material, and the references and anecdotes that come up as associations, is prepared during his car journey over (preceded by lengthy preparation, including certain eating habits, with the whole family involved), with a long preparatory stop outside my house. He is embarrassed if he bumps into another tenant on his way in: they might mistake him for a patient. He, like me, is a doctor. Certain circumstances, some of which he has only barely hinted at, shore him up in this belief: I was also a doctor; like his, my wife does the same job as I do; like him, I have two daughters (he saw a lot of things while he sat outside in his car).

ROSENFELD: The patient is very much attracted to the analyst, he is almost physically interpenetrated, but he is incapable of thinking on his own. So when the analysis is put off, he has an attack of haemorrhagic colitis. This is a very primitive way of saying: "I missed you", but he cannot express this and he does not know how to think it. As such primitive methods of reacting to the object are very violent, they do not allow the analyst to react in time, and they lead one to believe that the patient is not in touch. In reality, the patient is in touch, but only via these primitive ways of operating. Imitative aspects, such as, for example, offering his hand, don't mean anything; the patient wants the analyst to understand that they do not mean anything; and yet when he has the haemorrhagic colitis, this does mean something—this is not an imitation and it must be interpreted right away.

Establishing such an adhesive transference, enough to feel that he can control the analyst at his stomach or anus (to the extent that his intestine is lacerated when he is not there), the patient expresses a primitive and very violent way of relating. The patient has a physical mode of contact: he loves his little girls very much, but he does not know how to cope with them emotionally; anything that does not fit into one of his patterns is impossible for him to understand. For example, when he sees the other patient shaking the analyst's hand, he thinks: "So that's how it's done!" He knows nothing of the emotional world, he handles this sphere physically.

The patient appears to study closely what the analyst does, to prevent the analyst from understanding: whether the analyst understands or not, it is all such a shock to him that it sets off all his violent mechanisms for controlling and preventing the formation of what might be considered a normal analytic transference.

The patient's fear is that if he is not a colleague of the analyst's, he doesn't know who he is. This is too frightening: it would be like saying, "Who is this guy?" and descending into confusion. When he says: "I am a doctor, I'm a human being!", this reassures him. He could be a shapeless mass, a head with bits attached to it, a rather ambiguous entity.

We commonly say that one must locate adult and infantile aspects in patients; but with this patient the infantile aspects are not infantile, they are primitive: it is as if this patient was a concentration of flesh in his mother's side. Another patient might say, "I feel I am infantile and I am needy," but this patient is incapable even of saying this. All he can say is, "I am scared", and then he adds, "I am a doctor!" as his way of cancelling out the terror.

During the initial period of analysis, he decides to sign up for a specialization in psychiatry. When I considered his condition of total adhesion to myself, it is as if he felt he had been flushed out from a special position, which consisted of feeling himself to be some kind of copy of me, using me as a viewpoint from which he could observe a hypothetical patient and what I was doing with the patient. He continued to maintain attention formally, showing composure and emotional control even as I received signals of progressive hostility and intolerance from him. His interest in psychiatry lasts, he takes exams, and he begins to go to the psychiatric clinic as a visitor.

Then his father dies. He is back one week later.

At this point, he begins to sing his father's praises, to take on, perhaps a little clumsily, the role of the head of the family which his family has thrust upon him. He even starts wearing his father's suits to our sessions. Perhaps because of these aspects, but not just this, I gradually begin to feel the sensation that I am dealing with some kind of cadaver; his ever-weary attitude, the way he speaks in a monotonous and cavernous voice, his enormous inertia and passivity. This is an interminable period of pompous speeches and monologues, bereft of critical evaluation and personal experience. I begin to experience sensations of real physical unease, and during moments of exasperation I experience a strong impetus to break free.

Every now and then something crops up that allows me to undertake some kind of work; but as soon as any vitality creeps in to the analytic relationship, a new condition of asphyxia appears.

Separation and interruptions in the analysis have always been a critical moment (loss of constructive contact, numbing sleeps, awkward mistakes at work, with the risk of repercussions). Generally, we work best during the Tuesday session.

ROSENFELD: Tuesday seems to be the most secure moment, Wednesday is already nearer the end.

It is as if the patient were somehow glued to the object, meaning that there is no real sentiment that the analyst has missed. There may be a haemorrhage or some other physical symptom. It is not possible to draw nearer to his mental state by offering interpretations on infantile aspects—for example, by talking about a child who loses his mother.

The patient would only feel bombarded by this sort of interpretation; perhaps other interpretations focused on physical sensations might be more suitable.

Not long before the last Christmas holidays, Mario suddenly begins to drop hints about ending analysis. We are at the end of the fifth year: he has understood certain things, and he could be happy with that. The idea of continuing is becoming a real burden to him.

Without warning, just three days before doing so, he says he wants to suspend our sessions, to take time out to decide what to do (I believe, whether to stop or continue). During these days, a man arrives who requests going into analysis. Sent by Mario, he is the same age as the patient, a former fellow student at the university who is still studying medicine; the man has a ravaged appearance, a complex history of homosexuality, a recent psychotic crisis, hospitalization, excitement, and pantoclastia.

ROSENFELD: The patient is hoping for his double to undergo the analysis that he won't be doing himself.

After the break everything appears to have returned to normal, and analysis is once more a case of the usual hard slog. We get to February, just before my prearranged winter-break week. Mario tells me that he is very happy with this time off, because he can attend a major conference organized by the psychiatry clinic that he goes to. He daydreams about future work projects, he sings the praises of how things are going so well for him at home, and he says he has recommenced sexual activities with his wife. He can wind up the analysis!

He seems to me to be rather rambling. He talks about a patient taken in at the psychiatry clinic, a paranoid and violent man (domestic violence, public brawling with weapons, etc.): he has realized that this man is normal—it's all down to a lack of affection because in his infancy he was separated from his mother, who was hospitalized for mental illness. All the man was doing was trying to get some attention!

In a subsequent session, he tells me a brief dream: *a young child, the son of acquaintances, is sinking under water in a swimming pool. The patient wants to save him but he cannot decide whether to dive in. In the end, self-conscious about stripping off, he jumps in but thinks it is too late and is very relieved to see that his elder sister, Chiara, has also jumped in and is pulling the boy out.*

Prior to separation, he tells me that a few days earlier, after a session during which he "bunged up" his ears in order not to listen to me, he left and walked straight across a road without looking, forcing a lorry to brake sharply.

ROSENFELD: The dream is very significant. This return to the relationship and his need to stop up his ears has some affinities with the suicide situation sketched out in the truck episode. The patient talks about a relationship with a mother who may be dangerous; he may fall into the mother without knowing if he will live or die; this is the patient's central problem.

Here we have the problem of how to tackle the interpretation: one has the impression that a detailed interpretation of what is happening will not help the patient much, and may well upset him even more. Rather than making precise and detailed interpretations, one should offer an interpretation of feelings, as perhaps something will reach him.

This patient has the idea that if he is to trust the analyst, he must know and understand everything; his condition is always experienced as dangerous. If something is omitted, he falls to pieces.

[*The analyst confirms what Rosenfeld has said. Indeed, he has noticed that the patient becomes alarmed if the interpretation is brief and to the point, and responds with anxious questions; but when one talks to him calmly, it is as if he were much more relaxed about trusting the words.*]

However, this approach gives the patient the sensation that the analyst is thinking for him, and that he does not have to think. For this patient, birth is like a state of shock he cannot tolerate; the intrauterine environment (being inside his mother) is being cultivated by the patient after birth.

The patient is incapable of facing things as they are: it is as if he were pulled back inside his mother. This is the lethal condition he attempts to flee by blocking up his ears, but he is in danger of being run over by the lorry.

QUESTION: *I wonder if Mr Rosenfeld would agree that the primitive and violent part of him is increasingly being brought into analysis, and that after his attempts to stop analysis, his sending a patient-colleague to analysis, a concrete part of himself, his mention of the patient taken into the clinic, and his blocking of the ears—are these not an expression of coming closer to this very primitive part?*

ROSENFELD: The most striking material is the dream with the water, his sister who saves the child, and the material about the psychotic patient with a depressed mother. The patient feels that he has not been so ravaged, but he does mention patients he comes across who in some way may resemble him, as a means of communicating aspects of himself that he is incapable of verbalizing. The difficulty with this analysis is that because he is too scared the patient has put other people between himself and the analyst: he first must know if the analyst understands, and the only way he can do this is by projecting himself onto other people. Only if the analyst understands the situation interposed between them will the patient feel less anxious.

The patient offers a great deal of material, but it must be the analyst who deciphers it and brings it together. His life is in constant danger, but the right interpretations make this clear and bring it to light.

The analyst continues to feel that this patient is very primitive and is always difficult to reach. It is as if for him the birth event was impossible to deal with; it was intolerable and therefore very hard to represent. Such patients offer up this situation immediately, even before analysis begins, as is the case here. Other things in this analysis are less significant, but this primitive contact is very important indeed.

After five years of analysis, through consistency and continuity which have reassured him a little, the patient is attempting to fix this event in his mind, because it makes him more sure that the analyst will not allow him to fall.

[*At this point the analyst says that he feels that the verbal contact between the patient and himself is superficial and false, yet there is something deep and primitive that is hard to subsume under the term "contact".*]

Now I would like to look at the countertransference and how the analyst feels, to examine the almost physical type of connection that is established with the patient. The analyst may feel drowsy: there is a primitive and silent projection from the patient that insinuates itself into the analyst. It is important to be very much in touch with oneself, to feel and perceive inner conditions of unease or well-being. With patients such as this, there may be a sudden feeling of fear, without really knowing why. The impression one obtains is that the patient is in communication with both the analyst's mind and body, like a newborn baby can be with any non-depressed mother. The patient has spoken about a depressed mother through the "twin" sent into analysis. The more the analyst is capable of finding an answer within himself the better. The analyst does not know that much about how the patient functions, but this way of perceiving himself and perceiving the patient does make the patient feel better.

QUESTION: *I wonder whether the patient may be like an unborn twin, aborted by the haemorrhagic colitis.*

ROSENFELD: Something like this does take place, but we do not know whether the patient is identified with his twin and is the same as the twin. My impression is more that in addition to being perceivable as an external person, the patient is inside the analyst.

ANALYST: I would now like to bring up a dream I had about a year earlier, a dream which left me worried. *I was coming out of my house to run some errands when I found the patient standing by my car. Then, as I saw myself driving the car, a flashback took me back to having breakfast at home, with the patient sitting opposite me; I was in the bathroom shaving and the patient was there too. . . .*

ROSENFELD: This is a very realistic, very truthful dream which aids our understanding. Perhaps the analyst woke up very worried because before this dream he had not realized to what extent the patient was inside him. Finding him everywhere, he realized that the patient was inside him, though he had not noticed before: it is like having the patient so far inside that you don't know what to do.

ANALYST: The following sessions are from the week after the holidays.

Monday

[He strides in looking rather purposeful, and immediately starts talking, instead of his usual long introductory silence].

P: "I'm happy to be here again, back in my spot, which now seems familiar and intimate to me. I feel at ease, but that wasn't the way it was before the session . . . yesterday I was thinking how hard it would be to start up again. There were a number of famous psychoanalysts at the Conference *[he names them, showing how familiar he is with these people, leaving me rather surprised].* From the lectern they made important speeches, difficult ones. . . . I hardly understood a thing, except that psychoanalysis, true psychoanalysis, cannot be transferred into institutions, it has to be used in a different way, I don't know . . . here I am back to the psychoanalysis I understand a bit. We were sitting there and listening, a serious look plastered on every face, the look of people who are pretending to take it all in. . . . I was in the crowd, a lot of people there . . . but among us you just heard the same old stock phrases, empty words . . . it was just a bunch of pricks. . . . During the breaks when I went to the bathroom I was thinking that everybody else was going to the toilet . . . in the toilet I was using somebody else had done it, and then another . . . everybody's urine and faeces, all mixed up."

ROSENFELD: Finding it pleasant to be back in analysis, the patient's communication surprises us and allows us to appreciate how clearly this message is formulated compared to his usual highly confused and noisy manner of speech: it is direct speech. When the patient says that it was not like this before the session, he is asserting that he is still afraid of what may happen, but he acknowledges his pleasure at being back in a session.

It is interesting to note how the patient expresses himself: he perceives more detailed interpretations as incomprehensible, without meaning, like shit. Real analysis is also like a noise, it doesn't mean anything. It wouldn't make any difference whether it was conducted in English or in German, it still wouldn't mean a thing.

The patient wishes to communicate that he is afraid of perceiving this type of language, of receiving communication without meaning. In reality he is expressing himself in a highly articulated fashion when he talks about everybody being together, mixed up, at the conference, as if he always knew he was living in this confused and meaningless way; he also perceives that there is another way to live, a far cry from confusion and the throng.

He is happy to be out of this melée.

What is interesting is that in this situation the patient is capable of facing this emptiness, these omnipotent attitudes, and coming out without persecutory anxiety.

P: "In the midst of all those people I felt bewildered, a little dazed, but there was also something pleasant about the anonymity, without needing to think . . . my wife wanted to go out and about a bit, do some shopping; I couldn't tear myself away.

"Yesterday she wanted to leave before the end so we could be home early; I almost got angry . . . I didn't want to leave, I was thinking I had to start here again, all this mental work. . . . Well, I felt good and bad there . . ."

A: "That psychoanalysis was the analysis which, by leaving you, turned its back on you . . . it was as if you had stayed in touch with me, but with a part of me which speaks an incomprehensible and noisy language. You cannot pull yourself away, but you feel dazed, perhaps placed on the same level as my shit."
[*Long silence*]

ROSENFELD: He is putting things together, and the analyst is right to talk to him about incomprehensible and loud language, which alludes to the fear that might catch up with him and by which he may feel bombarded. He is looking for something that is more peaceful and non-violent. The analyst's interpretation about incomprehensible language is capable of reaching the patient. The patient appears to be able to express this without being too frightened.

P: "Well! . . . it has been a pleasure to be back here, but the hard work really has began again . . . [*another long silence, rather charged with tension*]."

A: "Perhaps you feel the need to be helped, supported in a tiresome quest."

[*He nods but remains silent*]

P: "The idea of finishing up the analysis was a bit absurd . . . a meaningless experience, which you jettison as soon as it is over, like military service. . . ."

A: "And you feel thrown away like shit yourself."

ROSENFELD: The analyst is experiencing and understanding the effort that the patient makes in the way he experiences the conflict between feeling good, feeling pleasant, and feeling bad. The patient is not able to do much when these things have to be brought together.

The analyst is very much on the button when he tells the patient that he needs to be helped and supported: the patient's fear is of tiring out the analyst and being discarded like faeces.

The word "support" used by the analyst is very important: given that he is not capable of communicating clearly, this patient does not believe that anybody can support him, or even that anybody is capable of staying with him for a long time and continuing to support him.

This interpretation helps him, and he remains silent as if to gather this up and into himself; then he communicates how stunned he is at the stupidity of wanting to wind up the analysis, how stupid it was to think of this meaningless solution. Before he was saying, "I want to finish the analysis," now he is saying he wants to begin it.

The patient is in touch with this empty thinking, which he associates with the stimulus to empty himself of all this empty faecal thought. The patient handles stimuli very badly, he does not know how to react.

We have all come across analysts who apply their theories, avoid contact with their patients, and talk emptily.

But the patient does not have a demeaning and scornful attitude towards all this. He thinks: this is reality, an opportunity that must be faced in some way. There is a possibility of emptiness, of an inability to get in contact. He must have thought this about his own analyst and feared that he was the only patient the analyst didn't understand, that he was one to be got rid of. At this moment he seems to emerge from this state of fear, and he manages to tell the analyst that this is happening.

Even though the analyst has not offered a detailed interpretation of all this, he has been sufficiently clear in communicating that he, too, may have been aware of the existence of this aspect on his part as well.

[*A participant refers to the type of communication the patient uses, one that takes place through an intermediary—such as when it was the wife who called the analyst to tell him that his father had died—and more direct communication too.*]

There are indeed two different types of communication. There is a way of communicating via the body, physically, not clearly, with which the analyst may feel uncomfortable and unable to find the words to describe what is going on. The patient flows into the analyst, not exactly in the way that Melanie Klein called projective identification; perhaps a more useful analogy would be to think of radio—we don't see the sound waves coming in.

It is very important to supply open answers with this kind of patient. One must not offer overly defined formulations. If you are too clear, the patient's perception and communication are killed off: he reacts negatively to overly explicit formulations.

The analyst's reply to his request for help and support is well formulated.

Tuesday

[*Today once more he starts talking right away, and unusually he does not offer an extensive prelude to the dream*]

P: "There is a dream I would like to talk about. . . . I don't know . . . one part of me would like to mull it over for a while . . . wait a little . . . but I seem to really want to tell you it; *there was a phrase . . . perhaps a concept . . . I don't know how it came out . . . it was: 'upset setting'. I can't even say what it really means . . . perhaps I heard it at the conference or, who knows, I may have read it somewhere. . . . Then I was here, but the dark throw on the couch wasn't there, perhaps you had taken it off, perhaps it was dirty and needed a wash . . . the couch was not here by your side, but in front, and it was not this one but a kind of white armchair. Your wife and an older woman entered, a woman I have seen here and thought might be your mother or mother-in-law. On that chair over there was a colleague of mine, someone about whom I have never talked, who wanted to go into analysis with Dr D [a very well-known analyst], but he didn't encourage her: he told her there was a waiting list. My colleague then went to Rome, to some Jungian analysts, and now all she talks about is psychoanalysis [I am amazed at the patient's ability to make these distinctions]. Your wife and the older woman were talking to you; you indicated to them that I was there too, and that they should include me in the conversation.*"

A: "It seems to me that there are many things you know, as if what is in your mind might be coming to light. . . ."

P: "It seemed to me that this dream did contain some kind of meaning, but I don't know what. What do these women signify

> ... and the other woman back there ... and the different position of things? I don't know if these things have a good or bad meaning."

A: "You want me now to talk to you like these women in the dream; you want me to confirm to you the different position you hold with regard to me, so that I help you to distinguish yourself from the position of your colleague, over there, all of which is in relation to the bad and dirty part of me ... the one you related to during separation."

P: "I was overcome by a kind of confusion, I did not know if this dream signified a rebellion, no longer accepting the couch and analysis, or if it meant the opposite. And then it was as if I was afraid of my head swelling, I thought about analysis and the influence it could have on somebody, and how it may have changed my relationship with work. I had wanted to work in the institution, following up certain interests of mine, and I thought about Dr A and Dr M at the hospital, who look after human resources within the hospital, using their analytic training ... [he is slightly excited].

"Now I feel physically uncomfortable, as if there was some inner tremor, palpitations ... it is a good thing, but it is also unpleasant. It has happened to me before, in the past, in moments of sincerity and contact with my father ... rare moments, moments I wanted to get away from. It is most definitely a sign of life; it's like taking a journey through a hilly landscape rather than a flat one, where everything is the same, everything is safe and makes me drowsy. But it's tough. . . ."

ROSENFELD: This material appears to confirm what was discussed earlier. The patient is seeking something, he is in an attentive state: it seems to him that the dream may mean something, perhaps for the first time, though he does not know what. The patient does not press the analyst and try to understand immediately; he can tolerate not knowing what it means, and he makes his enquiry in a rather calm manner.

The patient is conscious of being full of doubts and contrasting feelings; he is afraid that if something too clear emerges he may be overly influenced by it. He still does not trust becoming too clear, but what we witness is the emergence of a sensation of a little pleasure in becoming alive, of no longer being dead.

This is still an uncertain feeling, almost a dare, a threat to turn back. What is certain is that he is thinking, he is mulling things over, he is no longer urinating and defecating. Or, better still, there is a feeling of hope—the patient seems to want to dare to think.

The patient does not know what "upset setting" means (upset can, of course, be applied to the stomach), but this is something we do know: an upset setting, one which is up in the air, is an "up in the air" relationship with the mother.

When he recounts his dream, the patient remembers that there is a dark covering that needs to be washed, and then he talks about a white armchair. The patient is saying that there is something in the air, perhaps an analytic situation in suspension. The dream features a mother who is not upset by the baby's mess, she gets on with cleaning it up: the analyst is somebody who can differentiate and distinguish.

The white armchair seems to be there for the patient: it is the patient's opportunity to turn into a child who can sit on that chair, on condition that it is different from the confusion and filth on the couch. The analyst may be a highly reassuring figure because he does not suffer fear, he does not pull out his hair, and he is not upset by the filth.

The patient visualizes the analyst's mother inside the analysis-room. The analyst can stand having his mother around; this may mean that unlike the patient, the analyst is somebody who does not have a confused and upset relationship with his mother.

As for the colleague who couldn't wait, it seems that this particular patient wanted analysis and simply didn't care what kind; this she has achieved, and now she is confused. He is happy to feel different and says: "I am not in a state of confusion, I am not as messed up as this colleague. I know I must be patient, that if I move too fast I will get confused." It is as if he were beginning to understand that sometimes it is important to wait for something.

He does not know whether the things he observes are good or bad, but the analyst can assist him in this question as long as he does not pin things down too far; it seems that he wishes to forge more and more clearly ahead on his own.

In a case like this, comprehension may be established between patient and analyst if the analyst restricts himself to cleaning things up, rather than taking on board the patient's conclusions too strictly and then adding his own to arrive at a third viewpoint.

The patient's concerns become more alive. In this dream the patient, who had previously been confused by his aggression, seems to know the difference between faeces and something that is simply dirty, between something that really can damage and something that may simply be cleaned up. A more positive position may also be reached.

In the second part of the dream, what clearly emerges is that it is not impossible to take time as a means of avoiding confusion. Calm is required for him to think, unlike his colleague who, in a state of great upheaval, quickly looks around for an analyst.

Even though the patient is not sure whether this is a good dream or a bad dream, it is something that the patient appears to have cleared up. It appears that in his dream the patient is also conscious of what confusion may be created: not allowing himself time, he immediately becomes anxious. He has reflected on this problem and clearly highlights it in his dream. Helping him see that he has dwelt on this stimulates him to overcome this problem.

Wednesday

[*The patient arrives around five minutes or so late, and begins with a long silence*]

P: "This morning I feel like usual, a sensation of emptiness, not knowing what to say. . . . Vincenzo, the drug addict I told you about, comes to mind . . . he has stopped jacking up and taking other drugs . . . which is perhaps why he has moments of great emptiness. In the outpatients' department he is afraid people will think he's stupid . . . the first few times he came in he had a written list with him, but now he wants to take stimulants so as to have something to say. Often I feel I'm in a similar state. Perhaps I only managed to avoid drugs because of timing, because when I was a young boy they weren't around and I was too busy studying and playing sport, which worked as a drug for me. I was thinking about what we were saying yesterday . . . a sensation of something banal and strained . . . already said . . .

perhaps a sense of non-authenticity. This must be why I have these feelings this morning.

"Last night I went to bed as if I knew it would go like this; I slept badly. I was hoping to have some dreams, but all I remember is one scene: B [*his eldest daughter*] was complaining. But it was true, because I woke up and she was sitting there on the bed, with a cough.

"Usually my wife gets up—she has a special ear for it—while I sleep on. Last night I was the one who put the girls to bed, because my wife said enough was enough, that I shouldn't leave everything to her. I agreed with her.

"Perhaps, though, I did have a dream after all, with a scene that took place in Milan's main square, Piazza del duomo. *Liz Taylor was driving a bulldozer, she drove it right into a hole, got stuck, and then she managed to get it out.*

"I don't like Liz Taylor or characters who are just stuck-up little girls, trite roles [*he starts to tell me about a couple of these films*]. There was a photo of me and the family with grandpa in the garden. I was all decked out, with a grip in my hair, all nicely turned out. My grandfather was a tailor, he used to make us little clothes; he once made me a coat with a fur collar, and he always spruced me up when we went out.

"Last night on television I caught *The Odd Couple* [*he tells me what happens in the movie*]. I enjoyed watching it. In some ways, Jack Lemmon is like me: he's obsessive, attached to his possessions, and that's what makes him strong and successful. Perhaps despite everything I still believe that obsessiveness, tenacity, and persistence will win out in the end. . . ."

[*He suddenly falls silent after this stream of speech*]

A: "We are right at the end of the session, you have filled it all up. Now you can be silent and allow me a little space, because you have had a success. Your anxiety over withdrawal is behind you, you have filled in all the distance between yourself and me."

ROSENFELD: This patient partially analyses his manic attitude when he says that he does not like himself in Liz Taylor's place, like when he is in his nice clothes, all clean and elegant. He claims that he is undertaking this work, analysing himself and the repercussions, but in fact he is taking drugs. There is a danger that the patient does not realize what he is doing to fill the void. In reality, this emptiness should give him an opportunity to think, but he is so afraid of the void that he must immediately fill it up with something. He immediately feels magnificent, but in fact he becomes a drug addict. The most delicate moment for him is when he feels this emptiness. He hurries himself, he is overcome by the anxiety of immediately filling up this moment of emptiness. It would be important for the analyst to help him understand his horror at the sense of emptiness he has to fill up right away.

QUESTION: *Bearing in mind the material from the last session, I wonder whether this may not also be a reaction to the fear of becoming too dependent on the analyst?*

ROSENFELD: In yesterday's session, the patient became overexcited. It seems he tried to get rid of parts of himself and found the void. Instead of using his ability to think, he fills the void; this becomes a form of dependency, a kind of drug addiction. What was good becomes excellent, marvellous, and the relationship with the analyst is idealized.

The patient recognizes that he cannot stand emptiness, and he acknowledges that this is a feature of his personality. He wants to be helped to understand that this is part of him, so that he does not feel despair when it happens to him.

Yet he tends to become manic because he is so very afraid; he rescues himself in a false way and does not allow himself the opportunity to stop and truly move forward. He should be shown this need. When it occurs, the patient becomes excited and manic; something should be said straight away to interrupt the situation he is creating to fill up the void.

I recall a patient of mine—I presented his case at a seminar in Jerusalem—who had similar features. In session, one could tell from his voice that he became inebriated with words, words that seemed to have a meaning but actually prevented him from thinking. The patient believed that in this manner, on his own, he could become wonderful and alive, he could be born; what he did not understand was that in this way he had no relationship whatsoever with the analyst, and was not really going anywhere.

Like the patient discussed here, that patient was trying to give birth to himself, without the analyst's help. This is a kind of manic repair job that swings from emptiness to excitement, and then from excitement to emptiness. It can be very useful to show and describe this process, to communicate to the patient that the analyst can understand him, and that he is therefore not alone—he can fall back on a relationship with the analyst.

It would be important to succeed in making this kind of intervention a little before the session ends, so that the patient has some time to see if he manages to recover and offer another response. In such a case, the analyst must be as active with the patient as was his daughter who woke him up: one must therefore bring the patient to a halt, not put oneself in the position of somebody who is passively listening to the patient as he rambles on and on. . . .

It is important that the analyst does this, for the patient is not conscious of being in this situation. If one of the two is in a position to think, it is the analyst; the analyst alone can re-establish the conditions under which the patient is once more capable of thinking.

Here, too, it is important that the analyst does not launch into a great long speech, or that what happens is that big words line up to do battle against other big words. This intervention should be succinct, so that the patient has sufficient time to come up with a different response. The patient must understand that when this situation happens, it is as if the analyst weren't really there. The dream about the analysis-room, and the Elizabeth Taylor dream, show that he has more faith in the analyst and is happier, but that in this close relationship he can suddenly become highly excitable.

It is important that the analyst shows that this is a real danger, that this is the delicate moment when he may slip.

NINE

Crisis situations

This clinical situation here regards a young man who has his first psychotic breakdown three weeks after beginning analytic work, and who then makes a horrific suicide attempt.

The analytic events covered go up to the sixth year of analysis, including material from two sessions.

These sessions are followed by a dream the analyst had which— we later find out—occurs at the same time as a manic explosion by the patient, who is taken into a psychiatric hospital.

Rosenfeld emphasizes how useful it is for the analyst to build up a preliminary picture in his mind, which can then be modified as analysis proceeds, to serve as a fallback when a hard-to-manage crisis situation occurs.

An example for similar situations may be found in the analysis of this patient, revealing the need to rapidly become aware of the existence of a serious risk of suicide or of a psychotic crisis, fed by omnipotent guilt and identification with a destructive mother.

A great deal of caution must be used in the treatment of manic conditions. If handled precipitately, the patient's depressive state may worsen and push him to suicide.

Further interesting points come up regarding analysis of the various identifications operated by the patient; the need to understand the function of idealization which is typical of manic periods; and the care that the analyst must use in drawing onto himself all those aspects—critical aspects especially—that the patient picks up from him and then shifts onto other people.

Part of the supervision is focused on the effects of the trauma, and the development in traumatized patients of mistrust and suspicion, the fear of being "frozen" or killed.

A countertransference dream that took place during a crisis moment in treatment is also of interest.

ANALYST: When he begins analysis—it is now his seventh year—Giorgio is 33 years old, an engineer by training who works as a teacher at a vocational school. Right from the start, and this remains true today, he stimulates great liking in me, along with spontaneous affection.

What is attractive about him is the simple and casual way he dresses and lives: his hair is a little long, he has a "revolutionary" beard, but above all there is an imaginative lively quality to his speech—something I have often envied him—particularly the way he picks up on the most concrete images of everyday life, and, with a painter's flexibility transposes them to inner experiences. Another attractive feature is that he is a member of painting and theatre experimental research groups (at a later stage he refers to them as "his Myths"), which make up and compensate for the relatively humble nature of his work as a teacher. Another thing that arouses affection is the sad and unfortunate events that have accompanied him through life; this stirs up in me affectionate feelings of protectiveness and support.

His mother is a woman of modest cultural background, a woman whose religiousness is totalitarian, mystical, and sacrificial. She instilled in her child (and later, teenager) moralistic and mystical alliances of sacrificial love for one's neighbour, but she also punished him with terrifying moral reprisals, consisting of scorn for betraying common ideals. One such trigger event was when the child, aged 6, ate a chocolate behind her back. When he was 16 years old, Giorgio felt that the only way he could keep faith in these alliances was by becoming a Priest or Great Doctor, otherwise all he would ever amount to was the Great Betrayer.

He has a sister who is four years older than him, whom he loves dearly and idealizes. For him, she represents Free Intelligence, Culture, and a love of the things of life. With her he has experienced moments of enchantment and mutual understanding: mountain holidays, his first cigarette, his first free friendships outside the family. Then for many years he had to look on, impotent and "cowardly", as she descended and became trapped in a psychotic spiral, which took her to psychiatrists and analysts before she attempted suicide by drowning in the sea, clinging to her own child. She was imprisoned as a result of this. Currently she is suffering from grave consumption. His reaction? He runs away. . . .

His father, who died many years ago, is described as a big, corpulent man, a shopkeeper preoccupied by business and family concerns, perhaps the only one in the family with a sense of the practical, who looked on sullenly and silently from one corner of the table as the family quarrelled over ideas and ideals.

Giorgio attempts to make a break for freedom from this inner and outer setting by enrolling in electronic engineering (the faculty is renowned for what it does). His teenage religious ideals are channelled into the exultant revolutionary ideas of 1968, though even here he feels like "a parasite and a sham" ("What are you doing here with us?" asks one of his far-left comrades, "You're a softie!"). At the age of 22 he moves out of the family home and goes to live with "Eva", a woman twelve years his senior who has a daughter. For the next ten years, he is involved in a stormy relationship with her; this takes place against a background of aggression and adventure, heroism and unconventionality—and she, too, becomes another of his "Myths".

ROSENFELD: Listening to what the analyst has told us, one gets the impression that this patient is particularly adept at weaving an atmosphere around himself, and it is interesting to hear how he began to create this right from the start of treatment. This atmosphere is a guide to us, but we must also be careful: as well as helping us to understand, it may seduce us and distance us from several important aspects that are present here, aspects that the patient wishes to conceal. He is a charming and interesting fellow who gives the impression of being capable of establishing good relations with people he meets; he has the sensation that these people admire him, love him, and feel attracted to him. These same impressions applied to his mother, to whom he was attracted, and who evidently had an ability to charm the child. And yet she could transform from this pleasant situation and suddenly crush him with great destruction.

In other words, the most frightening thing was that his mother could inspire and idealize the child, but she could also crush him for some tiny mistake, until he didn't count for anything any more.

One may imagine that the child was constantly frightened of being cast down from the "heights" where she reigned, to become nothing at all.

In one way or another he felt he was pushed into a condition in which he never knew if there was room for him or not. Either he was a perfect child, or she would bring him crashing down. This is a terribly sadistic attitude; such a situation is impossible for any child, because one cannot live up to these expectations. It must have been the same for his sister, too.

Attributing her diabolic and destructive attitudes to the child, his mother also shows that she set herself up in an ideal role. Her children had no opportunity to fight back because she thought, "I'm going to hide my diabolic attitude" (which every now and then appeared, so overwhelming the children that they were powerless).

What I am suggesting is that it is appropriate to have a preliminary model in mind in order to be able to react and cope with periods of crisis, when one does not have sufficient time to think and the patient presents us with an "impossible" situation, such as a serious suicidal crisis.

On such occasions we must make use of the information we have already acquired. It is hard to think when we become anxious, and it is difficult to guide the patient through the crisis if we do not have sufficient elements from his history to draw upon.

In our first interview, he tells me that he broke things off with his partner a year earlier, and he is living now on his own. It seems that the equilibrium he had established through exciting ascetic, ideological, and political representations is no longer enough for him: he lives a lonely and squalid life; for a while he was drinking heavily. He has been advised to go into analysis (which he would like from a "great luminary"), so he is coming to me, he says, "to be reborn"; he wants to "have a shell", "a place where damage is made productive". We agree to start in September, four hours a week. Many years later, he acknowledges that self-delusion had a part to play in this too: psychoanalysis, the latest and greatest product of Science and Wisdom, seemed to him to be the final Myth he should sign up to, become a disciple of, to be able to tap into the heritage of a great cultural system and a great master.

Our relationship quickly develops traumatic and often upsetting moments. A few days after our agreement, Giorgio calls me up, rambling and confused. He asks to meet me because his sister has just died. The man I see before me is another man, almost a tramp, completely heedless of how he is dressed and of his appearance; his head is lolling on his shoulders, he bangs the table rhythmically, and he scatters tranquillizers pills over the tabletop: "She wanted milk, but with coffee, to distinguish it from her mother's; yesterday she had dinner at a friend's house, she wanted a soft-boiled egg, but it was rock hard; how could anybody give such a thing to eat to such a person?" I realize that he is going through a moment of delirium; he believes that everybody is part of this "cosmic" tragedy. He also manifests great fear that by asking me for this "unscheduled" meeting, he has definitively ruined his chance of starting analysis with me. There is a moment of frank contact between us. I tell him that the reasons, agreement, and potential for analysis have not changed, and he responds: "I'm glad, I was hoping you would say that." During the summer he is taken into psychiatric hospital for three days. I later learn that he has undergone a confused moment of manic and delirious excitement, during which he was convinced that his sister was not dead, and he had tried to persuade the police to exhume her.

Analysis commences in a climate of commitment and collaboration, confirming to me that I had made the right decision. In the first few weeks, I do not understand his complex and verbose reasonings, used to support interchangeable and changing identifications between himself and the characters in his life, who at that time were just names for me, bereft of any functional significance or representative role ("I am Eva . . . I am the mother . . ."). Predominating throughout is the issue of shame, the harm he has done to everybody, the contagion he is spreading; he rejects as "psychoanalytically theoretical" a comment I make about the (analytical) nourishment on offer. On the contrary, he accepts as comforting the representation of analysis as a breast (we both see this as a kind of safe haven, a port) at which he is now welcome.

ROSENFELD: During the psychotic episode associated with the death of his sister which took place between the initial interview and the start of analysis, the patient is overwhelmed by an enormous sense of guilt. He feels guilty for everything, he has infected everybody, he is someone who gave his sister so many horrible things so he is responsible for all this destruction. He contemplates suicide because he has become the mother, he has identified with the mother, in particular with the completely destructive mother.

In reality, it was his mother who spread the contagion in the family, not him.

If the patient is subject to such pressure from guilt, he really is at risk of committing suicide. These are conditions in which suicide can take place. Patients like this should stay in hospital until they are able to understand something—at least, this is what we usually do.

Treating these patients is very difficult. We are forced to assess very carefully when there is a risk of suicide. This risk is present if there is crushing omnipotent guilt; at this particular moment, the patient appears to be identifying with the mother who has destroyed everything. In addition, he has lost the good image of the mother; as a result, he has lost everything that could have provided him with nourishment.

Three weeks after our first interview, Giorgio makes a terrible—and, as far as I was concerned, unexpected—attempt on his own life. For four or five days in a row after work I go to what I refer to in my head as a "session", in a vigil next to this body in a coma, connected to tubes in the intensive care unit. I feel that his place within me has not been destroyed, in the hope (or faith?) that somehow he can sense my presence.

After he recovered from this incident, there is a clear manifestation of what, clinically speaking, we call a bipolar structure, with long periods of depression interspersed with brief periods of excitement or confusion. These latter periods take place particularly during the first two summer breaks: he spends everything he has in his bank account, he buys an unnecessarily large and powerful car, he goes to natural-remedy shops and therapists with whom he constructs a whole cast of characters. I too have my role: I am fantasized as some kind of demigod with a radiant appearance, who follows him from afar. At these moments—for reasons I have never understood—he buys a large number of cigarette lighters; this occurs every time he goes through a period of excitement.

For the first three years of analysis, I live in constant worry. I am concerned by the lengthy impoverishment that follows each period of depression and concerned about the alarming and euphoric solutions that he comes up with, mobilizing his friends, relatives, doctors, and the police.

ROSENFELD: The manic situation is highly interesting for us: although without doubt very serious, it is also highly common and typical.

In this case it is not so much a question of splitting, rather a series of mysterious relationships, a series of identifications—on the patient's part—that have the purpose of escaping the sense of being completely useless, not to mention racked by guilt.

Perhaps the sensation has been "distributed" not just to the analyst but to many other people. This, therefore, is "the mysterious thing"; "you" are the mysterious thing, "he" is the mysterious thing, everybody is a helper who must magically protect him, sort out the things that, deep down, he sees as having no solution. At least this defence, in which everybody is included, offers protection. This situation must not break down until it is sufficiently clear what the depression is—this horrible thing—or else the patient will try to commit suicide again.

At the same time, the patient knows he is dependent, and he says: "I had to depend on this state because it's the only thing that protects me. I have to have all these lighters because I have to be able to light one cigarette after another without a break." If he breaks off his dependency on this mental state, there is a danger that depression will return; therefore, from his point of view, having hundreds of lighters to maintain this dependency is worth while. The patient gives away a hint of this: "You must not interrupt me." The analyst must not tell the patient not to have all those lighters; he must accept that this is a very important need.

We continue meeting on a regular basis. We work with passion on the doors opened up with a total lack of distinction as he is invaded with and by others (these are referred to as "triumphant walks" through him by his mother and his partner); we work on these cultural "Myths" which deteriorate into megalomaniac delirium; we work on the small and inconstant self that is forced to cover itself up (this becomes the theme of his "Imitations"); we work on the slow intuition of being capable of bringing up this small-child self, maintaining a distance/distinction from others, surviving without these glittering garments. Giorgio seems to have readily nourished himself through this progressive orientation on the self, which he describes as a "small embryonic kernel" that has been found, even though it doesn't yet have "little arms" to use and to touch things with.

Another serious crisis and forced hospitalization follows at the beginning of the third year of analysis. What can I say about our reciprocal emotional relations? There is one very strange thing in particular that for a long-time has not ceased to amaze me. This is the patient under analysis with whom I thought I was undertaking important work, with great commitment and participation; I was certain that this was reaching him, and that the affection I showed was reciprocated by him. And yet—let me say that each time this amazed and hurt me—and yet it was he who, more than any other patient, accused me of scientific coldness, of theorization shorn of affection. He said that he did not understand or esteem my analytic methods (continuing to make comparisons with his Roman T-shirt-wearing psychiatrist), to the point that he located, attacked, and "damaged"—as Meltzer would have it—the things in my studio that were most dear to me (my doctor grandfather's old bookcase, a lamp that was full of memories for me, etc.), or what I wore, and how I acted: all of this was without any apparent wickedness; rather, with a painful, humble, almost affectionate and needful sincerity.

Meanwhile, holiday periods became more tranquil, and there are progressive attempts at realistic activities; his aesthetic culture and artistic production are channelled into applications that, though still conducted with *brio*, are more closely linked to his field of teaching. Sexual interest, something that had more less been wiped out, makes a timid reappearance (we are in the fifth year of analysis) when he is attracted to and starts going out with a pleasant girl. Three years have now elapsed since his moments of delirium; Giorgio refers to them as "a wrong turn", an illusion that, he thinks, will no longer deceive him.

At the end of his fifth year, after the summer there comes a point when we start broaching the issue of finishing analysis. This sets off a chord in both of us, a mixture of anxiety, and an underlying sense of satisfaction at how far we have come.

ROSENFELD: I find this commentary highly interesting. Of course it is important for the analyst to have a positive countertransference with this patient, because patients of this kind generate a great deal of worry. The patient must feel that there is something coming from the analyst, something that he can grab onto despite his "ups and downs". A number of elements worry the analyst: his work (as an analyst) has been slighted, belittled, and criticized, while the object running freely around is wonderful. This is typical of patients like this. Giorgio idealizes an "aleatory" object in which he sees something false; he idealizes people who do not have time to think (the analyst notes the patient's admiration for the psychiatrist who does not have any time).

It is vital to understand the meaning of this idealization of people who have no time to think. I am always interested in talking with colleagues who agree to take on difficult cases. Prior experience would have been very important for the analyst, because there are so many things about this patient that need to be understood, that can perhaps only be understood through experience acquired with other patients—otherwise, there is a danger of feeling lost.

It is very important to slowly acquire comprehension of the suicidal situation, as it lives on in a corner of the patient's mind. The patient is afraid that his manic nature will fracture if he doesn't have all those lighters to keep his cigarettes alight, and that the lure of suicide will return.

It is up to us to know this and to understand what the worst may be. You cannot wait for it to happen, you have to know beforehand in order to be able to keep him under control. If not, when it happens one is bewildered, as was the case with the analyst here.

If the analyst attempts to understand the patient's manic period, his mystical period, and his idealization of the psychiatrist—such an aleatory person—he runs the risk of thinking that it all hinges on the fact that he is attentive but the psychiatrist is not; and yet one must also consider the aspects that have been transferred by the analyst onto the other person (the psychiatrist), who seems to be superficial.

This is underscored by an accusation from the patient, who attempts to say to the analyst: "You don't want to understand what the problem is" (the depths of depression).

The analyst must focus on infantile transference, something that emerged forcefully in those initial meetings when the patient recalled that he is given solid food, that "Nobody understands I am such a little baby that I need liquid food."

We must bear in mind the time to which the patient regresses, as well as his consciousness of the mother's destructiveness, and the degree of damage she has caused to him and his sister.

To begin with, the patient is very much disappointed because he thought his mother was a queen; then he identifies with the destructive mother. This is in the transference.

One of the ways he can escape is through mania; the other is to try to return to his relationship with the nourishing mother. He is attempting to find his mother as she was when she looked after him and nourished him; he makes the analyst do the same thing, he places him in the position of the nourishing mother. This was a time when the persecutory sentiments were not as strong. Perhaps his mother's ferocious attitude appeared later on.

One may wonder how this baby was treated, if he was given to somebody else to be fed, if there was any anxiety, and so on.

What one may do in some cases is to talk to the mother and find out if there were prolonged problematic periods during early childhood. Sometimes one picks up information here; when you interpret, you need to know something about the period you are interpreting.

At the start of the sixth year of analysis—the first week after the summer holidays—Giorgio says in the first two sessions that he feels happy with how we have started up again: he feels he has brought me inside. These holidays were at last arranged around something interesting but not excessive: he travelled abroad, to W___, where he signed up on a course to learn German as a foreign language. He gives me a wide-ranging account of who he met, his friendships and their limitations, his satisfaction at doing well on the course, and also the moments of loneliness he suffered.

P: "Of course, analysis still is a strange thing . . . who can say if you'll ever really understand me. The French poet Antonin Artaud once said, "Not even a scholar, with the tyrannical exactitude of his theories, will ever be able to understand the prawn-pink feather Van Gogh draws, or that Van Gogh killed himself because evil people and society took incomprehensible infinity."

ROSENFELD: The patient senses that the temptation to commit suicide is still a strange thing, an unknown—this is something he communicates directly. The analyst is not oriented in this direction, he is happy and does not realize that the patient is saying to him: "Isn't it strange that you never analyse my attempts to commit suicide? Isn't it strange that you never come back to this event, that you are happy as things are? I think we should do this, otherwise I will kill myself, like Van Gogh did". Here we have what we were talking about at the beginning: the patient creates an extremely cordial atmosphere. Only if one listens more carefully can one hear that something isn't right. When he says that there are situations that cannot be completely understood, this may be a fact of life; but when the patient talks about Van Gogh, the act of understanding or not understanding becomes a question of life and death.

The patient is very acute, he explains this precisely; this is the explanation that must breach the analyst's optimistic mood.

The patient feels that nobody acknowledges that he may kill himself. He feels guilty about some important elements that have infected him. This is precisely why one must recognize and understand. When it comes to manic-depressive patients, one must be precise—not critical, but precise.

What is incomprehensible is not infinity, but the fact that Van Gogh committed suicide. This seems to be a very singular comment, but if we concentrate a little it becomes less strange, for it seems that something incomprehensible—containing important elements—has been taken away by a person of evil intent, or by the analyst who does not understand. In other words, these incomprehensible elements or factors must be viewed as comprehensible.

Often, an indication of what is killing the patient lies within these incomprehensible elements. This is the risk of suicide.

The maternal element reappears. The child was asking, "What is it?", and his mother replies: "Nothing". When somebody fails to understand something, the other person is transformed into nothing, he really is destroyed. The fear is that this nice and important thing is taken away tyrannically and sadistically. The patient is afraid that if his mother doesn't understand, she destroys his sense of being alive. The idea this patient has is that behind the person who helps him (the analyst) there is somebody who "freezes" with his scientific precision ("Yes, it is likely that you are somebody who helps me, you present yourself as an analyst, but I am afraid that with its scientific precision, analysis freezes something of enormous valuable").

It is important to bear in mind that for patients like this, who have lived through traumatic situations, the mother may have a lovely face but she also has a tyrannical attitude, and in a single moment she manages to completely annihilate the child by saying, "You are nothing," simply because he didn't do something the exact way she wanted.

The patient has said this explicitly. The analyst must analyse by looking at the question in transference, because the precise nature of tyrannical theory (the patient's theory) is connected with the fear of the tyrannical analyst.

The patient has worked on the basis of a positive transference of a mystical kind, distributed over a number of people, as we saw with the material concerning the lighters, which he uses as a kind of addiction-like shell for the underlying depression.

The problem is that beneath this manic covering the patient conceals not just the bad parts, but the good parts of himself too.

It is as if he were saying: "You have to concede me dependency on this good and 'vague' thing." Immediately afterwards, the patient presses further and says that good things are mixed up with "vagueness". He has hidden the good things because he is afraid that somebody will snatch them away from him; he must keep them in vagueness so that nobody can find out where they are, nobody can touch them.

There is a risk that if the analyst—as the source of scientific or theoretical precision—attempts to break through this manic carapace, he will kill (freeze) the good parts and leave only the suicidal depression.

The patient says that he has a fear: he is afraid that there are bad people who have a "precise" theory. We must take into account that these are psychoanalytic theories whereby manicality is considered to be a bad thing. In other words, I think that the manicality must be maintained for a certain time in order to understand what lies beneath it, which may be something either good or bad.

ANALYst: The material I am about to present covers two "optimistic" sessions—a catastrophic countertransference dream and a manic crisis immediately afterwards.

Thursday: third session of the week

P: "I have been thinking a lot about the nice evening I spent with K. I know she lives with her friend in the suburbs, but now she is in town alone, staying with an old couple [maybe Jewish architects? It's a den of a house, packed with antique objects, like a second-hand shop...]. For the first time, we said a bit about who we are; we didn't know much about one another.

"She tells me about her family; she has a special way of telling this, pulling faces, smiling at herself, attractive things, a little ambiguous. I tell her about myself that 'I am in analysis', though I don't know why I tell her—to show off? I also told somebody at W____, an Italian teacher, . . . he was talking about 'thinking all sorts of thoughts', while I [a reflection of analysis?] feel the need for 'a personal foundation to be laid down in order to do this'. Sometimes people react by saying that analysis is pointless. We talked a lot over dinner, we missed the movie; she wanted to buy me an ice cream. Fortunately there were no special sexual signals. . . . I would have happily slept with her, but there was an air of tenderness, because of the delicacy of the object [she is thin, svelte, . . .]. This is a first recognition of a different object, a subtle tenderness that makes me feel kind, well-mannered [and not just for seduction purposes!].

"But . . . perhaps it's best that I stay on my own. I don't want to be with somebody else: I only feel safe if there are differences. In W____, I met a couple from Venice [Greens] who asked me to go out with them. He was wearing dungarees, but I went along in a jacket, and I felt good about it because I retained my way of being, I was protected, I was myself with my differences; but with K I was a little less protected. For example, I was able to say no, with satisfaction, to a proposition to make love in a threesome; this straightened things out, and then we became good friends.

"What this really means is that people can 'be themselves' and feel perfectly ok about it! I feel like somebody who has handed over his ID to a policeman, feeling perfectly calm because he knows he has nothing to hide."

A: [*I feel a sensation of calm and of progress. I feel driven to evaluate his ability not to mix himself with others, indeed, his ability to say and take no*]. "I am happy to hear you saying this . . . the last few days we were talking about my distance, a not being there [in the summer, or after analysis]; at other times it is being different from you [because of my tastes], and sometimes it is even not being able to understand you [for example, the van

Gogh reference]. With this difference/distance accepted—by me and by the Venetian couple—you felt that your 'ID' is now clearer. . . . In the same way, I feel inclined to assess your meeting with K in a positive light; I was touched by the delicacy of your description; but in so doing I failed to take into account the fact that you have not been with a woman for a long time, your withdrawal into being alone. But I prefer to highlight that you were capable of coping with the disappointment of 'not sleeping together'."

P: [*Impetuously*] . . . "I was meaning to ask, how did your holidays go? I'm always talking about what I get up to! Yes, there is something wrong with analysis. The Venetian and his wife were saying: 'In a couple, one forestalls mutual suffering [too much!].' As for us . . . a one-way relationship, in my direction. But on a more human level, I do also care about your holidays, what's going on in your life; how did it go?"

Here I know I most certainly did not pick up on or interpret his aggressive response to my attitude, which he perhaps perceived as too conciliatory, which possibly fitted in with the "overly forestalling/concealing the couple's sufferings". What I feel most strongly is a sensation of pleasure at his interest in me, gratitude that he cares about what's happening in my life. I therefore reply with a few benign words, it was a good holiday, relaxing, and so on. I had a chance to enjoy nature, peace, and quiet.

P: "I didn't cut my hair this time: aggressively and vindictively just for my colleagues! I had my hair cut last time, when I was in a bad state, but now I want them at school to be able to say 'he's fine', that I am happy to go there, and that the analysis is going well. I intend to turn up in a fresh suit, looking much better, like a well-dressed Cinderella. So that they acknowledge that I am not well only when I am electrified, thin, jumpy, my eyes flashing (How weird! Yet they got on well with me even then, as if I was a welcome person!); I even managed to play a grown-up role, as analyst-daddy to the Venetians, who are certainly grown-up in age terms . . . I am amazed by this role, it is such a far cry from my fundamental lack of self-esteem!"

A: "It seems to me that this time you managed to cope with distances and differences, without turning them to a destructive use; you felt able to use this as a foundation on which to build your own sexual identity [with K], and a role as a father to yourself." [*Is there a fear of going too far?*]

ROSENFELD: I think that the issue regarding the ability to differentiate oneself and avoid fusion is handled well here. I agree with these aspects. The patient begins to realize that he does have friendly relationships; for example, he has a friendly relationship and feelings of tenderness for K. He felt sexually frustrated, but he is happy to have managed to control himself with her, as if he thought that sexual relations would have ruined the relationship of tenderness and friendship.

It seems he understands that friendly relations are not as frightening as he once thought; in similar situations in the past, he tended to lose his own identity and confuse himself with people. This is how he chose people: they had to be very different from him—in the way they dress, for example—so he could be sure that he would not fuse with them.

In describing the atmosphere of tenderness, he also says that he is better off alone, because being with others offers him nothing. A dangerous aspect evidently still exists, as he cannot see how he could maintain his own identity. He is afraid of becoming empty, vacuous; vacuousness is one way that he can protect himself from the fear of fusing into someone else.

He boasts of making progress, but he is still very much afraid. When he meets people for the first time, he is extremely circumspect, he treads softly because everything could be ruined and he might not enjoy the situation because of his hunger. It may be that he is hungry (he is frightened of swallowing others up), or that he attempts to fuse into others for other reasons, but there is no doubt that the patient is extremely anxious about this. He is happy he has made progress, but he felt very attracted by that girl; this implies not just fusing with destructive objects, such as his mother, but also with good objects. He is very clearly explaining that this fusion—this form of swallowing up—seems to be an extremely important feeling for him. He shows us that some progress has been made in analysis. Giorgio feels a manic element returning which

could ruin everything. The fact that he is anxious about the possibility of managing to keep himself in check may offer him help
in building relations with good objects.

At a certain point, the patient implements a form of collusion:
something he wants to be or aims to be is projected onto the analyst, who must therefore concur with him. All of a sudden, a kind
of fusion takes place.

This rather subtle distinction—between genuine identification
and projective identification—can only be sensed by following
shifts in transference.

It is interesting to hear what the analyst has to say: "I feel
drawn towards offering a positive assessment of the relationship
with K", as if he had really been in doubt, but then decided to
ascribe a positive value to it.

In other words, when one has a sensation, one must be aware of
not being sure, and therefore the interpretation must include the
fact that steps have been made, but that there is also a peculiar
atmosphere into which the patient is trying to draw the analyst; he
is trying to shift him from a position in which he thinks: "There's
something not right here" to one in which he says: "No, everything's fine, we're moving in the same direction."

It is a highly interesting fact that the analyst noted this, told us,
it but did not use it in the analysis or assess it from a countertransference point of view.

I would like to point out that it is only after the analyst acknowledges that there has been progress that the patient says: "By
the way, how was your holiday? I'm always talking about myself.
There must be something wrong with analysis, I am a human
being as well, I'm interested in your holidays, whether you had a
good time or not." This is one way of saying to the analyst: "How
nice of you to come towards me and agree with me that I'm so
much better! Why do you always have to be so analytical, always
look on from the sidelines at everything that's going on? Why
don't you relax a little and, like me, think that things are going
well? All I did was ask how your holidays went! That's all!" This
is the seductive aspect: the tone, how he presents the issue. He is
charming and seductive in order to bring the analyst closer to his
own way of thinking. It is not easy to find the right way to tackle
this point analytically. The analyst feels that it would be a mistake

to turn him down with a flat "No" because it would offend the patient. He thinks, "Why should I ruin his progress with my analytical stance? He would feel rejected. . . ."

This thought issues from the sensation that the patient is highly critical towards the analytic approach, and that it would be very difficult to find a different approach.

Another way he could have expressed himself would, for instance, have been: "I wonder how your holidays went; I realize I spend a lot of time thinking about myself, but I just thought I might ask you about your holidays." In so doing, the patient would have allowed the analyst the freedom to reply or not, and yet still have expressed his interest.

The main point about this form of patient communication is that it places the analyst in difficulty. The analyst does not want to answer aggressively, making explicit the fact that he is different from the patient: "I'm not manic like you, I had a restful holiday." The fact that he answered with a suggestive type of intervention, rather than an interpretative one, shows us that the analyst has been lured by the patient's powerful suggestion.

If we look back at how Giorgio's mother was, her ability to charm the child and to lure him into an atmosphere—making him lose his balance, making him feel that she knew the answers to everything, "dragging him back" so that she could reach him and make him lose his own identity—we can understand how, in winning his own separateness, Giorgio is trying to take it away from others. Right now he is doing precisely that with the analyst: the analyst seems to feel robbed of his consciousness as the patient attempts to reach him—and this occurs even though the analyst does not want it to.

If this diagnosis is correct, then later on in this session or soon afterwards there should be proof or evidence of the projection of an image in order to change the point of view: "You think I am like this; so I project this image and you have to look at me differently."

This is a means of communication whose profound meaning must be examined.

Immediately afterwards, the following communication arrives: "I didn't cut my hair this time, etc. . . . ." He says that despite being popular with his colleagues, he still feels the need to project this particular image that they must have had of him. Giorgio has also said, "I played the role of an adult, a father analyst, because the two Venetians are only adult in age terms."

This point in particular allows us to see what is happening: Giorgio is stealing the role of the analyst-father. It's not that he has grown: he doesn't grow in a natural way, he steals. The patient himself says as much.

Given that, stealing the father's role, he cannot become his own father, this is a narcissistic identification. In fact, Giorgio would feel stronger if he believed that the analyst is analyst-father to him. By stealing, in a narcissistic way he denies the existence of the father.

Let us now have a look to see if there is some allusion in the Friday session to the fact that things have not gone as well as the analyst thought.

This is a very subtle and difficult undertaking, but it is important because only through subtle in-session allusions can we distinguish the sensations that are felt; otherwise one risks merely feeling that one is rather content, as opposed to comprehending the full complexity of all these sensations.

If one follows this approach, there is less risk of making mistakes and interpreting destructively. It is a matter of interpreting the way he functions, what he does, and how he builds relationships.

One does not say to him: "Underneath it all I think you are very aggressive." This is not the issue. The seductive weaving of collusion with the analyst makes it very difficult to say "No", and it would be wrong for the analyst to say this.

When one interprets this, one way or another, it will be "a little" rather than "too much" rejection.

Friday: fourth session of the week.

P: "I'm a little disappointed with K: I was expecting to spend a few days together, at the Unità Festival, but now she says she's busy, she's heading back home. Am I falling into a stupid and boyish kind of dependency? I'm expected to ask, and I hope the answer is yes, perhaps just because I'm boring! In yesterday's session when you were talking about the identities and roles I take on, I thought about my 'analytical copying': I have always been a great verbal defender of my 'important relations'. I used to

defend the Theatre Group, the Left in 1968, the couple I was in
with Eva; years ago, I even stood up for analysis . . . but it was
rather artificial, protective, because I had an image of psychoanalysis as 'one of the sciences'; there was something unhealthy
about this defending, it was a little like taking sides. . . .

"In truth, even now I don't know you personally very well: I
know that the analyst is 'a scientist'. But now I have had real
experience with you: some things I have not 'taken from you
who knew them'; certain experiences, distances, organic
thoughts, certain flashes, are 'of good quality', thoughts that are
not just yours or mine but produced in common. This is different
from a persecutory science that always knows everything in
advance and therefore reduces values. . . .

"We have often dwelt on my mother, because her persecutory nature is evident. Less on my father, who may have had
his faults but who also had his own brand of humanity; he was
also a father who 'threatened to whip me hard', he was jealous
of the space we children took from mamma. Is there a phantasy,
envy, jealousy, being in competition . . . with mortal intentions
against the other, concerning my father?

"And why am I thinking about Eva right now? My certainty,
that people will like me with long hair. I feel uncomfortable
saying this to you here and now: you might make a hostile
judgement or ridicule me! Like looking one another in the eye,
a moment of embarrassment . . . like the first time alone with a
woman. . . ."

I point out that he has talked of "good-quality" thought conceived in
analysis. Basing himself on this, he has been able to improve, and
even to talk here about his feeling of aversion, his struggle against
this powerful father, perhaps even hatred towards him.

The patient responds by recalling a violent episode that he had
never brought up before. One day, his father asked his partner Eva
to go for a drink with him: as a daughter, or as a woman? Giorgio
himself behaved "like a hooligan", provocatively goading his partner to accept the invitation as a challenge. It appears that his father
tried to kiss her, but she pushed him away. All of this is experienced
as part of a tragic phantasy: a month after this episode, his increasingly depressed father became ill and died of pneumonia; the very

next day, Giorgio was awarded his degree with honours, "in front of prestigious architects".

Only a long time afterwards, when I looked back on these notes, did I realize the possible transference violence contained within these words, that this father "with the whip of power", who issues judgement of "ridicule" on his approaches with K might actually be me; that I could remove from him the relationship with his partner-analysis, and that all this might indicate a debate between us that was still so open and painful that it could be dangerously fatal, as it had been between himself and his father. At the time, however, I was seized by a sense of our common strength, and I told him that today he had been able to feel an important restoration of emotions—hatred for his father, destructive provocation, a guilty phantasy of having provoked his end—and that he had succeeded in facing the thought of ending analysis (graduating), and the associated phantasy that I, as father, could be made to violently disappear.

I believe that from this account of the first week in September, one can realize how calm we both felt about the progress he was making; we were serene about the possibility of facing the pain of separation, to the degree that the end of analysis was something we spoke about as a possibility. Indeed, this did not appear to provoke suffering, and I am certain that both of us emerged from the session feeling optimistic strength. I noted a mild bewilderment in myself regarding how the patient could contain fantasies so fraught with anxieties.

ROSENFELD: The patient realizes that he has felt a little like a teen-ager who was pretending to be older than he really is.

Giorgio felt inferior and uninteresting. Creation of an atmosphere of this kind, something at which he is so good, was an attempt to create yet another image of self, in such a way as to prevent you from seeing him as small and uninteresting. Indeed, if you addressed him in a more favourable way, he felt more grown-up than he really is.

Giorgio subsequently discusses his analytical understanding, demonstrating great consciousness of what he is doing: the fact that he imitates the analyst or another person is a matter of copying, it is not a good foundation, it is not constructive. The patient is drawing attention to this fact, and, very craftily, he does not attack the analyst. He simply indicates that he has noticed this mechanism, he believes it to be a defence of his, though it has never been very solid. Giorgio offers his version to the analyst, criticizing him, but also criticizing his own behaviour. In this way, he is acquiring even more control.

At the same time, he is aware of having had a realistic experience with the analyst. This much is true. He also says: "You haven't told me anything new; there were things that you knew and I didn't."

My interpretation is that the analyst felt the risk of being drawn towards a paternalistic position; the patient's fear is that the analyst, if he is in the paternal position, will attack him and hold him down.

Interpreting non-analytically, the patient's paternalism problem has been avoided, not treated.

Giorgio has always seen his father as the person who punished him with a whip, a father who was very jealous of the space the child had. Thus Giorgio is afraid of dealing with the analyst in the paternal role, afraid of accusing him of being the aggressive father. This problem has been buried "deep down", but perhaps one must add something else as well: his feelings of envy and jealousy towards others. Then Giorgio talks about his father's death and about how guilty he felt.

In this moment, however, what emerges is not so much guilt towards his father but fear: Giorgio's fear of looking down on his father, of feeling a sensation of superiority, of triumphing over him, killing him.

Even if Giorgio does not refer to his sense of guilt, we must realize that an issue of this nature engenders enormous feelings of guilt: there is a terrifying fear that everything will be taken away from him.

Giorgio is frightened of being left without space: he remembers that his father was jealous of his space; now, triumphing over his father, he feels he has taken space away from him, taken life away from him, and therefore feels that he does not have the right to live. This is without doubt the principal symptom of his depression—a feeling of not having the right to live—and therefore we must consider this revelation as of the utmost significance. His problem is connected to his relationship with his father, not his mother.

Earlier we were looking at his relationship with his mother. Then Giorgio presents the incident involving his father as something that created an enormous sense of guilt inside him.

The patient is afraid of analysing something that may actually have happened. His tactic is to try to "change" the analyst, persuade him to do something else.

In fact, what happens is that the analyst is afraid of ruining the good atmosphere between them by taking on the role of the father.

ANALYST: On Monday, three days later, I have a dream:

It is 1969, I have to leave Milan and move to Rome, where I am about to begin my analytic training. With sadness, I go to say goodbye to the head consultant and my colleagues, in the classroom where we have discussed so many cases together.

We are sitting around the usual table, only I am having an ECG. I manage to peek at the line coming out on the right of the machine, and I deliberately alter the occipital alpha waves; the technician, confused at first, draws a cerebral map and then points at a hyperfunctioning area. The diagnosis is an invasive formation (meningioma?) of the rear posterior cranial fossa.

We talk over this case, no longer me, but now Gassman. The consultant says: "This man who is condemned to death will now be around here without knowing. Only a clinician would be able to spot it: thinning hair and traces of tracheitis with catarrh (referring to a rare systemic syndrome which manifests itself in various organs, apparently without any connection).

A nurse brings in the medical report in a sealed envelope. A young man in a white coat reads the name on the envelope and then leaps to his feet, exclaiming: "But this is my ECG!" It seems that there was a mistake in writing down the name, and the ECG really is his, so we have been discussing terminal cancer in front of him! He has heard every single word—it's too late to do anything now.

In the morning, my dream is interrupted by a telephone ringing: it is Giorgio's mother. She says she is terrified by the explosion of hatred she reads in her son's eyes; he is sick, a poor wretch, it's all happening again, he could be up to anything; she begs me to do something, advise him to take medication, anything. I answer her with amazement, angry that she has called him a poor wretch and sick: this does not correspond to her son—he has been working so hard on himself! She answers in a wavering voice, but I can hear the stubbornness there too: "Ah . . . you cannot understand what I can see, you aren't a mother. . . ."

My irritation evaporates very quickly, to be gradually replaced by anxiety; without a shadow of a doubt I associate the dream and the phone call. I recall a "yellow Plasticine" dream I had had when Giorgio suffered his confusional crisis: is something like this happening now? I nervously await the afternoon session.

Indeed, Giorgio arrives seething with rage and resentment. Over the next few days this solidifies against "the holders of power, science and timekeepers; analysts with their little clocks". He soon starts to suffer from insomnia, and he protests in an increasingly agitated manner, until in session (the session with a pistol!) and later at school his behaviour becomes so apparently aggressive that everyone is frightened. In the end the police pick him up from school and he is put into a psychiatric ward, where he stays for a few days. Unlike on other occasions, he calls me at our session times to let me know that he is not yet able to come. I feel that everything that has happened is connected with something to do with our analytic relationship, and that for this reason it is something we could have worked on.

ROSENFELD: There is good reason to believe that these psychotic explosions are linked to an error by the analyst, to a countertransference problem.

The patient talks about something that he must deny right away in order to avoid a terrible situation, about which he speaks later on.

Giorgio mentions the business regarding his father, but this does not mean that he is really disclosing or analysing anything. This is a triumph over the analyst, who is reduced to an idiot because he has not picked up on the most important thing; Giorgio therefore kills the analyst, he destroys him. The resulting anxiety is intolerable to him, and so he slips into this psychotic episode.

When a patient feels like this, enormous anxiety and crushing guilty feelings are aroused by omnipotence.

We have been helped a great deal by the analyst who has brought us his dream. The dream shows the mechanisms that the patient mobilizes to convey that he has a very serious problem and that he knows it; this is precisely what has contributed to the formulation of a mistaken diagnosis.

The analyst has in fact altered his brain-waves because of what the patient has done to induce him to think he is getting better.

This ECG makes him believe that the patient is cured, which is not true: a serious manic problem remains.

The impetus to change the atmosphere derives from a manic attitude liable to influence the analyst's brain, to stop the analyst from functioning properly. The analyst is defeated when it comes to his ability to make diagnoses. Instead of saying, "Ah, there's something wrong here," he says, "Oh, everything's all right, things are going rather well!", mirroring the patient's line.

The patient's manipulation is not very clear, but it does allow one to intuit that something worrying is occurring.

Underlying the patient's manipulation is a fear of bringing the paternal transference into analysis. This would be dangerous to him: the analyst might say something to "knock down" the patient; or the patient might make the analyst feel that he is wrong, he has disappointed him, because he has caused the death of analysis; the analyst might feel so depressed he would not want to go on.

All this is present in the material concerning the patient's triumph over the father: this is not a fantasized death, it is a real death!

The patient remains with a huge sense of guilt and feeling of responsibility for his own father, but the analyst who fails to see this situation in some way destroys the sensation that they have both achieved something together.

The patient, however, is moving in the direction of a triumph over the analyst. He manages to take him for a ride by making him believe he has got better—through this "falsehood", both of them pave the way for the psychotic episode.

REFERENCES

Bion, W. R. (1954). Notes on the theory of schizophrenia. *International Journal of Psycho-Analysis, 35*: 113–118.

Bion, W. R. (1956). Development of schizophrenic thought. *International Journal of Psycho-Analysis, 37*: 344–346.

Bion, W. R. (1957). Attacks on linking. *International Journal of Psycho-Analysis, 40*: 306–315.

Clark, L. P. (1933). Treatment of narcissistic neurosis and psychosis. *Psychoanalytical Review, 4*.

Freud, S. (1937c). Analysis terminable and interminable. *S.E., 23*.

Klein, M. (1946). Notes on some schizoid mechanisms. In: *The Writings of Melanie Klein, Vol. 3: Envy, Gratitude and Other Works, 1946–1963.* London: Hogarth Press, 1975 [reprinted London: Karnac, 1992].

Meltzer, D. (1983). *Dream Life: A Re-examination of the Psychoanalytical Theory and Technique.* Perthshire: Clunie Press.

Pirandello, L. (1922). *Henry IV.* New York: Dutton.

Rosenfeld, H. (1965). *Psychotic States.* London: Hogarth Press [reprinted London: Karnac, 1985].

Rosenfeld, H. (1971). A clinical approach to the psychoanalytic theory of the life and death instincts: an investigation into the aggressive aspects of narcissism. *International Journal of Psycho-Analysis, 52*: 169–178.

Rosenfeld, H. (1978). Notes on the psychopathology and psychoanalytic treatment of some borderline patients. *International Journal of Psycho-Analysis, 59*: 215–221.

Rosenfeld, H. (1987). *Impasse and Interpretation: Therapeutic and Anti-Therapeutic Factors in the Psychoanalytic Treatment of Psychotic, Borderline and Neurotic Patients*. London: Tavistock.

Segal, H. (1956). Depression in the schizophrenic. *International Journal of Psycho-Analysis, 37*: 339–345.

Segal, H. (1983). Some clinical implications of Melanie Klein's work: emergence from narcissism. *International Journal of Psycho-Analysis, 64*: 269–276.

INDEX

abandonment, feeling of, 109, 162
abuse, childhood, 80, 83
acceptance, desire for from parents, 147
adhesion, to analyst, 186
Alexander, F., 24
analysis:
  allowing time in, to avoid confusion, 198
  as art, xiv
  as breast, 207
  control of by patient, xvi, 169
  desire to terminate, 16
  difficulties inherent in, xiii
  errors in, need to acknowledge, 155
  false, 184
  frequency of, 85
  by patient, 199–200, 223
  payment for, 58, 179–180
  by proxy, 187, 189, 190–191
  reciprocal emotional relations in, 209–210
  responsibility of analyst in, 134
  seduction in, 205, 218
  separations and interruptions in, 187
  sleeping during, 168
    see also drowsiness
  termination of, 187–188, 194
analyst:
  assessment of, by patient, 11
  choice of, 88
  confidence in, 190
  control of by patient, 184, 185–186, 223
  danger of idealizing patient, 41–42
  defeat of, 226
  desire of patient to impress, 14
  effect of absence of, 164
  errors made by, 147
  exasperation induced in, 187
  experienced as persecutory, 165
  exploitation by, patient's fear of, 15
  -father, 49–51, 220
    idealization of, 18
  fear of, 214

analyst (*continued*):
  interpenetration of, 185
  as male or female figure, 146
  -mother, 107, 113
  need to avoid patient's terror, 150
  needing time to digest information,
    177
  oedipal desires of patient for, 145
  as omnipotent protector, 123
  as persecutor, 123–124
  as person between mother and
    patient, 170
  as person who supplies the words,
    125
  paranoid rejection of, 8
  in paternal role, 223, 224
  patient's choice of, 85
  patient's love for, 142
  perceived failure of, 213
  representing non-confused
    parental couple, 170
  treated as child by patient, 171
  tyrannical, fear of, 214
analytic couple, concept of, 174–176
analytic relationship, 187
anger:
  within analysis, 95, 126–127
  analyst's, 163, 169, 170
  need of patient to find reason for,
    153
anxiety(ies):
  analyst's, 205
  and attack on self, 139
  catastrophic, 105
  created by working through
    transference feelings, 142
  death:
    within analysis, 21, 22, 23
    within transference situation,
      154
  depressive, 119, 137, 140–145, 149,
    150, 160
  exposed through dreams, 131
  intolerable, coping with, 127
  paranoid, 149
  persecution: *see* persecutory anxiety
  psychotic: *see* psychotic anxiety
  separation: *see* separation anxiety
attacks:
  destructive, 41, 44
  internal and external, 100

Benjamin, W., xiv
Bion, W. R., xvi, xix, 41, 43, 66, 67, 127
birth, 6, 7, 32
  analytic, 18
  intolerableness of, 189, 190
  of patient, without help of analyst,
    201
  premature, 26
blackmail, by patient, 61–62
blockage, 66, 67, 175
  developmental, 77
body:
  experienced as geometric shape,
    160–180
  image, 15
  intolerable, 19
  of mother/analyst, intolerable, 18–
    19
borderline patients, xi, xvii, xxi, 45–
    63, 64, 67, 153
boredom, 39
breast, analysis as, 207

Capozzi, P., xix, xxi–xxv
Caverzasi, E., xix, xxi–xxv
Clark, P., 64, 65
closeness, desire for, 88
colitis, haemorrhagic, 184, 185, 190
coming alive, fear of, 167–168
communication (*passim*):
  in analysis, xviii, xxii, 45–63
  behaviour as, 53
  complaining as, 96
  concrete, 59–61
  and countertransference, xviii
  defensive, 59
  and empathy, xxiii–xxiv
  infantile, 89, 122
  non-verbal, xi, 45–46, 66, 125
  placing analyst in difficulty, 219

pre-verbal, xi
through projective identification, 25
through smiling, 86, 172, 173, 185,
    215
symbolic, 51
via third party, 194
written, 53–55
complaining, 117
continual, 93, 95–96
confusion:
    aroused in analyst, 169
    state of in patient, 169–170
connections, 97
    made by analyst, signifying
        creation of couple, 94–96
container (Bion), 127
containment:
    by analyst, 19, 20, 31, 82, 153
    maternal, failure of, xxiii, 30, 42–43
    by patient, 60
contradiction, importance of
    revealing, 133
countertransference, 110, 121, 122,
    133, 139, 154, 218
    as defensive tool, xiii
    and dreams,
        analyst's, 203, 224–225
        patient's, 98
    drowsiness or fear, 190
    positive, 210
    and positive reception of
        interpretation, 47
    and use of phantasy, 65, 66, 68
couple relationship, patient's need
    for, 174

death:
    of analysis, 226
    anxiety, 154
        in analysis, 111, 226
    of baby, 26, 27
    of father, 157–158, 186–187, 223
        failure to work through, 157–158
    fear of, 142
    instinct, 25
    of parents, 119, 138

of sister, 207
situation, idealized, 137
defencelessness, 135, 158
defences:
    against dependency, 181
    early, 25
    evacuative, xxiii
    imitative, 222–223
    against insight, 77
    as means for survival, xxiv
    and psychotic islands, 42
    relative, and communication
        problems, 45
    and trauma in infancy, 77
degradation, 10
De Masi, F., vii–viii, xv–xix, xxi–xxv
dependency:
    in analysis, 62
        acknowledgement of, 123
    on mental state, 209
depression, 26–44, 142, 174, 211
    of analyst, 18–19
    suicidal, 214
depressive anxiety, 119, 137–140, 143,
    145, 149, 150, 160
    and development of ego, 150
depressive position, 25
depressive problems, need of analyst
    to make conscious, 150
destructive attack, 44
destructive narcissism, x, xvi, xvii
Deutsch, F., 24
dream(s), 5, 7
    analyst's, 191, 202, 203, 224, 226
    communication through, 48–51
    as instrument for contact with
        analyst, 112–113, 116
    in latent psychotic state, 28–44
    and persecutory anxiety, 166–174
    and primitive psychic structure,
        188–201
    and transference, 117, 128–144, 147,
        149, 154
    and trauma in infancy, 88–94, 96–
        100, 104, 110–117, 122–124
    and use of phantasy, 65, 70

drowsiness:
    analyst's feeling of, 163–164, 190
    during analysis, 68–69
    provoked in patient by
        interpretations, 163
Dunbar, F., 24
dying, fear of, 142

ego, infantile, 24
emotions, perceived as violent, 167–
    168
emptiness, 22, 37, 192, 194, 198, 200
    and excitement, swing between,
        201
    fear of, 217
    feeling of:
        within family, 122
        by analyst, 70–73
    manicality as protection against,
        182
    sensation of in patient, 21, 165
envy, x, xvii, 32–33, 39, 151, 153, 221,
    223
exploitation, by analyst, patient's fear
    of, 15

faeces, 81, 177, 192, 193, 198
false self, 10, 43
fantasies, 4, 9, 11, 13, 14, 38, 64, 69,
    102, 105, 108, 222
father:
    -analyst, 36
    death of, 186–187, 221
    identification with, 146–147
    powerful, 221
feelings:
    destructive and sadistic, 4
    of inferiority, 222
    of isolation, 39–40
    of madness, 174
    of panic, 164
    of terror, 53, 54
    see also drowsiness; emptiness,
        insecurity; jealousy
Freud, S., viii, xxv, 25
friendly relationships, fear of, 217

fusion, 60–61, 143, 170, 217, 218
    avoiding, 217
    fear of, 217
    interpretation of, 146

Gaddini, E., x
Galli, A., xix, xxi–xxv
Gammaro Moroni, P., xix, xxi–xxv
genitalization, early, 149–150
guilt, 29, 208, 213
    and death:
        of father, 222–226
        of sister, 207
    depressive, 131, 134–138
    omnipotent, 202, 207
    persecution by, 38
    and superego, 176
    transferred onto analyst, 47

history, of patient, 26, 118–120, 183–
    184
    ascribing too much significance to,
        78
    as basis for hypotheses, xviii, xxii–
        xxiii
    and blockage in analysis, 71, 205
    and communication problems, 46
    comprehensive, 79–89, 93
    insufficient, 71, 205
holidays, 162, 210
    asking analyst about, 216, 218–219
    and desire to end analysis, 187
    reaction to announcement of, 167
    sessions after, 165, 191, 212
    sessions before, 56–58
        final, 12–13
    summer, 34, 38, 122–123, 212
homosexual relations, 20–21
hostility, 31, 100
    felt by analyst as intrusion, 127
    towards analyst, 186
humiliation, 10

idealization, x, 18, 32, 33, 203, 210
    of psychiatrist, 211
    self-, xvii, 32, 42

identity problems, 184
imagination, 52, 67, 69, 70, 107
imitation, 185
impasse, xiii, xvi–xix, xxii, xxiv
impotence, 81, 97, 161
indecision, 169
infancy, trauma in, 77–117
infantile anxieties, 7, 25
infantile omnipotence, 174
infantile situation, regressive, 154,
     155, 171
infantile structure, 181, 182
inferiority, feeling of, 222
insecurity, 119, 148, 182, 184
     felt towards parents, 147
interpretations:
     brief, 189
     experienced by patient as an
          interruption, 95
     faulty, 154–155, 158–159
     fear of, 192
     of feelings, 189
     felt as incomprehensible, 192
     focus of, with primitive psychic
          structure, 187
     focused, difficulty created by, 189
     fragments of, 180
     mistimed, 146
     not tolerated, 153
     overly explicit, 195
     provoking drowsiness in patient,
          163–164
     provoking persecutory situation,
          167
     seen as intrusion, 167
     sense of danger aroused by, 100
     suffocating, 143–144
     too limited, 175
interpreting, as giving, rather than
     taking, 175
interrupting, 95, 99, 100
     by analyst, benefit of, 169–170
intervention, succinct, 201
introjection, 10
intrusion, patient's fear of, 167
isolation, feeling of, 39–40

Jaffé, R., xix, xxi–xxv
jealousy, 9, 151, 153, 221, 223
     of sibling, 9

Klein, M., x, xv, xvi, xvii, xix, 25, 194
     on projective identification, 127

Langs, R., 46
language:
     incomprehensible, 193
     metaphorical, 53–54, 57–58
libidinal defensive narcissism, x, xvi–
     xvii

madness:
     fear of, 132–134
     feeling of, 174
manic episodes:
     and fear and excitement, 200–201
     and idealization, 203, 206, 208, 211–
          213, 217, 219, 226
     and persecutory anxiety, 177
     as protection against emptiness,
          182
     self-analysis of, 199
manipulation:
     in analysis, patient's fear of, 122
     of analyst, 161, 168–170, 226
masturbation, 20, 80, 84, 149, 166, 172,
     173
maternal object, 65, 83, 84, 93, 94
     relationship with, 83–84
     search for, 93
Meltzer, D., viii, xv, 64, 65, 209
mental illness, fear of, 28
metaphorical language, 48, 51, 53, 57,
     61
Meyer, A., 24
missed sessions, 47, 48, 51
misunderstandings, between analyst
     and patient, xxii, 45
mother:
     of analyst, 197
     -analyst, 17, 36
     –child relationship, 17
     idealized, 14

mother (*continued*):
    dangerous, 188
    depressed, 189, 190
    destructive, 205, 211, 213, 217
        identification with, 202, 207
    insecure, 6
    nourishing, 211
    object, 113
    symbiotic relationship with, 165,
        170

narcissism:
    destructive, x, xvi–xvii
    and idealization of analytic couple,
        xvii
    libidinal defensive, x, xvi–xvii
    psychopathology of, xvi
    wounded, xxiii
narcissistic organization, 8–9
negative therapeutic reaction, xxiv
negative transference, 3, 4, 61, 119,
        150–152, 159
nightmare, 34, 163
non-verbal communication, xi, 45–46,
        66, 125

object(s):
    good:
        and bad, confusion of, 132–133
        building relations with, 218
    idealized, 123
    parental, 137, 142
    persecutory, projected onto analyst,
        123
oedipal situation, 145, 147
    analysis of male object in, 108
    conflict, 28
    desires of patient for analyst, 145
    and identity problems, 148–149
    precocious, 148
Oedipus complex, 148, 149
    negative, 16
omnipotence, 40, 192
    of analyst, 11, 123
    of destructive self, 37

and guilty feelings, 226
    infantile, 9–11, 15, 22, 23, 174
    need for analyst to avoid, 171
    of past and present figures, 11
    of patient, 11
    of predictive identifications, 161,
        170
omnipotent projective identification,
        25

panic, 164
paranoid anxiety, 149
paranoid–schizoid position, 25
parental object, 94
parents:
    desire for acceptance by, 147
    differentiating between positive
        and negative aspects of, 149,
        150
    feelings of persecution by, 141
    internal and external, 62, 63
    regression of, 170–171
paternal object, 79, 84, 112
patient:
    danger of cordial atmosphere
        created by, 204–205, 212
    destructive, 171
    fear:
        of being discarded by analyst,
            193–194
        of dependency on analyst, 200
    manic-depressive, 213
    need to emphasize healthy side of,
        136
    reliance of, on analyst, 175–176
    seductive, 218, 220
    suicidal, 205, 207
persecutory anxiety, 120–142, 160–
        181, 192
    and communication problems, 48,
        49, 53, 54, 61
    in latent psychotic state, 33, 36, 38,
        41
    and projective identification, 170–
        171

persecutory figure, 36, 125
personality:
    creative aspects of, xiv
    disintegration of, 7
    infantile aspects of, 11
phantasy, 19, 121, 146, 221, 222
    analyst's use of, 64–73
    and communication problems, 50
    danger of sharing with patient, 67–69
    to illuminate blockage, 66
    of merging with analyst, 145
    in psychotic transference, 19–20
    and separation, 107–108, 142–143
Pirandello, L., 160, 168
pregnancy, 32
primary object, need for, to survive, 60–61
primitive psychic structure, 181–201
projective identification, xxiv, 194–195
    as communication, 25, 66
    interpretation of, 33–34
    and genuine identification, 218
    omnipotent, 25
    and persecutory anxiety, 170–171
    vs. projection, 127–128
    and transference in psychosis, 126–127
psychic structure, primitive, 181–201
psychosomatic illness, and psychotic anxieties, 24–44
psychotic anxiety, 7, 25, 51
    and good and bad objects, 132, 217
psychotic breakdown, 202–226
psychotic islands, xi, xxiii, 25, 26, 41–44

reaction, depressive, 176
reality:
    attacks on, 41
    delayed contact with, after analytic session, 70
rejection:
    fear of, 55–56
    paternal, 27

repetition, 169
representation, symbolic, 24, 49
resonance, 65, 66, 67, 69
reverie (Bion), 43
Rosenfeld, H. (passim):
    contributions to psychoanalysis, xiii, xvi–xvii, xxi
    personality and supervisory style of, ix–xiv, xviii–xix, xxii
    running away, patient's desire of, 142

schizophrenia, 21, 22, 23
Segal, xvi, xvii
self, healthy part of, 9–10
self-sufficiency, 10
    omnipotent, 9
separation anxiety, 106–107, 139, 142, 146, 165
sexuality, anxiety concerning, 68
shame, 207
shyness, 119, 183
silence, 29, 125
    analyst's, 47, 49–50, 122
    communication through, 47–54, 56
    use of phantasy, 71
sister, death of, 204, 207
sleepiness. See drowsiness
smiling, and communication, 86, 172, 173, 185, 215
space, 223–224
    feeling of lack of, 153–154, 158
    internal, and development, 43
speaking, fear of, 53
splitting, 17, 34, 43, 44, 208
Steiner, R., ix–xiv
Stuflesser, M., xix, xxi–xxv
suicide, 202–226
    dream about, 28
    of sibling, 161
    threat of, to obtain treatment, 58–59
    and use of phantasy, 69
superego, 139
    destructive, 135
supervision, 5, 67, 68–70, 77, 161, 203
symbiosis, 166

symbolic language, 56

talking, incessant, 163
terror, 53, 54
theft of precious object, fear of, 166–168
therapist:
    aggressive feelings towards, 13
    loss of control, 18–20
    rejection by, 52–54
thinking:
    disturbances, 72
    empty, 194
    inability of, 39–40
    re-establishing conditions for, 201
transference, 78, 117, 218
    adhesive, 185
    and defences, 181, 186
    and dreams, 112
    eroticized, 71, 106
    idealized, 61
    infantile, 211
    interpreting, confusion caused by, 158
    maternal, 105–106
    negative, 3, 4, 119, 150–152, 159
        persecutory, 61

not interpreting in, 152
oedipal, 108
paternal, 226
positive, 214
psychosis, xxiiii, 29–34, 43–47
    in psychosis, 118–159
    psychotic, 3–23
    and psychotic islands, 25–27
    repetition, 122
    situations, importance of clarifying
        order of, 126
    violence, 222
traumatic experiences, infantile, 77–117

understanding, need for analyst to
    contain desire to, 171

vacuousness, as protection, 217
vagueness, 214
violent emotions, patient's fear of
    own, 167–168

weekend break, 78, 88, 102, 106, 123,
    145, 151, 156
    patient's feelings about, 104–111,
        113, 158